Early English Devotional Prose
and the Female Audience

Early English Devotional Prose and the Female Audience

Elizabeth Robertson

The University of Tennessee Press
KNOXVILLE

Frontispiece: Enclosure of an Anchoress. By permission of the Masters
and Fellows of Corpus Christi College, Cambridge, CCCC MS 79, fol.
96a (formerly fol. 72a).

Much of chapter 4 has appeared previously in *Seeking the Woman in Late
Medieval and Renaissance Writings: Essays in Feminist Contextual
Criticism,* edited by Sheila Fisher and Janet E. Halley (Knoxville: The
University of Tennessee Press, 1989), 109–34.

The paper in this book meets the minimum requirements of the
American National Standard for Permanence of Paper for Printed
Library Materials. ⊗ The binding materials have been
chosen for strength and durability.

Library of Congress Cataloging in Publication Data

Robertson, Elizabeth Ann, 1951-
   Early English devotional prose and the female audience/
Elizabeth Robertson.—1st ed.
      p. cm.
   Includes bibliographical references.
   ISBN 0–87049–641–7 (cloth: alk. paper)
   1. English prose literature—Middle English, 1100–1500—History
and criticism. 2. Christian literature, English (Middle)—History
and criticism. 3. Devotional literature, English—History and
criticism. 4. Women—England—Books and reading—History. 5. Women
and literature—England—History. 6. Women—England—Religious
life—History. I. Title.
PR275.R4R6 1990
828'.10809382—dc20   89–24836   CIP

To my mother and father,
sister and brother

Contents

Acknowledgments

I first became interested in the *Ancrene Wisse* in a graduate seminar at Columbia University in 1975, conducted by R. W. Hanning and attended for a week by a visiting professor, Linda Georgianna. R. W. Hanning directed my dissertation, which became the beginnings of this study; for his warm, generous, and intellectually stimulating support, then and now, I continue to be grateful. Linda Georgianna encouraged me to pursue this project and continues to inspire me with her intellectual energy, astuteness, and infinite generosity to junior scholars.

I would like to thank the University of Colorado for a Junior Faculty Development Fellowship and for a Summer Research Initiation Fellowship that allowed me to continue my research in Europe. I would also like to thank Carol Orr for encouraging this project from its earliest beginnings, Mavis Bryant for her careful copyediting, and the editors and staff of the University of Tennessee Press for their encouragement and support. Since 1975, a host of friends and colleagues has helped me bring this project to completion. To the chair of my department, Jeffrey Robinson, I owe thanks for his enthusiastic support of feminist studies and for the funding that allowed me to benefit from the meticulous editing and proofreading skills of Robin Martin, Beth Partin, and Sally Payson. I also am indebted to the following staff and colleagues of the University of Colorado for their support: Colleen Anderson, Donald Baker, Gerald Kinneavy, Anne Lyons, Marje Urban, and Constance Wright. I would also like to thank The Committee on University Scholarly Publications of the University of Colorado at Boulder for awarding me a generous publication subvention.

Several others have given me extended encouragement and advice. In particular, James Kincaid read early drafts of the entire manuscript with painstaking care, and his humorous yet astute comments were of immeasurable help. Elihu Pearlman's wit, eloquence, and intellectual precision continue to inspire me. I also benefited from the loyal support and fine scholarship of Karen Robertson and Dana Cuff. I would like to thank readers of individual chapters, including Thomas Head, Paul Kroll, Arthur Krystal, Grant Muter, Alan Nelson, Georges Rey, and Thomas Shippey. In addition, I am grateful to Jane Chance, Diane Lanier, and Cornelia Kammerer, and the myriad contributors to the Medieval Feminist Newsletter who so often have sharpened my thoughts about feminism and medieval literature. My parents, who have always encouraged intellectual pursuits of many kinds, deserve a special acknowledgment.

Finally, I would like to give special thanks to two scholars and friends who provided unflagging encouragement. Gerda Norvig continues to challenge me with the depth, range, and stubborn intellectual honesty of her own scholarly inquiries. David Benson, who was my first teacher of medieval literature, will always surprise and delight me with his tireless intellectual curiosity, his far-ranging scholarship, his flexibility, and his generosity in helping his students and friends shape and articulate fledgling ideas.

Publication of this book has been aided by a gift from the Office of the Dean of Arts and Sciences, University of Colorado at Boulder.

Take me to You, imprison me, for I,
Except You' enthrall me, never shall be free,
Nor ever chaste, except You ravish me.

JOHN DONNE

CHAPTER I

The Implications of Illiteracy for the Development of Middle English Literature

Enthralled by God and voluntarily imprisoned for life in a cell attached to a church, the unworldly thirteenth-century English female recluse—the anchoress—inspired the creation of a significant body of Middle English literature. That corpus is comprised of six major prose works, all written in the first quarter of the thirteenth century. Named by Tolkien the "AB texts" for the dialect they share, the six are: the religious rule for anchoresses known as the *Ancrene Wisse* ("Guide for Anchoresses"); a homily, "Sawles Warde" ("The Guardianship of the Soul"); three female saints' lives, the lives of Saints Katherine, Margaret, and Juliana; and a guide to virginity, *Hali Meidenhad* ("Holy Virginity").[1] Thanks to Linda Georgianna's ground-breaking study of the relationship of the *Ancrene Wisse* to continental developments in notions of the self, this Middle English work has been recognized for its literary and psychological sophistication.[2] The remaining AB texts, known as the Katherine Group, although acknowledged for their unusual dialectal similarity to the *Wisse*, have been valued primarily for their historical significance as some of the very few early Middle English works that remain, and are generally viewed as possessing little literary value.

What scholars have ignored in studies of the AB texts is the fact that both the *Ancrene Wisse* and the Katherine Group were written for women. According to E. J. Dobson, the *Ancrene Wisse* was originally composed in about 1215 A.D. for three anchoresses living in the Deerfold near Wigmore Abbey in Herefordshire.[3] While the precise audience of the Katherine Group is still unknown, these works, too, are addressed, if not to the anchoresses of the Deerfold themselves, at least to a similar group of female contemplatives. That fact that the AB texts all share an address to women readers is crucial both to our understanding of the distinctive style that the works share and, more generally, to the proper appreciation of the ways in which audiences untrained in Latin shaped the development of early Middle English literature.

It may seem peculiar that such a small and specialized audience, a handful of anchoresses, should have played an important role in the development of Middle English. But this group became significant in part because of the unusual effects of the Norman Conquest on English literary production. Between 1066 and the flourishing of that literature in the fourteenth century, the history of English literature is obscure.[4] Few texts from the period 1066–1350 exist. What works remain are saints' lives; homilies; religious guides; medical texts; a major debate poem, "The Owl and the Nightingale"; and a few alliterative romances. Many of these English works are translations of earlier Ælfrician works or are pale versions of more colorful continental texts. Some believe that the small number of surviving manuscripts suggests that the production of English texts was severely curtailed by the Norman Conquest. Although there is no reason to believe that English writing ceased as a result of the Conquest, it is important to realize not only that fewer English works were produced, but also that the audience for whom English works were written changed. Literary historians do recognize that the eclipse of vernacular poetry was due to a displacement of audience.[5] The circumstances affecting the production of prose works are harder to assess. As Wilson has explained in his survey of Middle English prose, English prose was threatened by the dominance of both French and Latin in the land. Latin, the language of the reformed Norman church and initially the most prominent literary language, was joined after the twelfth century by French, partly because of the power of the Angevin empire of Henry II.

Nonetheless, the production of English works continued. Much of what remains is western in origin, suggesting that the West remained or became a center for English writing. The character of the extant works suggests that they were intended for lay audiences who had little schooling, and often for women. The literary productivity in the West has led some critics to argue that there existed an unbroken English prose tradition, but the scarcity of primary material from this period, among other things, makes the argument for continuity dubious.[6] In any case, what is of greater importance is the fact that an audience that was relatively insignificant before the Conquest—those uneducated in Latin—became afterward the primary audience for English literature. This uneducated audience plays a crucial role in both the survival and the development of English prose.

The content of extant manuscripts from the twelfth and thirteenth centuries is consonant with the idea that female readers formed an important part of this audience, although further work needs to be done on the provenance of these works. For example, Royal 17 A XXVII and Cotton Titus D 18 both contain several works of the AB group as well as several of the so-called Wooing Group. We shall see that the AB texts were originally intended for female readers. The Wooing Group, too, was probably written either for or by women. Of course, many of these works, including the *Ancrene Wisse,* were revised to address larger groups of male and female readers, but the proliferation of works originally intended for female readers suggests that after the Conquest, women were a significant audience for English literature.

The AB texts share not only a common female audience, but also a common and distinctive style. Characteristic of the AB texts is what can be called a quotidian psychological realism—that is, the texts detail the circumstances of the everyday life of a specific audience, anchoresses, in order to explore the psychological conflicts inherent in that life. The texts are written by men, however, and for this reason the exploration of anchoritic life is controlled by male assumptions about both the material and the conceptual nature of female religious experience; the concrete imagery employed is that which these male authors considered appropriate specifically for female readers. Consider, for example, the following images. In "The Life of St. Margaret," the dragon who tempts Margaret is described as a lumbering, clumsy animal with eyes as big as washbasins—a simile tied directly to the domestic circumstances of female contemplatives. Employing a similarly domestic image, the author of the *Ancrene Wisse* compares the anchoress to the common sparrow outside her window, spiraling towards heaven and yet inevitably returning to earth. *Hali Meidenhad* celebrates the virgin's marriage to Christ by contrasting it to secular marriage, giving a detailed Dickensian portrait of marriage in which a wife sweats over the fire with the cat at the flitch, the hound at the hide, and a baby squalling at her side. Such distinctive images deserve greater attention than they have been given.

Most studies of the AB texts have undervalued or misrepresented the psychological realism of the works. Many of these studies are influenced by Latin-based textual criticism; that is, these critics, including many of the recent editors of the AB texts, devote most of their critical attention to the identification of the specific Latin sources of the AB texts. In so doing, they underestimate the important ways in which the works differ from those sources. In addition to these editors, another group of critics, the exegetical scholars, inspired by the work of D. W. Robertson, also views the AB texts in terms of their sources. Viewing patristic masterpieces as the key to understanding all medieval vernacular literature, these critics overlook both the problems of the transmission of such sources and the complexity of specific cultural adaptations of those sources to particular audiences. In their search for sources, this last group of scholars dismisses the psychological specificity of medieval works, such as that found in the AB texts, stressing instead a more abstract Christian context. Such strategies assume that theological works play the same role for all audiences. But those not fully trained in Latin, particularly women and lay audiences, had a different relationship to theology and therefore fall outside the reach of this critical framework. While Robertsonianism has been largely abandoned (sometimes with detrimental effects) in studies of later fourteenth-century literature, many Robertsonian assumptions persist in studies of the AB texts. These studies reveal a misogyny, doubtless unconscious, that undervalues the psychologically complex stylistic innovations of literature written for or by women, as well as an elitism that persistently subordinates English style to what is perceived as a more developed and sophisticated Latin style. Both editors and critics who emphasize Latin sources neglect the importance of a particular history and psychology as keys to understanding the AB texts.

D. W. Robertson has warned readers to avoid taking too modern and psychological a view of medieval works. Urging us to abandon our nineteenth-century Romantic notions of imagination in interpreting medieval texts, Robertson argues that it is primarily theology which informs the psychology of the medieval period. He tells readers of medieval texts not to look for rhetorical figures "inducing a spontaneous emotional perception."[7] We should instead use as our guide Augustine, who "saw that if the figures are regarded as problems capable of an intellectual solution it is possible to recognize the fact that they conform to an abstract pattern which harmonizes with the pattern of a useful idea. . . . the affective value of this figurative language lies in what is found beneath the language and not in the concrete materials of the figures."[8] Medieval texts offer the Robertsonian critic an intellectual puzzle whose solution lies in identifying the theological sources that constitute the abstract, heirarchical frame for any given text. Robertson warns, "Medieval man, who inherited the implications of Augustine's doctrine of illumination, looked inward, not to find the roots of emotion, but to find God."[9]

While it is true that medieval texts, including the AB texts and medieval psychology, are certainly conditioned by their Christian framework, the AB texts' insistence on emphasizing the context of concrete, everyday experience, in which religious ideals can be realized, renders these texts stubbornly resistant to monolithic and abstract theological allegorizing. The Robertsonian leap to abstract and moral meanings, the easy translation of images into "figures," ignores entirely the subversive imagistic force of the hound at the hide or those wonderful washbasin eyes. Robertsonianism has been unable to give quotidian imagery its due, partly because such an approach rarely considers texts written for audiences who do not participate fully in the Latin tradition. Robertson, in his survey of medieval literature, nowhere mentions the AB texts, works written for readers both untrained in Latin and denied access to scholasticism—that is, women.

The continental context of the AB texts, therefore, must be considered with caution and must be qualified by an understanding of how those continental sources have been adapted for a specific audience. Linda Georgianna's study of the *Ancrene Wisse* has corrected Robertson's dismissal of psychology and has explained the complex relationship of that text to developments, on the continent, of notions of the self.[10] Her work is clearly applicable to the other texts in the AB group as well. As she, R. W. Hanning, R. W. Southern, and others have discussed, several twelfth- and thirteenth-century theological movements had important implications for the development of both literature and psychology.[11] The psychological richness of the AB texts owes much to the twelfth-century continental development known as the affective movement, in which religious writers exhibit a new interest in the emotions and in the self. Equally important are the related "scientific" movements of the Chartrians and the Victorines which contributed to the close scrutiny and celebration of the physical world as a way to understand God. The significance of all of these continental developments for a particular female English audience must be considered.

An older critical approach to the AB texts has argued that continental influences and sources are less significant than the works' indebtedness to a native tradition of English prose.[12] If we reconsider that tradition, we do in fact find that many late Anglo-Saxon and early Middle English works also make use of the distinctive quotidian imagery found in the AB texts. Yet such studies, too, have their limitations. First, they tend to view the AB texts as throwbacks to an earlier tradition rather than as developments of it. Second, they assert that the English prose tradition is homogeneous and continuous, an argument that, like Latin-based criticism, neglects the importance of the specific historical circumstances of a particular audience on the production of a work. Indeed, if we review the English tradition, we find a significant variation in style directly dependent on the kind of audience for whom the works were written. In general, it appears that the further the vernacular audience is from the Latin tradition, the more common is the vernacular texts' use of quotidian imagery. At the beginning of the vernacular tradition is Alfred, a writer who tells us that he is translating Latin texts into English specifically because Latin learning has declined in England, and whose work is permeated with concrete imagery drawn from everyday experience.

The pragmatism of works such as those by Alfred and his school raises questions about the relationship of certain kinds of imagery to social structure. Alfred wrote for a decentralized, nonfeudal, warring community, organized according to the ideal of the *comitatus*. The monasteries were the primary centers of learning, though Alfred himself became unusually well-trained outside of a monastic center.[13] Continual wars with the Danes chipped away at the organization of his kingdom, destroyed monasteries and libraries, and threatened the Christian hierarchy, necessitating texts that explained and reinforced the fundaments of that hierarchy. In Alfred's view, human beings struggle with dual angelic and bestial natures that pull them away from spiritual understanding. Rather than assuming that his audience simply needs training in abstract theory, Alfred uses imagery that relates to their dual nature.

By the tenth century, cultural conditions and the nature of the audience had changed. Anglo-Saxon kingdoms were at relative peace with one another. Often they united against their common enemies, non-Christian groups like the Picts, the Scots, or the Welsh. Monasteries prospered, and books multiplied. The kingdom enjoyed frequent and easy communication with continental centers of learning. It is not surprising, therefore, that the works of Ælfric, most often addressed to monks, eschew the kind of concrete imagery found in Alfred's writing and favor abstract, intellectual argument. Ælfric particularly avoids the literal level in his interpretation of images. Ælfric's interests were shared by his contemporary, Wulfstan, but Wulfstan wrote for a larger lay audience and consequently made some limited use of quotidian imagery.[14] As a bishop concerned with addressing large audiences, Wulfstan avoids the kind of particularized and individualized everyday imagery that we find in the AB texts. Stylistically, Wulfstan is located midway between Aelfric and the authors of the AB texts, for, although he writes for lay audiences, he is so firmly ensconced in the Christian establishment that his writing tends toward the conservative. Indeed, he often merely translated Aelfric's sermons as the basis for his own presentations. Nonetheless, as we move from audiences secure in their

Latin learning to less educated audiences, concrete, pragmatic imagery becomes more common.

This relationship of style and audience is even more pronounced in another strand of homiletic writing, the apocryphal homilies. Parallel to the more learned works of Ælfric and Wulfstan runs a stream of vernacular apocryphal homilies. This tradition began as early as the eighth century and continued through the thirteenth century. These homilies characteristically employ a high percentage of images drawn from everyday life, as well as alliterative, adjectival descriptions designed to inspire strongly emotional responses. Although we know little about the audiences to whom these homilies were addressed, we can infer that those who listened to these texts were not the erudite monks for whom Aelfric wrote. Indeed, Ælfric frequently criticized the use of apocryphal material like that found in the anonymous homilies.

Latin illiteracy—and illiteracy in general—thus has implications for the development of literary style which are as significant in their own way as are the implications of literacy.[15] It is not surprising that a quotidian style continues to occur in literature written later for popular audiences—for example, the audiences of Middle English drama. This singular style, moreover, is congruent with the Christian world view of nonfeudal, Anglo-Saxon communities. Society, according to this conception, is divided into three groups—those who work, those who pray, and those who rule. The leader of the kingdom is the head, and the workers are the limbs. It is fitting that laborers, as limbs, are trained not through abstract ideas but through concrete, sensual imagery.

In order to appreciate the realism of the AB texts, then, we must consider them intrinsically and in their own context, one which includes but is not dominated by an indebtedness to continental literature and to Anglo-Saxon precursors. Finally, it is the condition of the particular audience, in its precise historical moment, that must take precedence. One would expect post–Norman Conquest texts to reflect the influence of a revived Latin tradition. The hierarchical Christian order became codified with the establishment of feudalism, a major consequence of the Conquest. In addition, the Normans brought with them the well-established Latin learning of the continent. Admittedly, the AB texts do depend on Latin sources; almost all the works are based on Latin originals which were imported from the continent. Yet the relationship of early Middle English religious establishments to the Norman regime was complex. The placement of Norman leaders in almost all the centers of power stripped the monasteries of their autonomy and their money. In England, Latin learning suffered in the monasteries and, more significantly, in the convents. What indirect records we have suggest that very few women contemplatives had the books, time, or opportunities to devote themselves to Latin learning.

The group that needed English texts most, oddly enough, was an apparently small group: anchoresses. Despite their small number, these women created a demand for literature, not unlike the well-documented demand that followed the arrival of the Franciscans in England. Like that later audience, these readers needed texts that describe the individual's relationship to Christian ideals within the context of everyday experience. For a variety of historical reasons, including the fact that the Normans had appropriated Anglo-Saxon convents, anchoritism became especially popular among women in twelfth- and thirteenth-century England. These women had a complex relationship to the Christian tradition: while firmly embedded within it, they were denied access to positions of authority; they were dependent on visiting priests for confession; and they had little or no training in Latin. Furthermore, their physical mobility was highly circumscribed. An anchoress was bricked up for life into a room or rooms attached to a church. As an anchoress, she was expected to forget the world, devoting her life to prayer and contemplation. Although many anchoresses occupied themselves with weaving or sewing, they were discouraged from even these activities. They therefore spent the majority of their time reading, but the books that they could read were limited. Clearly they needed vernacular texts such as saints' lives, sermons, and religious guides; but these works needed to be adapted to their circumstances as women who led unusually restricted lives. These texts also had to address the fact that the female anchoritic life was dictated by established Christian traditions and yet rested paradoxically outside of that establishment. Thus, a body of English texts arose that exhibit an unusual degree of psychological sophistication in their concern for the peculiar needs and circumstances of the anchoress.

More than history is at issue in interpreting these texts. Clearly those writing for anchoresses were guided by their view of a woman's place in religion and in the world, particularly by a pervasive view of women as grounded in their bodies. This view and those associated with it have their roots in Aristotelian categories which differentiate men and women as active/passive; form/matter; completion/incompletion; act/potency; perfection/imperfection; possession/deprivation.[16] These categories in turn inform Christian commentaries in which Eve is identified with will and the body, and Adam with wit and the mind. As daughters of Eve, all women inherit Eve's dependence on the senses, her inability to think abstractly, her fundamental willfulness, and, most importantly, her sexual guilt. Inescapably bound by these categories, a woman must be trained accordingly. Associated with the "limbs" of society rather than with the head, Eve must be trained to control her limbs. Texts written for women therefore focus on training the willful body through the body. Rather than seeking to deny or to escape her sexuality, a woman must redirect her sensual and sexual self to an appropriate object, Christ. Like her male counterparts on the continent, the anchoress celebrates her betrothal to Christ, but, because she is a woman, this marriage is literalized. The focus on the concrete in the AB texts arises from an unstated controlling principle that women are locked into their sinful bodies.

The use of a quotidian style in the AB texts thus is both practically and theoretically appropriate to the perceived needs of their female audience. In addition, the emotions portrayed in the AB texts reveal what men think women feel. They see women as particularly suited by nature to two kinds of experience: an identification with Christ's suffering and an expression of that experience through tears. While these elements appear in male affective texts, they are central to texts written for women. Blood and tears are particularly frequent images in the AB texts. Because women are presumed to contain in their bodies more moisture, which is then purged through menstruation and tears, they are considered biologically suited to an empathetic response to Christ's passion.

In addition to a focus on emotions, the texts can also be described, to use Carol Gilligan's terms, as relational rather than hierarchical—that is, the female contemplative is defined through her relationship to others, rather than through her commitment to an abstract ideal.[17] The works stress the virgin's relationship to Christ. A relational emphasis is also viewed as theoretically appropriate because a woman is seen as being by nature dependent on Christ, and, as we shall see, her place in religious life is to be defined by her relationship to Christ, not by her place in an abstract hierarchy. Women, even more than the uneducated lower classes, are altogether outside the hierarchy, both practically and theoretically.

The psychologically astute, pragmatic spirituality of the AB texts seems, then, to be a product of both English and continental traditions and to be a peculiar result of combined historical and theoretical forces. The move to incorporate psychologically effective images drawn from everyday experience within an instructional framework was a fruitful contribution to the development of literature. Yet, as I will show, the style itself sprang from patronizing attitudes towards those persons who did not know Latin. Concretion and pragmatism were deemed appropriate for the limbs of the king, but when the texts turned to women audiences, these attitudes became particularly confining. These authors not only assumed that women were motivated by sensual willfulness, but they also denied women access to the abstract hierarchy available to men. The emphasis on concrete, pragmatic reality, while positive in its unusual concern for the needs and circumstances of women, also seemed to reinforce women's isolation from centers of power. Paradoxically, however, the stylistic focus on the everyday experience of women had the positive aspect of centering women. Indeed, the tendency to draw attention to the world for the sake of vilifying it—a technique advanced by the church fathers—had the potential to undermine its own purposes. Ultimately such a focus resulted in the "scientific" scrutiny of the world that eventually undermined Christianity.

This study will begin with a consideration of the historical circumstances of the anchoress. Arguing that the religious experience inscribed in the religious works of the period differs for men and women, I shall describe the conditions and motivations of female anchoritic life. Women's restricted options in both secular and religious life after the Norman Conquest contributed to the surprising popularity, especially among English women, of what might seem an eccentric and marginal movement. The anchorhold, primarily a woman's space, offered women unusual opportunities but also posed particular problems. The peculiar enticements and challenges of the English recluse inspired the creation of a literature that addressed her unique situation and celebrated her role. The particular realism of the literature written for the anchoress is in part a response to her physical environment.

Yet the AB texts' authors' understanding of those circumstances and indeed the anchoress's own understanding of herself were also influenced by contemporary views of female sexuality. Through a discussion of Christian commentary on women and the Aristotelian and Galenic medical views that inform those commentaries, I argue, in chapter 3, that the perception of women as daughters of Eve—inescapably trapped in their bodies, essentially willful, dependent on the senses, and incapable of theorizing—informs not only the themes but also the structure and imagery of these works.

In the following chapters, I shall show how the dialectic between material circumstances and misogynistic views of women influences the style of English works written for the anchoress. All six AB works exhibit a style (often associated in recent times with literature written *by* women rather than *for* women) that is pragmatic, nonteleological, and emotional. It is a style that stresses the concrete and personal over the abstract and the universal. As a group, these works set forth, within the context of a specific environment, a masculine vision of a particularly feminine spirituality.

Because critics have failed to take into account the influence of the audience on the production of these works, they have misunderstood the place of these works within the English tradition and, in turn, have failed to appreciate the varied nature of the Anglo-Saxon tradition itself. I argue that the style of the AB texts has features in common with those texts of the Anglo-Saxon tradition addressed to audiences with similar needs—that is, audiences uneducated in Latin or those located far from established religious centers. Through an analysis of works of Alfred, Ælfric, Wulfstan, and the anonymous homilists in the context of their audiences, we shall see how Anglo-Saxon religious works emphasize the pragmatic or the theoretical according to the needs and education of the specific audience. Such an analysis suggests that attitudes toward women and toward the uneducated often coincide and that they engender similar styles.

Next, I examine the continental context of the AB texts, drawing out the implications of continental developments for female audiences. While previous critical discussions have explained the pervasive influence of the affective movement upon the AB texts, they have overlooked the fact that these developments had different implications for women than for men. A comparison of the AB texts with their sources, such as those of St. Bernard or Hugh of St. Victor, reveals differences between mystical texts stemming from an intellectual and masculine Latin tradition and those written for a more restricted and less informed female audience.

These differences suggest that we must reassess the affective movement itself in terms of audience. Indeed, female audiences played an unrecognized role in the development of affective piety in such works as Anselm's letters to women and Abelard's letters to Heloise. While these writers developed affective imagery available to both men and women, when they wrote for women, they carried affective piety into a new area by arguing that women are more biologically suited than men for certain kinds of affective meditation. Influenced by the Aristotelian attribution of excess moisture to women, these writers consider blood and tears, for example, to be natural to female mysticism. A "pathetic" strain of affective piety particularly designed for women thus emerges. A recognition of the ways in which male ideas about women determine notions of feminine spirituality forces us to reassess the influence of continental sources on the representation of female spirituality found in the AB texts.

Once we recognize the crucial influence that the perceived nature of the audience exerts on the character of the AB texts, we must reexamine the role that not only women but all readers uneducated in Latin play in the development of the resources of the English literary tradition. By considering the ways in which audience and gender influence the production of English works, I suggest that we may also be forced to reconsider our understanding of the production and nature of later Middle English works, including Middle English drama as well as the canonical works of Chaucer, Langland, and the Pearl Poet.

CHAPTER 2

An Anchorhold of Her Own:
The Anchoress in
Thirteenth-Century England

In *Sir Gawain and the Green Knight*, Gawain, the hero, armed with a shield whose underside portrays an image of the Virgin Mary, sets forth into the wilderness in fulfillment of his promise to uphold courtesy by standing a fatal blow from the Green Knight. The real spiritual and secular test of his courtesy takes place in the bedroom of a castle, though that confrontation is conditioned for him by his yearlong wanderings through a wilderness filled with beasts and dragons. For women in the Middle Ages, personal quests, whether historical or literary, religious or secular, took place in much less rarified and exotic landscapes. Most often they occurred at home. Because women of religious vocations were not free to travel, they necessarily pursued their religious goals in a symbolic rather than a literal wilderness. The English religious woman who in particular wished to replicate the spiritual quest of the desert fathers in the wilderness could do this only in a small and enclosed place, in the anchorhold.

Anchoritism was one of the most popular forms of religious life available to women in Norman England. Although we unfortunately know very little about the personal histories of these women, we do know an occasional name of an anchoress and sometimes a few details of a life.[1] For example, we know of Loretta, Countess of Leicester. After her father fell out of favor with King John, her family was in precarious political circumstances, and several family members suffered exile or death as a result. She herself fled into exile but later returned to England and, in 1220, retired into solitude in an anchorhold in Hackington, Kent.[2] We also have a few details of the early fourteenth-century Katherine of Ledbury, the wealthy wife of Nicholas, Baron Audley, and the mother of three children. Twelve years after her husband's death, she gave up her lands and became an anchoress in Ledbury, supported by revenue from her own lands. More familiar, perhaps, is the late fourteenth-century anchoress, Julian of Norwich, known particularly for her account of the revelations that inspired her pursuit of an anchoritic life.

These scanty details portray a group of women who were determined and independent, who had in common a strong desire, despite odds and resistance, to pursue the anchoritic life. Why should women like these have chosen such a demanding form of the religious life? By any standards, anchoritism was a peculiarly extreme form of the religious life. Bricked into a room for life, cut off from contact with her sisters, and discouraged from fraternization with the world outside, the anchoress's daily life excluded the human distractions which might divert her mind from contemplation and prayer. In this way she lived in virtual isolation and anonymity for decades. Considering the austerity and rigors of anchoritic life, anchoritism was surprisingly popular—especially among post-Conquest English women. To us, a choice to pursue an anchoritic life is difficult to comprehend. As Ann Warren writes, "The psychological impact of the walling up of the recluse forces the modern mind to thoughts of incarceration as punishment, the cell as a prison, and the anchorite existence as a living death."[3]

The common explanation for the popularity of anchoritism in twelfth- and thirteenth-century England is that the anchoritic movement itself was simply a response to the growing religious fervor of the period, and that anchoritism becomes more comprehensible when set against the background of the general ascetic idealism of the twelfth and thirteenth centuries. The period was marked by the establishment of new institutions devoted to especially ascetic forms of the religious life.[4] The founding of the Cistercians was a typical response to the religious climate of the period. Reacting to what they saw as the corruption and self-indulgence of the Benedictines, the Cistercians dedicated themselves to an austere life, with contemplation as the primary goal of the monastery. The spiritual fervor inspired by Cistercians such as Bernard of Clairvaux led to the establishment of numerous particularly ascetic foundations, such as those of the Carthusians and the Premonstretensians.

In part because the new orders preferred to admit adults rather than the children raised in their own houses, the ascetic life was made available to a larger and more varied group of people than ever before.[5] This larger group, however, did not include women. The most influential group, the Cistercians, refused for almost a century to admit women. Although, on the continent, groups organized specifically for women, such as the Beguines, did spring up in response to reawakened interest in asceticism, these groups founded only a few houses, if any, in England, and those were open to only a small number of women. As a result, women in England who wished to follow the ascetic life may have turned to anchorholds simply because no other religious foundation offered them a place to pursue a rigorous ascetic practice.

While such an analysis provides a general answer to the question of why English women found anchoritism an attractive form of the religious life, it fails to consider the particular issue of how gender may have influenced such choices. Why should women choose anchoritism? In order to appreciate the female anchoritic movement in England, it is necessary to consider the broader context of choices available to English women as a whole. Since many of the women who became anchoresses had previously been lay women rather than religious women from the convent, we must consider both secular and religious options. I shall argue here that a woman's choice to become an anchoress was governed not only by the strength of her spiritual vocation, but also by the limited number and restricted nature of other options available to women in both religious and secular life in thirteenth-century England. That thirteenth-century English women should have found anchoritism an attractive form of life is not so surprising when we consider this choice in the light of the diminished legal and intellectual opportunities available to women after the Conquest.

Early Anglo-Norman anchoresses, those of the late eleventh and early twelfth centuries, may well have been motivated to enter anchorholds by their desire to retain the independence that the native Anglo-Saxon social organization had allowed women before the Conquest.[6] Some became anchoresses simply for political expediency, entering anchorholds when their families were out of favor and leaving them when the political climate changed. Others, however, may have chosen anchorholds as places where they might retain some of the legal and intellectual freedom they had previously enjoyed. Because specific information about women in these early periods is not available until bishops' registers begin in the thirteenth century, surviving evidence which documents women's position in both Anglo-Saxon England and early Norman England is fragmentary.[7] Existing legal and literary records suggest, however, that English women at the time of the Conquest were relatively independent. As in any patriarchal culture, Anglo-Saxon women were very much subject to the control of men. Yet legal records suggest that women had considerable flexibility in marriage choices, were able to divorce, could represent themselves in courts, and could make wills.[8] In addition, the large number of place names based on women's names suggests that women often possessed land. Anglo-Saxon wills also indicate that land could easily be left to a woman.[9] Furthermore, the queens who reigned in Anglo-Saxon times were powerful figures. It was not unusual for a queen to rule after her husband's death, and often she subsequently led men into battle. Women under the early Norman regime had been used to a considerable degree of autonomy in secular life.

Anglo-Saxon women also had a significant degree of autonomy in the religious life. Christianity was first introduced into England because of a woman, Bertha. In the late sixth century, Æthelberht of Kent married the Frankish Bertha, who brought with her to England the Frankish bishop Liudhard and continued to practice her religion despite her husband's continuing paganism. The religious fervor of Bertha and her bishop led Æthelberht to welcome Augustine in England; in 597, therefore, Christianity gained its foothold in England. By the mid-seventh century, women were able to participate in intellectual life through religious establishments. Women were expected to acquire a high level of proficiency in Latin. Aldhelm's abstruse letter of guidance to the nuns of Barking is one indication of the high degree of Latin proficiency at least these nuns were expected to have attained. England was known for its double monasteries, centers of learning open equally to men and women. Besides participating in learning, women also were allowed to take on high level administrative positions; many women headed not only nunneries, but also double monasteries of both men and women. Among the most famous of these was Whitby, headed by Hild. Not least among Hild's accomplishments was her influence on the development of English vernacular poetry, for it was Hild who encouraged the first English vernacular poet, Caedmon, to write, not only by providing him a place in her monastery but also by providing him with the Latin texts on which his poetry is based. Anglo-Saxon nuns not only encouraged others to learn, but also wrote themselves. Hygeburg, for example, is known for recording the recollections of Willibald, bishop of Eckstalt. This book was the first travel book written about the East, and the first book known to have been written by an English woman.

The positions of power in both secular and religious life, the educational opportunities, the rights to land, and the relative freedom in marriage rights of Anglo-Saxon women were all drastically reduced after the Conquest. The effect of the Conquest on the status of women was dramatic, though the enforcement of laws may not have been as rigid as the code suggests. Nonetheless, the Conquest brought with it feudalism, a system that radically redefined women as first and foremost the property of men. The Conquest thus instituted a shift from a horizontal clan system to a vertical and hierarchical system of primogeniture. It also brought with it a well-established and narrowly-defined religious concept of women—a subject treated in the next chapter. Furthermore, the legal system imported by the Normans denied women status under the law. The popularity of anchoritism, then, can be explained partly as a reaction to a new and repressive system, and the anchorholds themselves offered a partial escape from that system.

Perhaps the most significant influence on the status of women was William I's establishment of the rule of primogeniture, which meant that daughters, like younger sons, were entirely dependent on their fathers' generosity for financial support. The rule of primogeniture as well as the related system of feudalism carried with it a new attitude towards women, as they were placed perpetually under the control of men. Women were subject to the authority of their fathers or their husbands, and ultimately to that of their lords. It was common for a woman to be married off at an early age and to be pressured into remarriage by a lord. Often the presence of a marriageable daughter occasioned a battle between the girl's father and the father's lord.[10] The cavalier attitude the lord took towards a marriageable woman is illustrated by the story of Grace. The child of a villager's wife who was disguised as a noblewoman's offspring, Grace fell under her lord's power. He first married her at the age of four to Adam Neville, a forester's brother. She was later sold to the lord's chamberlain for two hundred marks, and, at the chamberlain's death, she was sold again for three hundred marks to her third husband, Brian de Lisle.[11] After the establishment of feudalism, women lost any power to control the circumstances of their marriages. Although divorce was still common in this period, as it had been in the earlier Anglo-Saxon period, the earlier practice by which women chose to divorce for their own personal reasons seems to have been lost. In the later period, divorces were most often enacted by men for their own advantage. Because of the obscurity of the consanguinity laws, marriages could be dissolved fairly easily.[12] Although these laws do not limit divorce to men, the fact that women had no legal status in Norman England suggests that men rather than women were the ones most likely to turn to consanguinity laws as justifications for divorce.

Legal records suggest that within marriage too women were completely under the power of their husbands, for marriage meant that women lost control over their own property. The Norman marriage laws, as summarized by Pollock and Maitland, included the following strictures: "In the lands of which the wife is tenant in fee, whether they belonged to her at the date of the marriage or came to her during the marriage, the husband has an estate which will endure during the marriage, and this he can alienate without her concurrence. If a child is born of the marriage, thenceforth the husband as 'tenant by the curtesy' has an estate which will endure for the whole of his life, and this he can alienate without his wife's concurrence. . . . The wife has during the marriage no power to alienate her land without her husband's concurrence."[13] By custom, a husband was not supposed to alienate his wife's land without her consent, but because she could not act for herself in court, she had little recourse if she objected to his actions.[14] After the Conquest, women also lost the right to act as jurors or judges.

Women not only lost power over their land and their legal status in court, but also lost their right to possess their own goods. A wife had no possessions while her husband was alive, could not purchase goods with her own money, and whatever goods had belonged to her before her marriage, after marriage belonged to her husband. There was also some question about a woman's right to keep her own clothes and jewelry.[15] She was legally entitled only to her necessary clothes. In addition, women seemed to have no power to incur a debt and thus had no credit.[16] Because women had no right to their goods, they also had no right to make wills without the consent of their husbands.[17]

Marriage was one of the few choices available to women, and, indeed, marriage was one of the few options that guaranteed a woman some degree of financial security. Yet under Norman law, marriage surely was much less attractive than it had been under Anglo-Saxon law. Women had little or no say about whom they married, and, once married, they could not object if they were beaten or if their husbands committed adultery. The wife and all her property were under complete control of her husband.[18] It was also common for men to maintain mistresses, and, as mentioned earlier, it was easy for a man to dissolve a marriage on the basis of consanguinity.

There is indirect evidence that husbands often beat their wives. Legal records suggest, "The king's court would protect the life and limb of the married woman against her husband's savagery, if he killed or maimed her. If she went in fear of any violence exceeding a reasonable chastisement, he could be bound with sureties to keep the peace; but she had no action against him, nor had he against her. If she killed him, that was petty treason."[19] What society or the law considered reasonable chastisement is hard to judge. The Norman Somma says that "a husband may not put out his wife's eye nor break her arm, for that would not be correction."[20] The fact that this law was necessary suggests the degree of brutality to which women could be subjected. If they resisted such treatment, they faced potentially severe punishment, since women who plotted against their husbands were guilty of treason. The reverse, however, was not true. The differential categorization of a wife's attack on her husband makes clear the imposition of feudal hierarchical patterns in marriage. The wife becomes subject to the husband, as man is subject to his lord.

In both the Anglo-Saxon and Norman periods, as indeed until recently, the dangers women faced in childbirth were extensive.[21] Infant mortality was high, and the risks to the mother were serious. A woman's chances of dying in childbirth or of being exhausted by motherhood to the point of death were great, especially given the fact that women often had ten or more children. The laws governing the relationship of parents and children, moreover, illustrate the father's complete dominion over the child's welfare. In the seventh century, a father could sell a child of seven or under into slavery without the child's or the mother's consent. There is no reason to believe that the father's power diminished after the Conquest.

Even a woman who was content with her husband and had survived the hazards of childbirth faced a difficult and demanding life as a housewife, for the medieval housewife was responsible for the maintenance of the house, servants, supplies, and often the lands as well. Only as a widow did a woman gain some legal independence. She was able to sue and be sued, and she could make seals and bonds without any guardianship.[22] Being a widow was clearly legally desirable, even though, at the point of widowhood, she might lose a great deal of land. At her husband's death, a woman could claim one-third of her husband's land, although, as Pollock and Maitland observe, "from the frequency with which a *dos nominata* is mentioned, we should gather that many widows of high station had to be content with less."[23] Furthermore, this third could be disputed if the marriage had not been conducted at the church. Widowhood had both advantages and disadvantages, from a legal standpoint. Although a widow had no right to goods other than her necessary clothes, she nonetheless inherited both her husband's debts and his responsibility to provide goods to others.[24] Despite the widow's legal standing, at the outset a new widow's legal freedom was tenuous. She was subject to the authority of her lord, who could marry her off to his advantage at any time. And widows who were not harassed in this way nonetheless faced the considerable responsibilities of running their new property. They had to make sure their acreage was well stocked, keep control of the granges, control servants, and supervise disposal of alms, storing of the harvest, and a host of household activities.

Such a picture suggests that, whether married or widowed, women in the middle and upper classes in secular life were exceedingly constrained.

Clearly, there were exceptions. Eleanor of Aquitane influenced more than one king, but it is important to recognize that Eleanor was a woman who turned the constraints upon women to her advantage.[25] For example, she turned a marriage in which she had no choice—her marriage to Louis of France—into a means to reinforce her lands and power, and then, claiming consanguinity, abandoned that marriage for an even more powerful one to Henry II of England. Her attempts at independence often resulted in disaster, as, for example, in the case of her attendance on Louis' crusade. Finally, she overstepped the bounds of a woman's role so extensively that she ended her life as a prisoner of her second husband. This imprisonment can be seen as simply an exaggeration of the constraints that post-Conquest society imposed on women.

Ironically, it was the upper-class woman who was most subject to such oppression. Lower-class women, although of course subject to the same restrictions in marriage and the same dangers in childbirth, gained increasing mobility and autonomy as the middle class grew in power and size. Women in the lower classes were able to pursue a number of alternatives to marriage, including weaving, cloth-making, dying, and brewing. In fact, brewing seems to have been primarily in the hands of women.[26] It was far more desirable for a lower-class man to set his daughter to a trade than to provide a dowry for her. It must not be forgotten, however, that under the feudal system, even these tradeswomen were subject to a male hierarchy that had ultimate control over both their lands and their money, for a tradeswoman who married became subject to her husband and his lord.

Several scholars have criticized *Hali Meidenhad*, a text we shall consider in detail later, for its harsh and unrealistic portrait of marriage. They argue that the text's picture of a harassed housewife—one who fears the brutality of her husband and is anxious about the safety and welfare of her children, who might well die before they reached their teens—was a rhetorical exaggeration designed only to enhance a contrasting celebration of the virgin's betrothal to Christ. However, both Anglo-Norman law and records of marriage practices suggest that, despite its rhetorical purposes, *Hali Meidenhad's* portrait of marriage is much more accurate than some suppose. Marriage to Christ, then, was set against a realistic rather than a hyperbolic portrait of marriage. Given the legal restrictions of marriage, the unpleasantness of married life, and the constant surveillance of widows, it is not surprising that many women preferred to enter the religious life. As Power writes, "Such women as left husband and children to take the veil must have been moved by a very strong vocation for religion, or else by excessive weariness . . . as [suggested by] the misguided realist of

Hali Meidenhad."[27] Often fathers discouraged their daughters from marrying simply because they could not afford the marriage dower. It was less expensive to send a daughter to a nunnery, and it was common for daughters to be sent to nunneries even in infancy. The post-Conquest population explosion exacerbated this problem, since population studies suggest that there were many more single women than men in the thirteenth century. A very few women pursued the alternatives of becoming doctors or witches—both liminal roles. Those women who did choose such courses guaranteed themselves an unparalleled independence and intellectual autonomy. Yet these choices denied women participation in the social order and put them at risk of persecution and death.

For those who were unwilling to rebel entirely and eager to participate in the central belief system of the age, and who yet found marriage or widowhood unappealing, the Christian life was the only other alternative. The religious life was an obvious choice for women. It was a socially acceptable alternative, and women could be controlled within the patriarchal system. The status accorded to women within Christianity should not be overlooked. Although medieval Christianity, as developed by the Roman Catholic hierarchy, was ultimately a patriarchal religion and hence oppressive to women, Christianity did offer women a place. Women were celebrated as handmaidens of the Lord. Thus, to a certain extent, as nuns, women possessed an authority that they lacked in secular life. Given the quality of medieval married life, it is not implausible to think that women might find the religious life, in either a convent or an anchorhold, an attractive alternative.

The social advantages should not obscure the spiritual reasons which moved many women to choose a religious life. Many women undoubtedly entered the convent because of a deep sense of religious vocation. Many others, however, may have entered for other reasons. Often girls were placed in convents in childhood or even in infancy, regardless of the child's spiritual convictions. Some children were put into a convent because they were illegitimate or because a parent had no money to support them. Older daughters were probably encouraged to join convents, since it was often less expensive to place a girl in a nunnery than to get her married. Women often found it possible to escape particular marriages, if unconsummated, through entering the religious life.[28] Often women fled to nunneries simply to avoid an unwelcome marriage offer. As noted earlier, some women became nuns or anchoresses for political reasons. Given the political turmoil that surrounded these women and the dubious security of secular life, the religious life may well have been appealing. Stenton describes what appears to have been an attractive, stable life led by the recluse Loretta and another woman: "These ladies were able to live a simple life in a modest two- or three-roomed house attended by a couple of servants with a man-servant to look after their business. They were fed by alms."[29] Clearly, both convents and anchorholds offered women a life that would be attractive from a secular point of view.

The life of a nun might well have seemed enviable. Nuns had educational opportunities unavailable to women outside the convent.[30] They were trained in some Latin and were expected to read or to listen to both vernacular and Latin texts as part of their daily lives. The church also encouraged many nuns to write religious works themselves. Such intellectual opportunities were not available to the married woman. Upper-class women, as we have seen, were restricted both physically and intellectually. These educational opportunities, of course, were not what they had been in Anglo-Saxon times; after the Norman Conquest, for reasons that are not clear, women in the convents lost their earlier facility with Latin. Letters written to women after the Conquest still were often written in Latin, but the correspondent often urged the receiver to have the letter translated into French or English. Nuns did acquire some training in Latin in the convents, since their daily routine included recitations of the Latin psalms, but the level of learning required to master these simple texts was rudimentary compared to the level of learning expected of nuns in the earlier periods. Rote learning and reiteration of prayers does not necessarily imply an ability to read and write in Latin. Whether trained in Latin or not, nuns were expected to spend a part of each day reading or listening to religious texts. In addition to Latin, women were taught a variety of crafts, such as gardening, sewing, weaving, and manuscript illumination. In fact, women were involved in the production of some of the finest manuscript illumination of the age. Although skills taught to women were primarily those involving manual dexterity, such crafts also demanded mental discipline. While it is true that domestic supervision, cooking, and the preparation of herbal concoctions, as well as the range of crafts expected of women in secular life also required mental discipline, the convent offered a clear structure of mental discipline in addition to consistent training. Thus, a nunnery was easily attractive to a woman who wished to train her mind.

Despite the appeal of convent life, the precarious condition in which the Conquest left convents explains why some women might prefer anchorholds in which to pursue the religious life to convents. Post-Conquest English nunneries were small and poor. Stenton tells us that after the Conquest, only nine fully established nunneries existed. Power concludes that even during the later Middle Ages, there were only 138 nunneries, and 73 of these received less than one hundred pounds a year in income. Sixty-three of the 138 had less than ten members.[31] The Norman Conquest also reduced the power and influence of the abbesses. Abbesses in this period ceased to be religious leaders. Double monasteries were abolished, and abbesses were subject to the authority of the local bishop, a Norman, who was most interested in reorganizing the religious orders to support Norman needs. Formerly autonomous communities of nuns were now under the control of the bishop and were subject to frequent visitations.

The attractions of convent life might have been outweighed by its difficulties; for those wishing to pursue an especially rigorous ascetic life, the condition of the nunneries also, if somewhat paradoxically, might well have served as a deterrent. Because convents were supposed to be virtually self-supporting, every woman in the community had to fight to maintain its precarious financial balance. Thus, a woman who entered a convent to escape the world might find herself more involved in the world than ever before. She might, for example, be responsible for running the home farm or for managing the clothes or food budget. Such worldly concerns were time-consuming and anxiety-provoking. Ironically, the more ascetic a nun was, the more likely it was that she would be put in positions of increasing power. The title of abbess or prioress brought with it increasing involvement for its bearer in the world outside the convent. Among the duties of the prioress described by Power are visiting royalty, supervising manors, presiding at legal disputes, and attending funerals.[32] As the recorded complaints against them testify, prioresses were thus subject to a variety of temptations, ranging from the desire for luxury to sexual involvement.

Even the ordinary nun was rarely free to concentrate on contemplation alone. The small size of the convents suggests that each member was assigned a time-consuming and demanding role in the convent, perhaps as a cellaress or chamberess—duties that obviously did not enhance contemplation. A sacrist or a chantress, on the other hand, might more easily be able to integrate her convent duties and her contemplative goals.

For the ascetic, an anchorhold would offer an attractive alternative to convent life. An anchorhold, I shall argue, offered a woman a medieval version of Virginia Woolf's "room of one's own," because there a woman could find privacy, autonomy, and a chance for intellectual development unavailable even in the convent. Because an anchoress was supported by grants from the mobility and alms from local inhabitants, she had minimal financial concerns. One must be cautious, of course, in presenting the life of the anchorhold as a positive option for women. The anchorhold was a place defined and strictly controlled by men, and anchoresses were subject to frequent visits from priests and bishops. The limited Latin training offered to a post-Conquest woman within the anchorhold also limited her intellectual freedom. Finally, an anchoress's intellectual inquiries were also conditioned by her Christianity.[33] Despite its limitations, an anchorhold may well have offered a haven to women.

Unfortunately, we know little about the details of anchoritic life in thirteenth-century England, except that it was popular among both men and women. The word "anchorite" derives from the Greek word *anchoreta,* to withdraw, and the idea of anchoritism derives from the experiences of the early church fathers who withdrew to the desert to be free of the cares of the world and to enter into an active confrontation with the devil. In England, the anchoritic condition was replicated in the anchorite's cell, intended as an imitation of the desert caves of the Egyptian saints St. Anthony, St. Paul of Thebes, and St. Mary the Egyptian. Embodying an ideal that was both external and internal, the anchorite chose to live in a cell or cells attached to a church in order to prepare the mind for confrontation with the devil. A primary goal of the male or female anchorite was to control the inner life, based on extensive self-scrutiny and self-knowledge.[34]

Men could pursue this ideal by being either a hermit or an anchorite, but women, because they supposedly needed protection, had to become anchorites. In England, the anchoritic life was particularly appealing to women. As Warren concludes in her study of anchorites in England, "Women were anchorites more commonly than men throughout the entire period, but the degree to which this was true varied considerably from century to century. In the twelfth century there is a rat... of about five women to three men; in the thirteenth century about four to one; in the fourteenth century about five to two; in the fifteenth, about five to three again. . . . Thirteenth-century anchoritism was both a growing phenomenon and one with an increasingly feminine bias."[35] In the period in which the AB texts were written, records tell us of 198 known anchorites at 175 sites, 123 of whom were known to be women.[36] Anchorites came from a variety of classes and circumstances, but Warren tell us that "in the main, male anchorites tended to be clerical and female anchorites lay. . . . Only 2 of the 123 female anchorites known for the thirteenth century can with confidence be counted as former nuns."[37] While many of the female recluses of the twelfth century came primarily from the upper classes—a reflection, as Warren tells us, of the upper-class woman's reaction to the Normanization of the country—anchoresses of the thirteenth century came from the upper and middle classes. Furthermore, servants of anchoresses often took over anchorholds after their mistresses' deaths. Warren tells us, "Thirteenth-century data not only yield aristocratic women as anchoresses but reveal one who was the sister of the lord of the town, another who was the daughter of a cordwainer, and another who was the niece of a yeoman."[38] Most were maidens, but some were widows who preferred the anchoritic life to remarriage.[39]

Theological sources, especially letters, tell us that generally a woman could not decide on her own to pursue the anchoritic life, nor was anchoritism a profession that she could enter easily. Her credentials were carefully scrutinized, not only by her own superior, the prioress or abbess, but also by that woman's superior, a priest or bishop. In a letter to a nun at the convent of St. Marie de Troyes who wished to become an anchoress, St. Bernard emphasizes that a woman with such desires had to be highly recommended for her asceticism.[40] Even then, she might not qualify. St. Bernard urges the nun to put aside her desire to be an anchoress, arguing that she will be more subject to sin in an anchorhold than in a convent in which she is checked by her superiors and companions. Furthermore, St. Bernard argues, the woman is running away from her responsibility to overcome the temptations and petty angers so often found in convent life. The restriction of approval to become an anchoress to those with successful convent experience was not always necessary—at least not for women who entered the anchorhold from secular life. Christina of Markyate and Julian of Norwich all entered anchorholds without prior convent experience. Nuns who wished to be anchoresses may well have faced greater restrictions than the lay women who desired such a life.

Women who chose the anchoritic life were ultimately under the control of the bishop, who first ruled on their personal qualifications, scrutinized their finances, performed the rite of enclosure, and then supervised them for a number of years.[41] Thirteenth-century episcopal legislators in their synodal statutes address two issues repeatedly: the hasty establishment of underendowed anchorholds and the large number of sexual transgressions among anchorites.[42] Men were warned not to allow women into their cells at night; women were warned not only against visitors but against the dubious morality of their own advisors.[43]

Anchoresses not only had to meet the ascetic ideals of the episcopate upon entrance into an anchorhold, but also had to prove their financial stability. The anchoress was sometimes self-supporting, but in most cases she was supported in a variety of ways, including alms generated from bequests, anniversary arrangements and indulgences, pensions from lay individuals and from ecclesiastical officials, and regular alms or corrodies from religious houses. Sometimes the anchoress received more alms than she needed, and then she acted as a benefactress herself, an activity that both Ailred of Rievaulx and the author of the *Ancrene Wisse* warn against. In addition to alms, many anchoresses were supported by royalty who provided regular payments, usually amounting to a penny a day, the average wage earned by a manual laborer. Often the anchoress received goods such as beer, bread, or firewood instead of money.

Those who were considered suitable by the authorities, then, were women who were both exceedingly devoted to contemplation and considered well-balanced and responsible. The *Ancrene Wisse* praises the three anchoresses of the Deerfold for just these qualities.[44] Once a woman chose the anchoritic life, she faced further restrictions. Unlike male hermits who could set up hermitages wherever they chose, dismantle them when they wished to change residence, and live as far from civilization as they desired, the anchoress, like any woman of this period, was not allowed to wander far from the observation of men. Therefore, anchoresses were forced to set up their anchorholds near cities, and that dwelling became their permanent residence.

Female anchorholds most often consisted of a room or rooms attached to a church.[45] Usually the women were boarded up or bricked into these rooms and the mass for the dead was said over their door. Warren describes the following, probably typical, twelfth-century pontifical service for enclosure:

> The barefoot postulant lies prostrate in the church (in the west end if female, at the entrance to the choir if male, and in mid-choir if a cleric). Two clerks recite the litany while the bishop (or his appointed delegate) and his entourage bless the candidate with holy water and incense. The postulant then receives two lighted tapers. One is given to him by a priest, the other by someone he himself has chosen. The tapers and their bestowers represent the love of God and of one's neighbor. There is a scriptural reading. Then, while the sponsors of the postulant lead him to the foot of the altar, the clergy chant the *Veni creator*. Kneeling at the altar the postulant recites the verse *Suscipe me Domine* three times and then places his tapers in a candelabra on the altar. Following an explication of the scriptural text by a priest, the congregation is invited to pray for the individual who is about to become enclosed, the *recludendus*. A mass of the Holy Spirit is then celebrated. If the postulant is himself a priest, he may be the celebrant. After the mass the recluse is conducted to his reclusorium while the entourage chants antiphons and psalms drawn from the Office of the Dead; the reclusorium is sanctified with holy water and incense. The officiant then proceeds with the Office of extreme unction followed by prayers for the dying. Now the recluse enters the house; the officiant sprinkles him with a little dust to

the continued singing of the antiphons and psalms; all then withdraw save the priest, who remains with the recluse to tell him to rise and to live by obedience. On the emergence of the officiant the command is given to block up the door of the house: *Obstruant hostium domus.* Two final prayers are said and all then depart in peace.[46]

In one enclosure ceremony, the anchoress is carried into the anchorhold in a coffin while the mass for the dead is sung for her.

Anchorholds varied in size and arrangement. Often they were single-celled dwellings built into the side of a church, but sometimes the anchorhold was built for a group of anchoresses and they therefore contained a number of rooms. As this fact indicates, although anchoresses usually lived alone, they sometimes lived in groups. The three anchoresses for whom the *Ancrene Wisse* was written shared a group of rooms which included their own bedrooms as well as servants' quarters that housed two maids and a kitchen boy. Sometimes the anchorhold was a group of adjoining cells separated from the church. Some had kitchens, servants' quarters, sanitation rooms, and gardens. A set of early rules for anchorites set out the following specifications:

> Within the interior of a convent or attached to a church there was to be a room twelve feet square which communicated with the world through three narrow windows. One window was to look into the church and through it the recluse could watch mass, receive communion, speak with his [or her] confessor . . . A second window was for service: through it food and other necessities for his [or her] living was provided. A third, to allow light was to be covered with a horn.[47]

Some anchorholds included an enclosed garden or servants' quarters. Some anchorholds were very small: "One excavated at Letherhead church in Surrey was eight feet square and its window into the church was twenty-one inches square. A cell at Compton, also in Surrey, had a cubicle 6'8" by 4'4" plus a loft where the anchorite slept."[48]

Daily anchoritic life is hard to reconstruct. The most detailed description of a female recluse's experiences that remains from this date is that of Christina of Markyate.[49] Christina was both a nun and a recluse at various times in her life. Although she is by no means a typical anchoress, her early life as a recluse was anchoritic. We can discern from her story that she was motivated to adopt the reclusive life both because of her strong sense of vocation and because of her equally strong desire to escape the marriage her parents wished her to make. After escaping from her parents and her would-be husband, Christina lived for many years in a cell adjoining that of Roger the Hermit. Under his guidance, she led an extremely ascetic life.

Roger protected her from her family and from the religious establishment, who, influenced by her parents, initially refused to admit her vocation. As an anchoress, Christina suffered many physical indignities. Her Latin *Vita* describes the toads that infested her cell. She suffered from thirst and from extremes of heat and cold and had to wait until nightfall to crawl out of her cell to urinate so as not to disturb Roger's meditations. Because most anchoresses did not need the direct male protection Roger the Hermit provided Christina, they may not have suffered such excruciating physical indignities, but the emotional pressure of physical confinement and virtual solitude must have been considerable for any anchoress, as it was for Christina. Furthermore, partly because she was so continuously subject to the scrutiny and criticism of men, an anchoress, like Christina, no doubt would feel continual pressure to prove herself to male authorities as worthy of the reclusive life through an extreme asceticism far in excess of that of her male counterparts.

Christina's life testifies to the strength of religious vocation among women. Despite the physical hardships Christina experienced for many years, she longed for such a life. She felt her vocation when she was a young child but had to overcome the resistance to it both of her parents and of the religious establishment. Christina's parents tried to force her into marriage by locking her into a room with her suitor. In this story, we see a dramatized representation of the choice women faced between a secular husband and betrothal to Christ. Given the vanity, self-interest, and insensitivity of her suitor, Christina's choice of Christ as her betrothed seems logical. Christina's life also dramatizes another Christian maxim, common in religious texts, that a recluse should "forget thy people." Christina had to escape both her family and her would-be husband. Her need to escape her family was only the beginning of her problems, however, because, without the approval of the male religious establishment, she was unable to lead her chosen religious life openly. Once accepted by Archbishop Thurstan of York, Christina was able to pursue a rigorous ascetic and politically powerful life, although she was still unable to make official her religious profession until nineteen years after her professed vow of virginity. Average anchoresses were presumably not interested in or capable of such political notoriety, since no record of their lives or even of their deaths remain. We may surmise, however, that they, too, must have felt that the strength of their vocations outweighed both the difficulties they faced in establishing an anchorhold and the difficulties they endured within it.

It is possible that Christina's life was written in part to provide women with a model for the pursuit of the reclusive life. Although female saints' lives were popular during this period, manuscript evidence suggests that Christina's life is one of the earliest lives written in post-Conquest England to celebrate the life of an English female recluse. The story of Christina's life provided a model both for women wishing to leave their families, and for women who were discouraged by the local religious establishment from following a religious path. Her life shows how women, despite the considerable restrictions imposed upon them by the Norman regime, nonetheless could maintain autonomy. Christina's life both justifies and celebrates the female anchoritic life.

Most anchoresses, of course, led a less varied—and consequently less exciting—life than Christina. The routine of the anchorhold is difficult to recover, but the one prescribed by the author of the *Ancrene Wisse* suggests that life there was akin to life in a nunnery; it included the alternation of prayer, divine service, reading, and manual labor. Ailred of Rievaulx, in his guide to the reclusive life written for his sister, objects to the anchoress's involvement in activities other than contemplation.[50] From his complaint we learn indirectly that an anchoress often busied herself with a variety of chores not directly related to contemplation. He forbids the anchoress to weave or embroider, to make her own clothes, to grow her own food, or to sell her handiwork. Many anchoresses, then, were far from idle. The anchoress's primary occupation, however, was contemplation. The anchoresses of the *Wisse,* for example, were praised for their rigorous life and were criticized only for being overly conscientious, thereby risking the possibility of pride.

Paradoxically, those who had chosen to become dead to the world were often those most alive to its temptations. Ailred's letter suggests that women pursuing the anchoritic life often failed to maintain its strict and isolating rigor. He warns his sister not to succumb to the contemptible behavior of some anchoresses who became local gossips and business dealers, or who were absorbed by their interests in spinning, in food and drink, or even in the company of men.[51] Even women following the less ascetic routine of convent life were sorely tempted to abandon chastity. The scandal involving a nun of Watton, who became pregnant by a monk who shared her double monastery, is an outstanding example of what must not have been an uncommon event.[52] In fact, the collapse of morality in double monasteries and convents was later used as a reason for closing those establishments. Later the buildings were reopened for men only or were redesigned as male colleges.

Those nuns who overcame these more obvious temptations still faced the problem of structuring their time within the anchorhold. Nuns were specifically warned about *acedia,* or the sin of Sloth, in the wake of long hours of unvaried convent routine.[53] The nun had less to fear in this respect than the anchoress, however, for the nun was busy with the complex maintenance of the convent. The anchorhold, on the other hand, did not require such care. The very freedom from responsibility that an anchoress gained by entering an anchorhold might lead her into unexpected spiritual dangers. Without the responsibilities of caring for the anchorhold or contributing to production within it, the anchoress could face many idle hours and therefore had to be especially conscious of her susceptibility to sloth and the despair that results from it.

The one occupation that was encouraged as an alternative to daily prayers was reading. Books therefore must have played a very important part in the life of the anchoress. Her daily reading probably included the rule she followed, the Bible, saints' lives, sermons, and other religious tracts. Her reading was limited, however, by her limited training in Latin, for, as we have noted, most evidence suggests that women of this period could rarely read little more than a smattering of Latin. The Herefordshire anchoresses for whom the *Ancrene Wisse* was written presumably had a scanty knowledge of Latin, since the author chose to write his rule for them in English rather than Latin. Also, we know that nuns in the area a generation later knew very little Latin, because in 1277 Bishop Cantilupe wrote to the nuns at Limebrook in Herefordshire in Latin, but he expected them to find a translator: "You are to cause this our letter to be expounded to you several times in the year by your penancers in the French or English tongue, whichever you know best."[54] Among the limited vernacular texts available to women were the popular French romances, and that the anchoresses were at least familiar with popular romance is suggested by the *Wisse* author's reference to them.[55] The probable lack of Latin proficiency among anchoresses suggests a need that English works addressed to their circumstances and concerns be written for them. The centrality of reading and contemplation in the anchoritic life to the exclusion of all other activities might well have contributed to a woman's desire to pursue such a life. Given all the other options available to women at this time—marriage without choice, the risks of childbirth, political activity that often led to imprisonment or death, entrance into a nunnery suffering from poverty and overly fastidious male supervision—surely an anchorhold offered women not only the negative freedom from these other options, but also the positive advantage of having a room of her own. An anchorhold offered a woman privacy, autonomy, and the opportunity to develop her mind. Clearly, the anchorhold was a positive space for women of this period.

A view of an anchorhold as a liberating alternative for women is, of course, subject to a number of criticisms. To begin with, the anchoress was very much under the control of men. Priests visited her often to administer the sacrament and to admire her asceticism—visits riddled with danger of sexual temptation, as the *Wisse* author points out. Furthermore, the intellectual freedom to be found in the contemplative life was extremely limited. First, women without Latin could not learn from or participate in the extensive theological debates of the age. A few exceptional women did engage in scholastic debate—Heloise is the foremost example—but such involvement was rare for the anchoress. Second, whatever intellectual stimulation women did find through Christian contemplation was limited by the nature of Christianity itself, a religion that was both liberating for and oppressive to women. I shall turn to this subject in the next chapter.

We have seen, then, that anchoritism, although a demanding and rigorous form of the ascetic life, was an attractive option for women. Establishing an anchorhold of her own gave a woman an economic security and an intellectual and emotional structure unavailable to her either in marriage or in the convents. The mental space that contemplation opened up for these women also created a need for guides to that contemplation. The potential richness and variety of the mental life offered by the anchorhold inspired the great majority of texts written for and by women in this period. How that literature addressed the needs of the female anchorite, how that literature relates to the continuity of English prose, and how that literature responded to the new focus on the self generated by the twelfth-century renaissance—these are the subjects of the chapters to come.

CHAPTER 3

Medieval Views
of Female Spirituality

The anchorhold, primarily a woman's space, and one both physical and psychological in nature, gave women unusual opportunities but also posed particular problems. The psychological dimension was defined in part by the nature of Christianity itself. Christianity, as an ideology, was far from gender-neutral. The fact that the anchoress was not only a contemplative but also female meant that her spiritual role was circumscribed by her femininity. The AB authors' understanding of a woman's spiritual role— and probably the female contemplative's understanding of herself as well—was thus heavily influenced by contemporary views of the relationship between gender and spirituality. To understand the nature of AB authors' investigation of female spirituality, we must consider how medieval views of women in general shaped medieval notions of female spirituality.

Medieval views of female spirituality were influenced by classical attitudes toward both the soul and the body. The Middle Ages inherited two opposing views of the nature of the soul, the Platonic view of the soul as gender-neutral and the Aristotelian view of the soul as gender-determined. To Plato, the body was a hindrance to the freedom of the soul, but was relatively unimportant in comparison to the sexually undifferentiated soul.[1] For Plato, it was excellence, or virtue, that mattered above all, and virtue was viewed as equally available to both men and women, although it was more often found in men than women.[2] Aristotle, on the other hand, was much more interested in the body and believed that sexual differentiation was a primary distinction among individuals. That differentiation was more than merely physical to Aristotle, and his misogynistic views of women's physical nature extended to the nature of their souls as well. Conceiving of the soul as possessing nutritive, sensitive or appetitive, and reasonable faculties, Aristotle saw women's souls as deficient in all three aspects but especially in the faculty of reason.

Biblical commentators thus inherited a dual concept of women's souls. In general, the eastern and western Church Fathers, respectively, followed the Platonic and Aristotelian lines of thought.[3] Christian discussions of the nature of the soul focused on the gender attribution of the human soul at creation and at resurrection. The eastern Father, Gregory of Nyssa, for example, argued for the gender neutrality of the soul after death. The western Church Fathers, particularly Augustine, while adopting some Platonic ideas, in the end assumed sexual differentiation of the soul.

Whatever the patristic view of the soul, however, the Church Fathers were less divided about the nature of the body, which in general they viewed as the bestial aspect of human beings that drew them away from God.[4] More often than not, the carnal was closely associated with the feminine. Thus, in discussions of the nature of the feminine, Christian commentators adopted Aristotelian rather than Platonic views of the body, primarily because Aristotle had written extensively about the nature of the female body. Thus, although neo-Platonism allowed for the possibility that a woman's soul was not by nature dissimilar to a man's soul, and although some theologians argued for the equality of souls after death, Aristotelian biological views of women combined with Galenic and Hippocratic views of the nature of the female body dominate medieval thought so completely that even positive inquiries into the nature of a woman's soul as an image of God were qualified by Aristotelian misogyny. In order to see how such attitudes may have affected not only the images of women presented in religious works written for women, but also the style of these works, I shall survey briefly the essential features of these views.

Thirteenth-century views of a woman's role in spiritual life were determined by the dominant scholastic synthesis of Aristotelian biological views and biblical commentaries on Genesis. Because Aristotle's works were not readily available until the thirteenth century, it is generally assumed that Aristotle had little direct influence on medieval theology until the time of the faculty of theology at the University of Paris. However, those who have investigated the rediscovery of Aristotle in the West have been concerned primarily with the rediscovery of Aristotelian logic. It was Aristotle's philosophical writings that were lost, not his biological writings. We need not look to Paris for a source for Aristotelian thought, because Aristotelian concepts of femininity were inculcated in Christianity from an early date. Whereas the eastern patristic influence was primarily Platonic, western Christian thought showed an inherent bias towards Aristotelianism.[5]

Aristotle's medical views were fundamental to the development of medieval views of female spirituality because they defined women first and foremost through their bodies. Aristotle's reproductive theory associated women with matter.[6] For example, he wrote, "The female always provides the material, the male that which fashions it, for this is the power that we say they each possess, and this is what is meant by calling them male and female."[7] Moreover, a woman's primary impulse is "a desire for completion by intercourse with the male."[8] A female child is simply a defective, incomplete male child; as Ian Maclean summarizes the Aristotelian argument, "Nature would always wish to create the most perfect thing, which is the most completely formed, the best endowed with powers of procreation, and the hottest. Such a creature is the male, who implants his semen in the female to the end of procreating males. If, however, there is some lack of generative heat, or climactic conditions are adverse, then creation is not perfected and a female results."[9] These Aristotelian reproductive views, in conjunction with Galenic views, dominated medieval medical theory. Although Galen argued for the existence and efficacy of female semen, Galen's views are otherwise in keeping with Aristotelian misogyny: "In Aristotelian and Galenic terms, woman is less fully developed than man. Because of lack of heat in generation, her sexual organs have remained internal, she is incomplete, colder and moister in dominant humors."[10]

The association of women with matter, as well as with cold, moist humors, led to psychological and ethical conceptions of women which persist to this day. Because women were believed to have less body heat, they were also believed to have less courage, liberality, and moral strength.[11] It is important to recognize that in Aristotle and in subsequent medieval views, women are defined not by opposition or by otherness but by deprivation, a conceptualization which has determined the dualities traditionally associated with men and women: "active/passive, form/matter, act/potency, perfection/imperfection, completion/incompletion, possession/deprivation."[12]

These defining characteristics led Aristotle to ethical conclusions about a woman's role in public life. He argued, in his *Politics*, that because men have greater reasoning powers than women, they have a natural right to rule women.[13] The physiological differences Aristotle identifies in women led him to argue that women also possess a diminished capacity for moral virtue.[14] Men, because they are rational, are therefore free to engage in abstract mental processes from which women are excluded. A woman's "assumed frailty of body, which best befits her for the care of the young and makes her unsuited to exposure to the dangers of the outside world, is accompanied by mental and emotional weaknesses which are the natural justification for her exclusion from public life, responsibility, and moral fulfillment."[15]

Aristotle's reproductive theories further determined his view of a woman's character. Assumptions about female character have their roots in the following passage from Aristotle's *Historia Animalium:*

> With all other animals the female is softer in disposition than the male, is more mischievous, less simple, more impulsive, and more attentive to the nurture of the young; the male, on the other hand, is more spirited than the female, more savage, more simple and less cunning. . . . The fact is, the nature of man is the most rounded off and complete and consequently in man the qualities or capacities above referred to are found in their perfection. Hence woman is more compassionate than man, more easily moved to tears, at the same time is more jealous, more querulous, more apt to scold and to strike. She is furthermore more prone to despondency and less hopeful than the man, more void of shame or self-respect, more false of speech, more deceptive and of more retentive memory.[16]

That women are by nature talkative, compassionate, and cunning are commonplaces in Christian discussions of the Fall.

Another central psychological characteristic attributed to women by Aristotle was changeability, resulting from a woman's menstrual cycle. Because women have uteruses (from the Greek *hysteria*), they were expected to behave hysterically, and hysteria and weakness of mind were viewed as natural to women. Moreover, as previously noted, the humors, as seats of psychological characteristics, were implicated when women were seen as less spirited and subject to mental changeability and inconstancy. Softer flesh also predisposed women to psychological softness and, because they were weaker in rationality, they were also more subject to the passions. The idea of softness led Isidore of Seville (d. 636) to the following etymological explanation of the genders: "Vir nuncupatus, quia maior in eo vis est quam in feminis: unde et virtus nomen accepit . . . Mulier vero a mollite. . . . ideo virtus maxima viri, mulieris minor." ("He is called 'man' because there is greater 'strength' in him than in women; whence 'virtue' takes its name. . . . But 'woman' comes from 'softness' . . . therefore there is greater virtue in man and less in woman.")[17]

Later writers refined the Aristotelian views about softness and moistness in women, in conjunction with Hippocratic notions about the effects of the humors, leading to the additional association of women with moisture, and especially with blood and tears. As Bullough summarizes, "The author of the Hippocratic work entitled *Regimen,* for example, taught that females were more inclined to water than men, and so grew from foods, drink and pursuits that were cold, moist and gentle."[18] Excess moisture further reinforced a woman's association with desire, for, to commentators such as Adelard of Bath, humidity in women caused desire.[19] Menstruation and coitus were seen as cleansing operations necessary to reduce excess moisture. In addition, all excess moistures, whether blood, milk, tears or semen, were seen as physiologically equivalent.[20] This excess moisture defined not only physiological characteristics, but also psychologically determined behavior.

Aristotelian definitions of women, along with Galenic and Hippocratic theories of the humors, were crystalized and developed in Christian theological commentary on women. The texts crucial for medieval views of women were Genesis, the Pauline epistles, and the Gospel accounts of women, although Old Testament women, especially Judith, were often singled out as additional role models for women. The nature of woman was developed particularly in discussions of Genesis, for the relationship between man and God that is represented in the creation story was seen as extending to the relationship between man and woman. As Maclean writes, "The 'spiritual signification' (or anagogical meaning) of sex difference lies in the parallel between woman and the soul and man and the Godhead."[21]

Theologians commented on the two versions of the creation story—one which states that "God created man, male and female he created them," and the other, which describes how God first created Adam from soil and then created Eve from Adam's rib. Although some theologians did consider the egalitarian possibilities inherent in the earlier story, most often they subordinated the earlier account to the later one. Although the second story, in which Eve was created in Paradise, allowed some theologians to argue in favor of woman's inherent perfection, most theologians focused rather on Eve's role in the Fall and on the implications of that behavior for the nature of women generally. Theologians commenting on Genesis generally agreed that because Eve was created from Adam's rib, she was associated with the body rather than with the head and that she was naturally subordinate to men. The association of women with the body persisted in later medieval glosses, where "Man is the *spiritus* (masc.), the higher rational soul, woman the *anima* (fem.), the lower sensible soul."[22] Isidore of Seville carried forward Aristotle's reproductive theory, also associating women with matter. As he wrote in the *Etymologies*, "She is called 'mother' . . . because from her something is effected; for mother is the matter, father the cause."[23] Bonaventure also based his discussion of reproduction on Aristotelian ideas. Although Bonaventure followed Galen rather than Aristotle in adopting the idea that both men and women have reproductive seeds, that of the father and that of the mother, he nonetheless sustained the idea that a woman's contribution is matter alone, writing, "The former acts as 'efficient' cause of conception, the latter as 'material' cause."[24] Biblical interpretations of the implications of Eve's creation from the rib of Adam thus reasserted Aristotelian notions of the material nature of woman.

Because Eve was associated with matter, she also became linked with sense perception. This idea was developed by Philo, who, as Bullough comments, "defined the female as inferior to the male since the female represented sense perception, while the male represented the rational soul."[25] Discussions of the Fall elaborated the essential sensuality of women. To Ambrose, for example, "The serpent symbolizes lust (*delectatio corporalis*); woman represents sense perception (*sensus*); man is intelligence (*mens*)."[26]

Aristotelian concepts of a woman's inferior, appetitive, and irrational nature were extended by Pauline injunctions about a woman's natural position. For Paul, the fact that Eve was made from Adam's rib seemed a multivalent symbol indicating that Adam is the head, Eve the body; Adam the authority, Eve the follower. As Paul wrote: "But I would have you know that the head of every man is Christ and the head of the woman is man and the head of Christ is God," and "Let the woman learn in silence with all subjection. But I suffer not a woman to teach nor to usurp authority over the man but to be in silence. For Adam was first formed, and then Eve."[27] Women's submission and lack of authority were thus deemed to be necessary consequences of her status in creation. A woman's lack of authority also extended to her use of language, partly because of Eve's garrulity in the temptation scene and partly because Adam was put in the special position of naming things: he had been given a privileged power over language.

This kind of allegorical explanation of a woman's nature further shaped medieval attitudes toward the nature of a woman's mind. As Maclean points out, "Another biblical text associated with Genesis 2:21 is 1 Pet 3:7 (woman the weaker vessel) from which scholastics deduce diminished mental powers (especially reason) in the female."[28] Women, as followers of Eve, the weaker vessel, were thus viewed as weak, changeable, willful, irrational and lacking in control. The Church Fathers elaborated these views. For example, as Ferrante summarizes, "Throughout the *Moralia* Gregory personifies the mind, which he connects with Job's wife, as female because it is changeable, easily alarmed and agitated and open to surprise and deception. . . . . The minds of men who serve God with yielding purpose are, he says, not undeservedly called women (III, 40), whereas those who follow the ways of the Lord with firm and steady steps are men (XXVIII, 12). The mind is the door-keeper of the soul; if it is female, that is given to carnal thoughts, it allows evil to enter. (III, 61)"[29]

Eve's temptation by the devil, as well as the punishment she received, was closely linked to Eve's association with the body. Her temptation by the devil was successful because of her irrational, appetitive sensuality.[30] In addition, a woman's punishment to bear children in pain was seen as a logical consequence of her bodily nature. Unlike Adam, who received a punishment which was divorced from his body and was therefore gender-neutral, Eve and therefore all women, because of their perceived inherent bodiliness, received a gender-determined punishment. Carrying forward Aristotelian notions of essential female nature, commentators also argued that, because of the Fall, women not only suffer the pains of childbirth but also experience continual sexual desire for the male.[31]

All women were seen by these writers as subject to the curse of Eve and as inheriting her fault. As Tertullian wrote, "Do you not realize, Eve, that it is you? The curse God pronounced on your sex weighs still on the world. Guilty, you must bear its hardships. You are the devil's gateway, you desecrated the fatal tree, you first betrayed the law of God, you softened up with your cajoling words the man against whom the devil could not prevail by force."[32] Temptation and seduction were specifically associated with woman's speech. Furthermore, the Fall allowed theologians to develop a model of woman that emphasized her capacity for suffering, her endurance, and her passivity. To Bonaventure, for example, "Man is oriented to action, while woman bears suffering better; but in human life leadership belongs to action rather than to suffering."[33] Because she endured suffering, woman was also by nature more compassionate. As daughters of Eve, all women were alleged to inherit Eve's rootedness in the body, her incapacity for theory, and her dependence on the senses.

Because commentators were divided about the nature of a woman's soul, her spiritual potential was a matter for debate. Augustine's influential commentaries, especially on Genesis, exhibited a tension between neo-Platonic egalitarianism and Aristotelian misogyny.[34] On the one hand, Augustine interpreted the creation myth in Aristotelian terms, concluding, as he does in his essay, "On Continence," that where woman may be said to symbolize the flesh, man symbolizes reason. In "On the Trinity," he suggests that woman symbolizes appetite, the portion of the human mind that should be controlled by reason, whereas man symbolizes reason itself.[35]

On the other hand, Augustine sometimes supports a Platonic and gender-neutral ideal of the soul, except that spiritual freedom from gender determination does not affect a woman's earthly role. As Rosemary Reuther writes, Augustine attempts to distinguish "between what woman is, as a rational spirit (in which she is equivalent to the male), and what she 'symbolizes' in her bodily nature, where she stands for . . . that debasing carnality that draws the male mind down from its heavenly heights. But he thinks that what she thus symbolizes, in the eye of male perception, is also what she 'is' in her female nature."[36] A woman's experience of spirituality was thus inevitably intertwined with the experiences of the body. As Tavard summarizes Augustine's position: "As souls, both man and woman are equally the image of God. As bodies, however, only the man is made in the image, for only he expresses in his body the power and superiority of God, the female body expressing, on the contrary, passivity and inferiority. Thus, man experiences no conflict between his soul and his body from the point of view of being God's image, whereas woman is caught in a permanent squeeze between her soul—image of God—and her body, which cannot image God."[37] Given these attributes, how was a woman in the religious life expected to perceive her spiritual role?

These negative notions of the nature of woman are mitigated to some extent by the redeeming figure of Mary. The fact that Mary was historical allows the possibility that actual women have redemptive power.[38] Mary offers a model of a woman who redeems the physical in women because, as Ferrante puts it, "She was able to bear fruit, physically as well as spiritually, body and soul."[39] Yet, because Mary is extraordinary and unique, "alone of all her sex," as Marina Warner calls her, ultimately she can do little to alter conceptions of a woman's essential nature. Unlike Eve and all other women, Mary is not defined by her body. As a model for women, therefore, she cannot help women overcome the problems of their femininity; rather, she offers a model for behavior that can only mitigate rather than alter that essential nature. Mary has been seen as the antithesis of Eve: where Eve was garrulous, Mary was silent; where Eve was disobedient, Mary was obedient and submissive; where Eve suffered in childbirth, Mary did not. Thus, a woman can never rise above her body as did Mary, who gave birth "without breach" and conceived without sin, but she can at least imitate Mary's silence and obedience. She can follow Mary in humility, obedience, silence, modesty, prudence, and mortification as well as in compassion and endurance of suffering.

While Mary may have provided a model of behavior for women, her image did little to alter male views of woman's essential nature. As Bynum

points out, the fact that Mary did not figure prominently in female meditative works suggests the lack of range of meditative possibilities opened up
by this unique, essentially unwomanly figure, and indicates that Mary actually offered women little in the way of a redemptive model.[40]

It might be argued, and often was, that women could transcend their
sensual natures through virginity. An anchoress might be turned to as one
who, because of her chosen life, need not contend with the sins of Eve. As
Warner writes, "Through virginity and self-inflicted hardship, the faults of
female nature could be corrected."[41] Some medieval biblical commentators
lauded virginity as a state which allowed women virtually to alter their
gender—that is, as Jerome writes, "As long as woman is for birth and
children, she is different from man as body is from soul. But if she wishes
to serve Christ more than the world, then she will cease to be a woman and
will be called a man."[42] To many commentators, progress for women
"meant giving up the female gender, that is, the passive, corporeal and
sense perception, for the male gender that is the active, incorporeal and
rational thought."[43]

More often than not, however, for the woman in the spiritual life, virginity was not a means of escaping her femininity, but rather was the ultimate fulfillment of her femininity. Female saints, for example, models of
virginity, often exhibited Aristotelian female characteristics. As Bynum
observes, "Both men and women saw female saints as models of suffering
and inner spirituality, male saints as models of action."[44] The preservation
of chastity was indeed the central issue of these female saints. Yet the very
centrality of this issue raises some questions about a woman's ability to
transcend her bodily nature. In most male saints' lives, where sexual temptation might be one problem for the male contemplative, it was subordinated in a progressive series of temptations, usually culminating in a temptation to pride. In female saints' lives, sexual temptation was either the
saint's sole or her central temptation. The preservation of virginity, then,
was not presented in women's lives as a means to transcend the demands
of the flesh, as it was in men's, but rather as a reflection of the view that a
woman's sanctity was intimately connected with her sexual identity. Male
biographers, according to Bynum, "were also far more likely to attribute
sexual or bodily temptation to female nature than to male (men's sexual
yearnings could always be blamed on the presence of women as temp-
tresses) and to see women struggling unsuccessfully to overcome the
flesh."[45] The centrality of sexual temptation in female saints' lives thus
reflected the prevalent view of women as bound by their fundamentally
guilty sexual natures. Unlike men who could climb an allegorical ladder to

God and thereby transcend the body, women remained rooted in their bodies.

Physicality was not only a woman's problem, however, it was also her solution. Physical suffering was the primary corrective to sexual tempta-tion.[46] Through fasting, a woman's sinful body could be controlled: "Fast-ing, like chastity, was prescribed for both sexes; but, like virginity, fasting has a particular character in women that enhances the symbolism of whole-ness and purity."[47] Indeed, for many women, fasting did help erase their essential femininity by impeding menstruation. Even so, despite the tri-umphs of virginity and fasting (indeed, perhaps because of them) the fe-male contemplative was expected to be continually aware of her body. A woman's spiritual experience was thus determined by a self-consciousness about the body, rather than by a transcendence of it.

Aristotelian views of women, as crystallized in Christian commentaries on Genesis, also suggested that women had a different experience of desire than men. Because man was created in the image of God, while woman was created from the rib of Adam, man's fundamental motivation was de-sire for God, but women's primary motivation was desire for man. Thus, in the contemplative life, women's spiritual desire was concretized. Bynum has written extensively on the importance of the humanization of Christ for female contemplation. That importance stems in part from these biologi-cally based notions of creation, for, according to these theories, there is no way for a woman to experience God except by experiencing God in his humanity. For women, renunciation of desire is impossible; instead, desire must be transferred to Christ.

Positive accounts of women in both the Old and the New Testaments were utilized in commentary as figures praised primarily for overcoming their essential sensuality. However, more often than not, positive views of women in the Bible were transformed in such a way that their historical reality was ignored and the figures instead became impersonal abstractions. As Ferrante writes,

> Those women to whom the Bible ascribes, instead, great moral strength—Ju-dith, Esther, Ruth—are divested of their human nature by commentators and are made to represent impersonal abstractions like the church; even the bride of the Canticles is identified in early exegesis primarily with the collective church . . . bad women, like Delilah or Potiphar's wife, represent lower human characteris-tics, weaknesses of the flesh; good women stand for impersonal abstractions like the church.[48]

Celebration of the Virgin Mary and the femininity of the image of the bride of Christ became central to exegesis in the twelfth century. St. Bernard's commentary on the Song of Songs, which celebrates the marriage of the soul to God, employs the language of compassion, tenderness, and tears, terms usually associated with women. In some respects this approach represented a feminization of exegesis. Yet, despite its eroticism, this commentary did nothing for actual women; instead, qualities associated with women were appropriated by men. For example, Bernard's celebration of motherhood in his commentaries did not change attitudes toward real motherhood, but, rather allowed Bernard to identify himself as mother to his monks.[49] In his treatment of the marriage metaphor, man stands in relation to God as woman to man. So the writer must identify with the woman, the bride, in his relation to God, the bridegroom. Ferrante comments on Bernard's exegesis:

> Although Bernard speaks here and elsewhere of a love that strongly suggests the physical union of male and female, even at times with sexual overtones, and although he acknowledges our need for the body in order to prepare our spirits to reach salvation (V, i.1), the love he intends us to understand is purely spiritual. Despite his remarks about marriage and his use of sensual imagery, Bernard has no feeling for the love between man and woman. His sermons are written for men, even more narrowly for those men already vowed to a religious life, and his views on women, whether dictated by his audience or by personal preference, do not differ markedly from those of the Gloss.[50]

What implications do these attitudes have for a woman's spiritual role? Bynum argues that the idea that women were not created in God's image was "not absorbed by medieval women . . . as a prohibition of their approach to God."[51] I would argue that, although women were allowed equal access to God, their approach was fundamentally different. We have seen in the previous chapter that a woman's choice to become a recluse was conditioned by the options available to her in secular life and that her experience within the anchorhold was further conditioned by the fact that she was a woman in the religious life. The anchorhold is a specifically feminine space—almost a womb—where women were both severely restricted and unusually free. A woman's experience within that feminine space was also determined by her culture's view of women in general and by women's roles in the spiritual life in particular. Like the space offered to her, these views both circumscribed and liberated the anchoress.

The AB texts specifically address the nature of female spirituality, both proscribing and describing the anchoress's role. Indeed, the AB texts have been thoroughly feminized. As we shall see in discussing the texts, despite her choice to lead a virgin life, a woman's religious experience was very much determined by her reproductive role. In the religious life, woman could not have authority, and she was seen as dominated by desire—biologically. All the AB texts are in effect women's stories—stories of a woman's experience of spirituality, as conceived by men. Such stories differ from men's stories of their own experience not only in a thematic emphasis on sexual temptation and bodily weakness, but also in structure and imagery. These authors believed that a woman must experience spirituality through the body; moreover, she can overcome the body only through the physical and mental resources determined by her female nature. Thus, the writers saw her as needing religious works that addressed her appetitive, changeable, sensual nature. In accommodating women's perceived inferior grasp of reason, the creators of these works used nonteleological structures. The assumption that a woman's nature was sensual led these writers to focus on tactile and sensual images, as well as on other images emphasizing such "female" characteristics as moisture, blood, tears, suffering, endurance, and compassion. In addition, specialized syntax and imagery were employed to lead women toward an emotional and physical realization of religious truths. Intended for the female reader, models such as the three saints' lives focused on sexual temptation, torments of the flesh, and the issue of desire—desire transformed into desire for Christ. All the texts dramatize a woman's literalized marriage to Christ. Thus, medieval attitudes towards female spirituality profoundly affect not only the images of women, but also the style and structure of the works themselves.

CHAPTER 4

The Rule of the Body: The Female Spirituality of the _Ancrene Wisse_

The thirteenth-century Middle English religious guide, the _Ancrene Wisse_ ("Guide for Anchoresses"), is the best known and most highly praised of the AB texts. It is acknowledged for its psychological astuteness, for its unusual imagery, and for the liveliness of its examples, drawn from everyday life. Despite this recognition, the role gender played in the production of this work has never been investigated. The _Ancrene Wisse_ offers an unusual opportunity to investigate the ways in which the existence of a female audience shapes the development of a text, because, unlike many other medieval works, it tells us of its intended audience. The _Wisse_ author, a male cleric, originally wrote his work at the request of three female recluses in Herefordshire, and the writing was later revised to address larger groups of recluses.[1] One of the work's special features, its pragmatic spirituality, therefore derives in part from the author's concern for the precise material circumstances of his female audience. Moreover, the _Ancrene Wisse's_ peculiar style, we shall see, was shaped by its author's culturally determined assumptions about women. The creation of this apparently gender-neutral text, I believe, was governed by its male author's view of women as daughters of Eve, inescapably rooted in their bodies.

Characteristic of the _Ancrene Wisse_ is its quotidian psychological realism, a realism that includes consideration of such varied problems as the anchoress's thoughtless anger at her cook's boy and the spiritual dangers of excessive asceticism. Both Linda Georgianna and Janet Grayson have praised the text's literary and psychological sophistication in exploring such problems.[2] As Georgianna has explained, the author takes a radically new approach to the idea of a religious rule, by emphasizing an inner rule—the right ruling of the unruly heart—over an outer rule focused on instructions about dress, prayer routines, and other external circumstances. Janet Grayson has shown how the _Wisse_ interweaves its discussions of external rules with analyses of inner experience, through the use of imagery which links Christian precepts with illustrations drawn from everyday life. Grayson also notes the fact that the work is structurally innovative, in that it urges the reader to dip into the text at random and to use it only insofar as it applies to everyday experience. This psychologically sophisticated integration of everyday experience with abstract religious precepts permeates the work.

While Georgianna and Grayson have recognized the psychological and literary sophistication of the *Wisse,* they have overlooked the ways in which its psychological specificity is especially tailored for women and, further, the ways in which its spirituality reflects a circumscribed view of women's spiritual potential. The *Ancrene Wisse* is clearly a response first and foremost to the highly specialized needs of the female recluse. Although little is known about the particular women to whom the work was addressed, Dobson has at least been able to identify them conclusively as the three unnamed anchoresses who lived in the anchorhold of the Deerfold near Wigmore Abbey.[3] From the *Wisse* itself, we learn that they were women deeply committed to their profession. That they did not know Latin can be assumed: not only is the book in English, but also every reference and biblical quotation is translated. The intended readers probably could not read Bernard or Hugh of St. Victor, although, given the popularity of these authors in England, it is likely that they knew of them. It might be argued, then, that the author's repeated emphasis on daily life rather than books may be simply the result of his belief that the anchoresses were unfamiliar with books. In any case, as we have seen, the anchoritic life also offered peculiar enticements to the flesh and challenges of socialization; consequently, the anchoress needed a guide appropriate to her circumstances, one that focused with psychological acumen on the pressures and distractions of everyday life. The author's pragmatic treatment of anchoritic life thus derives in part from his sensitivity to the restrictions that life imposed upon women.

More than external circumstances, however, shaped the *Wisse* author's treatment of female anchoritic experience. Clearly the author's understanding of the anchoress's situation—and, indeed, the anchoress's understanding of herself as well—was influenced by the contemporary views of female sexuality which we have just reviewed. The style of the *Ancrene Wisse* reflects its male author's assumption that the spiritual potential of the women for whom he wrote was circumscribed and defined by their femininity. For example, the style of the work is accommodative, emphasizing the temporal and interactive rather than atemporal and static, focusing not on timeless Christian ideals but on the exfoliation of those ideals in daily life. The work also focuses on the personal and the contemporary rather than on the universal and the historical; it is nonteleological, concrete rather than abstract, and practical rather than theoretical. Such stylistic emphases, we shall see, reflect the author's organization of his discussion around his underlying belief that female sexuality leads to the downfall of mankind and that a woman can achieve union with God only by recognizing that her body is responsible for that *poena damni*.

In identifying the *Wisse's* distinctive features, critics have not fully taken into account medieval attitudes toward women. Neglecting what is particular to women, those who have studied the *Wisse* have read the book as if it were written for the general reader. This dismissal of the text's particularities leads critics to study the *Wisse* primarily in terms of its indebtedness to the continental affective movement. Clearly, the psychological sophistication of its exploration of the inner life does reflect the new interest in the self found in works by such writers as Anselm, Abelard, and Bernard. In the English work, the emphasis on feeling falls in line with the Latin affective movement in general.[4] Indeed, Bernardine mysticism, especially the lyricism of the *sponsa christi* motif developed by Bernard in his commentary on the Song of Songs, pervades the text. In a later chapter, I shall consider the specific ways in which twelfth-century theology may have shaped the author's representation of spirituality in the *Ancrene Wisse*.

It is a mistake, however, to characterize the mysticism of these works simply as an outgrowth of the affective movement. Despite affinities with continental mysticism, the *Ancrene Wisse* shows, interestingly enough, as Geoffrey Shepherd notes, a fundamental "aversion from mysticism."[5] Like continental contemplatives, the anchoresses who read the *Wisse* presumably believed that their ultimate goal was union with God. Yet these women were taught that they could achieve such union only through full awareness of the pressures and demands of the world, rather than through a traditional dismissal or denial of such worldliness. Because, as Grayson and Georgianna have discussed, the *Wisse* focuses so insistently on the boundary between inner and outer experience, the outside world is as important as the inner life in the meditative sphere of this English work. Continental affective texts, on the other hand, are primarily concerned with inner meditation. In addition, whereas continental texts take the contemplative from the earth to mystical union with God, the imagery of the *Wisse* constantly draws the attention of the contemplative back to earth. We must look away from the continent for a source of this unusual and particular spirituality.

It might be argued that the pragmatic focus of the *Ancrene Wisse* has more in common with the English tradition—that is, with works written for audiences similarly removed from continental centers of Latin learning—than with continental sources. Like other lay audiences, the anchoresses needed a work that explained Christian precepts in the terms of everyday experience. Indeed, the work's essential "Englishness" has been praised by early critics of the work, although what is particular to its Englishness has never been investigated in any depth.[6] It is possible that part of the *Ancrene Wisse's* representation of a spirituality that emphasizes the integration of the everyday with spiritual goals reflects a characteristically English emphasis. Indeed, Wolfgang Riehle in *The Middle English Mystics* has shown how English mystical works characteristically employ concrete imagery to communicate theological concepts.[7] Yet comparisons of the *Ancrene Wisse* with other English mystical works written for men suggest that there are aspects of the author's representation of spirituality that cannot be accounted for by its English context. *The Cloud of Unknowing*, for example, follows the male mystic's hierarchical ascent to union with God, a progressive ascent that is conspicuously absent from the *Wisse* author's account of spirituality. The exact relationship of the *Ancrene Wisse* to other English works will be considered in a later chapter, but it is important to recognize that the English context in part accounts for its characteristic pragmatism.

The worldly focus of the *Wisse* might be accounted for by the influence of both the affective movement and the English tradition. In addition, it might derive from other continental theological developments rather than from medieval theories about women. Indeed, the text's discussion of the outside world as an appropriate focus for meditation does reflect the Chartrian investigation of God's presence in all things.[8] And the Victorine exploration of the literal interpretation of the Bible also influences the text's emphasis on the physical world.[9] There are indeed many reasons for finding in Victorine thought a major, but hitherto unnoticed, influence on the *Ancrene Wisse*. After all, Wigmore Abbey, the abbey associated with the *Wisse*, was led by Andrew of St. Victor, an abbot who wrote extensively about the need to recover the literal sense of the Bible. Another Victorine whose work is quoted frequently in the *Ancrene Wisse* is Hugh of St. Victor, whose effect on exegesis in general was profound, for his philosophy encouraged exploration of history, archeology, and literary criticism as disciplines necessary for the understanding of the literal sense of the Bible. Because his exegetical techniques suggested that the world itself was particularly worthy of the contemplative's attention, Hugh's emphasis may have had an effect on the attitudes of the *Wisse* author. Both the Victorines and Bernard clearly figured in the *Wisse's* rendering of spiritual goals, but, as we shall see, theoretical assumptions about women ultimately were more important in forming the work's rhetoric and imagery and accounting for the particular character that makes it so very different from mystical works written for men.

The relationship of the *Ancrene Wisse* to both its Anglo-Saxon and its continental contexts is complex; yet, if we look closely at the *Wisse* author's use of continental sources, bearing in mind his consideration of his female audience, we find significant differences between his work and that of continental writers—differences suggesting that his views of female spiritual potential were foremost in his mind. To see some of the ways in which the *Wisse* author's attitudes towards women affected his use of continental sources, let us compare a well-known passage of the *Wisse*—the discussion of the dangers of sight in section 2, "The Custody of the Senses"—to two of its sources: (1) Bernard's exegesis of the dangers of curiosity in chapter 10 of *De Gradibus Humilitatis Superbiae,* and (2) Hugh of St. Victor's commentary on Noah's ark, *De Arca Noe Morali.*[10] All three texts discuss the dangers of sight, with reference to biblical exempla. Although the English passage closely follows both Bernard and Hugh, the differences between the *Wisse* and its sources, which have previously been considered small and insignificant, point to a major difference in the English author's understanding of spirituality. This major difference originates in his view of his audience, in his belief that his women readers, as daughters of Eve, must guard constantly against their sensual willfulness. This willfulness, the English text implies, can be controlled only through confrontation and analysis of the female contemplative's sensual experience of the world. Books and the theories that spring from them— essential as guides for the male contemplative—are seen as peripheral to the female contemplative's meditative frame, both because women have little experience with books and because women's alleged descent from Eve dissociates them from the theoretical realm.

Before considering the *Wisse* author's direct quotation of Bernard, it is important to recognize that Bernard was not unaware of audience need— that is, of his male monastic audience's needs. At the beginning of chapter 9 of his commentary on the Song of Songs, for example, Bernard justifies his exegesis:

> Accedamus iam ad librum, verbisque sponsae rationem demus et consequen-
> tiam. Pendent enim, et praerupta nutant absque principio. Ideoque praemitten-

dum cui competentur cohaereant. (It is time for us to return to the book [the Bible] and attempt an explanation of the words of the bride and their consequence. For there they are, swinging precipitately out of nowhere, suspended before us. But we must see if there is something antecedent to them, to which we may suitably connect them.)[11]

The diversity and sophistication of Bernard's explanations provided his monks with something which they could use to save themselves from what he calls "animi arentis languore atque hebetudine stolidae mentis, quod Dei scilicet alta atque subtilia penetrare nequirent" ("the langor and dryness of the soul, an ineptitude and dullness of mind devoid of the power to penetrate the profound and subtle truths of God").[12]

The *Wisse* author clearly adopted some of Bernard's concerns; he, too, recognized the dangers of routine and dullness of mind. Yet Bernard's different audience, composed of monks who were well trained in both the Bible and a wide range of biblical commentaries, allowed him to utilize references to such works. When Bernard looked for antecedents to which he could connect things, those antecedents could be found in the intellectual world of the monks; he links his words to words of other writers. As we shall see in examining his changes in Bernard's commentaries, the *Wisse* author, when writing for women, also looked for things to connect words to. Sometimes he, too, connects words to the words of other commentators. More often than not, however, he connects words to things—objects or events taken from the everyday experience of the anchoress. The *Wisse* author also was trying to save the anchoress from mental stagnation. For her, however, staleness arose not from overfamiliarity with biblical texts, but rather from the stark and restricted routine of the anchorhold, a routine that precluded access to many of the books known to her male counterpart. Dullness of mind could lead the anchoress to sin by drawing her, paradoxically, out into the world rather than into herself; such external absorption could lead to unease of conscience (an impediment to meditation) and eventually to despair. In order to guide the anchoress to proper meditation, the writer needed to draw the outside world safely into the meditative frame by reinterpreting it for her. Thus, instead of providing the anchoress with antecedents and contexts for words, as Bernard does, the *Wisse* provides spiritual contexts for physical objects and actions. Whereas Bernard leaves the outer world far behind, the *Wisse* redefines the outer world as part of the inner world. The ultimate meditative goal of the two authors may have been the same, but the different audiences dictated radically different methods of reaching that goal.

These general differences in purpose affect, for example, the two authors' otherwise similar exegeses of the dangers of curiosity. The *Wisse* author bases much of his discussion of the anchorhold and its dangers on chapter 10 of *De Gradibus,* which discusses the dangers of sin that begins with the eyes. Both Bernard and the *Wisse* examine this sin by discussing the circumstances, motivations, and results of the actions of three biblical figures, Dinah, Eve, and Lucifer. The most extensive discussion in both is devoted to Dinah and the sin that resulted when Dinah went out to see the strange women. The *Wisse* author's shift from theory to practice is clear in his use of Bernard's exegesis. Lamenting Dinah's actions, Bernard writes:

> Dina namque dum ad pascendos haedos egreditur, ipsa patri, et sua sibi virginitas rapitur. O Dina, quid necesse est ut videas mulieres alienigenas? Qua necessitate? . . . Etsi tu otiose vides, sed non vitiose videris. Tu curiose spectas, sed curiosius spectarius: Quis crederet tunc illam tuam curiosam otiositatem. vel otiasem curiositatem, fore post sic non otiasam, sed tibi, tuis hostibusque tam perniciosam. (PL, 958) (For when Dinah goes out to feed her kids, her father loses her and she loses her virginity. Oh Dinah, why is it necessary for you to see the daughters of the land? What is the need? Even though you see them idly, you are not idly seen. You look curiously, but you are seen curiously. Who would believe that this curious idleness or idle curiosity would not afterwards be idle to you, but would be pernicious to you and your friends and enemies?)

The *Wisse* author begins his passage by quoting Bernard, but he continues by spelling out the dangers that will face the anchoress if she looks out of her anchorhold or allows anyone to visit her:

> Egressa est dyna filia iacob ut videret mulieres ali enigenas. z cetera. A Meiden as dyna het iacobes dohter as hit teleð i Genesy. eode ut to bihalden uncuðe wummen. ʒet ne seið hit nawt þet ha biheold wepmen. Ant hwet come wenest tu of þ bihaldunge? ha leas hire meidenhad z wes imaket hore . . . þus eode ut hire sihðe . . . ant nim þer of ʒeme þ tis uvel of dyna com nawt of þ ha seh sichen emores sune þ ha sunegede wið. ah dude of þ ha lette him leggen ehnen on hire.[13] (Dina, the daughter of Jacob, went out to see the strange women. There is a story told in Genesis of a maiden called Dina, the daughter of Jacob, who went out to look at the strange women. It does not say that she looked at men. What happened, do you think, as a result of that looking? She lost her maidenhood and became a harlot . . . That is what came of her looking . . . And observe that Dina's evil was not the result of seeing Sichem, the son of Hamor, with whom she sinned, but the result of her allowing him to look upon her.)[14]

Bernard uses the biblical reference to Dinah to support his theological argument that the first step in pride is curiosity. The *Wisse* author, on the other hand, has a concrete and immediate purpose, rather than a theological argument, in mind. He is warning the anchoress of the specific danger she faces, losing her virginity, as a result of either looking out her window at men or, alternatively, allowing men to look at her. Dinah is invoked by the *Wisse* author not to provide a biblical context for a discussion of curiosity, but to provide a negative female model for the anchoress. In both the Latin and the English versions, women are blamed for enticing men to rape, but, for the *Wisse* author, this is a danger of which the anchoress immediately must be conscious, for her beauty could entice even a visiting priest. The example thus suggests that women are in peril whether they are the subjects or objects of action. In a reference to Bathsheba, which immediately follows this example in the *Wisse;* the sexual dangers facing women are made even more explicit:

> Alswa Bersabee þurh þ ha unwreah hire idaviðes sihðe. ha dude him sunegin on hire se hali king as he wes z godes prophete. Nu kimeð forð a feble mon. halt him þah ahelich ʒef he haveð a wid hod z a loke cape z wule iseon ʒunge ancres. loki nede ase stan hire wlite him liki. þe naveð nawt hire leor forbearnd i þe sunne.z seið ha mei baldeliche iseon hali men. (Tolkien, 33) (Bethsabee also, by unclothing herself before David's eyes, caused him to sin with her, even though he was so holy a king and a prophet of God. And after all this, a weak man comes forward, thinks himself formidable in his wide hood and closed cloak, and wishes to see some young anchoresses, and must needs look, as if he were made of stone, to see how the beauty of a woman whose face is not burned by the sun pleases him, saying that she may look without fear at holy men. [Salu, 24]

Although men, too, are implicated in the *Wisse* author's censure, women not only are blamed for being vulnerable to sexual sin, but also are held responsible for inspiring it in men. Returning to Dinah, the author concludes his discussion with the following warning:

> ʒe mine leove sustren ʒef ei is anewil to seon ow. ne wene ʒe þer neaver god. ah leveð him þe leasse. Nulle ich þet nan iseo ow bute he habbe of ower meistre spetiale leaue. for alle þe þreo sunnen þ ich spec of least. z al þ uvel of dina þ ich spec of herre. (Tolkien, 33) (Ah, my dear sisters, if anyone insists on seeing you, believe no good of it and trust him the less for it. I do not want anyone to see you without the special leave of your director, for all those three sins I have just spoken of, and all the evil that came about through Dina, of which I spoke above. [Salu, 24])

The English author thus moves his discussion continually out of the realm of the theoretical and historical into that of the practical and immediate. A subtle but significant difference in Bernard and the *Wisse* author's versions is that, whereas Bernard's argument progresses from a biblical event to the general, abstract, and theoretical nature of curiosity, the *Wisse* author avoids the general and returns continually to the immediate, practical concerns of daily life. Furthermore, whereas Bernard asks a rhetorical question of a biblical figure, the *Wisse* author steps out of the context of books by addressing his question directly to the contemporary anchoress, thereby giving his discussion a paternalistic rather than an egalitarian tone. His reference to Dinah is in fact presented as an answer to a hypothetical question posed earlier by the anchoress: "Me leove sire seið sum z is hit nu se over uvel forte totin utwart?" (Tolkien, 31) (" 'But, dear master,' someone may say, 'is it so excessively evil to peep out?' " [Salu, 22]). The female voice that the author here constructs indicates his view of women as naive and further belittles what could otherwise be viewed as a legitimate question. Female logic is thus dismissed in favor of male logic.

A similar shift from the theoretical to the practical occurs in the *Wisse* author's use of Bernard's discussion of Eve. Of Eve's fascination with the apple, Bernard says:

> Quid illo tam crebro vagantia lumina jacis! Quid spectare libet, quod manducare non licet? Oculos, inquis, tendo, non manum. . . . Etsi culpa non est, culpae tamen occasio est et indicium commissae et causa est committendae. (PL, 958– 59) (Why cast wandering glances so frequently hither? Why does sight of it delight thee, when to bite is not allowed thee? It is my eyes, thou sayest, not my hand which I reach out . . . Though it be not a crime, yet it is the occasion of crime, the mark of one committed and the cause of one to be committed.)

The *Wisse* author, on the other hand, allies Eve's experience directly with that of the anchoress, Eve's daughter:

> Of eve ure alde moder is iwriten on alre earst in hire sunne inȝong of hire ehsihðe. . . . Eve biheold o þe forboden eappel. z seh hine feier z feng to deliten iþe bihaldunge. z toc hire lust þer toward. z nom z et þrof. z ȝef hire lauerd. low hu hali writ spekeð. z hu inwardliche hit teleð hu sunne bigon. þus eode sunne bivoren z makede wei to uvel lust.z com þe dede þrefter þæt al moncun ifeleð. þes eappel leove suster bitacneð alle þe wa þ lust falleð to z delit of sunne. Hwen þu bihaldest te mon.þu art in eve point. (Tolkien, 31) (Of Eve, our first mother, it is recorded that at the very beginning of her sin its entry was through her eyes. . . . Eve looked upon the forbidden apple and saw that it was fair, and she began to take delight in looking at it, and to desire it, and she plucked some of it and ate it, and gave it to her lord. Observe how Holy Writ speaks of this, telling how sin began in an inward manner; this inward sin went before and made way for evil desire, and the deed followed, the consequences of which are felt by all mankind. The apple, my dear sister, symbolizes all those things towards which desire and sinful delight turn. When you look upon a man, you are in Eve's case. [Salu, 23])

As in the Dinah sequence, the *Wisse* author places the anchoress in a long line of sinful women. Once again, instead of leading into a discussion of the abstract nature of sin, the biblical example leads directly back to the experiential and to an emphasis on the temporal and interactive rather than the atemporal and static. His discussion of Eve thus reinforces the immediate concern raised in his discussion of Dinah, a concern about the anchoress's susceptibility to the temptation offered by visiting priests.

Although both authors consider temptation from Eve's point of view, for the *Wisse* author, the relationship between Eve and his readers is real rather than theoretical, literal rather than figurative. He presents this hypothetical response to the anchoress:

> Hwerof chalengest tu me. þe eapple þ ich loki on. is forbode me to eotene z nawt to bihalden. þus walde eve inohreaðe habben iondsweret. O mine leove sustren as eve haveð monie dehtren þe folhið hare moder þe ondswerieð o þisse wise. (Tolkien, 32) ("Of what are you accusing me? I am forbidden to eat the apple at which I am looking; I am not forbidden to look at it." Thus Eve would have answered readily enough, my dear sisters, and she has many daughters who, following their mother, answer in the same way. [Salu, 23]

Although the *Wisse* author draws the reader into the experience of sin by recreating a scene of Eve's temptations much like the one in Bernard's exegesis, the *Wisse*'s Eve reference is applied specifically to the daily life of the anchoress by warning her not to look upon a man. Later in the passage, the *Wisse* author makes this connection even clearer by framing another hypothetical question from the anchoress: "Me wenest tu seið sum þ ich wulle leapen on him þah ich loki on him?" (Tolkien, 32) (" 'But do you think,' someone will say, 'that I shall leap upon him because I look at him?' " [Salu, 23]). The author's hypothetical response indicates his assumption that women are unlikely to formulate consequences outside of the immediate and circumstantial; once again, the hypothetical response of the anchoress contains a strong point that is being denied and ruled out of legitimate consideration.

Both authors refer to Lucifer as another example of the dangers of curiosity, but, where the *Wisse* author mentions him only in passing, Bernard saves the fallen angel for the culmination of his argument. Bernard urges his monks: "Sta in te, ne cadas a te" (PL, 959) ("Stay in yourself lest you fall from yourself"). He continues, "Per curiositatem a veritate ceciderit quia prius speravit curiose quod affectavit illicite speravit preaesumptuose" (PL, 963) ("Through curiosity he [Lucifer] fell from the truth because he first curiously observed what he then unlawfully coveted and boldly aspired to."). The *Wisse* author, however, makes only one reference to Lucifer: "Lucifer þurh þ he seh z biheold on him seolf his ahne feiernesse. leop in to prude. z bicom of angel eatel ich deovel" (Tolkien, 31) ("Lucifer, because he looked upon himself and saw his own beauty, leapt into pride and from being an angel he became a loathsome devil." [Salu, 22–23]). Both authors refer to Lucifer in the course of making an argument that it is necessary to guard the heart, but the *Wisse* author's primary concern is to remind the anchoress of the relationship of an abstract example to her daily experience. His substitution of the word "beauty" for Bernard's word "truth" further suggests his assumption that a woman's sphere of sin is more narrowly circumscribed. Whereas male spirituality includes the moral, philosophical, and intellectual realms conveyed by the abstract word "truth," female spirituality is circumscribed in the word "beauty," which, although also abstract, is realized sensorily. Her experience of sin is thus determined by and confined to her essential corporeality. The *Wisse* author uses Lucifer as an example primarily to turn the female reader's attention yet again to contemplation of her own sinful body, warning her to beware of pride in physical asceticism (a virtue of the anchoresses which he had praised earlier) and asserting once again her culpability in the dangers her physical beauty poses for men.

The placement of this example illustrates differences between the authors' meditative plans. Bernard's argument follows an ascending progression moving back through scriptural time from Dinah to Eve to Lucifer and from historical example to eternal archetype. The examples the *Wisse* author employs—first Lucifer, then Eve, Dinah, and Bathsheba—move in the opposite direction, from the otherworldly to the worldly. Interestingly, Lucifer becomes a less direct negative example than the wayward women. But even omitting consideration of Lucifer as the pinnacle of a series of negative exempla, the order of the *Wisse* author's discussion of women is not hierarchical. Although it might be argued that his discussion charts the historical progress of women's victimization—although in each story it is female rather than male guilt that is emphasized—the *Wisse* author's discussion does not suggest that any one incident is worse than another. Each example in his discussion contains the whole argument. On the other hand, Bernard, for whom sexual sin is less important than the sin of pride, arranges his examples so as to suggest an ascending order of temptation. Indeed, this order is a rhetorical device that reinforces his stated overall purpose, to discuss the steps of humility that lead to truth. The *Wisse* author's nonprogressive, and apparently random, order is typical of his overall design. He is not interested in logical progression to higher truths but rather in the fluctuating process of spiritual education in which the female contemplative must always be reminded of the spiritual as she falls from her path.

The *Wisse* author's overriding concern for the practical, quotidian realization of religious ideals underlies his alteration of Bernard's conclusion. Bernard writes:

> Utquid audes oculos levare ad coelum qui peccasti in coelum? Terram intuere, ut cognoscas teipsum. Ipsa te tibi repraesentabit quia terra es et in terram ibis. (PL, 957) (How do you dare lift your eyes to heaven, when you have sinned against heaven? Look at the earth in order to know yourself. Only it will show you an image of yourself: "For dust thou art, and unto dust shalt thou return.")

The *Wisse* author, on the other hand, concludes:

> Ha schulden schrapien euche dei þe eorþe up of hare put þ ha schulien rotien in. Godd hit wat þ put deð muche god moni ancre. for as Salomon seið. Me morare novissima tua z in eternum non peccabis. þeo þe haveð eaver hire deað as bivoren hire ehnen þ te put munegeð. (Tolkien, 62–63) (They should scrape up earth every day out of the grave in which they shall rot. God knows, the sight of her grave near her does many an anchoress much good, for as Solomon says: "Remember thy last end and thou shalt never sin." She who keeps her death as it were before her eyes, her open grave reminding her of it.) [Salu, 51]).

Bernard's advice is much less literal and concrete than that of the English author. His words are the culmination of an argument designed to facilitate meditation. The *Wisse* author's advice also will lead to meditation, but his words are not the key; for his female audience, a literal, physical contact with the earth by digging a grave is a more effective key to understanding. Although Bernard's reference to the earth is also to a physical thing, his concept is general and impersonal, whereas the *Wisse* author's concept is specific and personal.

Clearly, the *Wisse* author's attitudes toward women govern his use of Bernard. What, then, of his use of Hugh of St. Victor? The way in which the English author discusses the dangers of looking out of the anchorhold's window could perhaps derive from Hugh's exegesis of the ark's window and door in his *De Arce Morali,* which has a similar emphasis on the connection between physical things of this world and spiritual meditation. Hugh argues that through contemplation of the outside world, the contemplative gains inner understanding: "Plena est omnis terra majestate ejus per terram omnis corporea creatura significatur quae plena est majestate Dei" (PL, 622) ("The whole earth is full of His Glory, which means that every corporeal creature on earth is full of the glory of God."). Earthly experience is significant to Hugh as a meditative focus, just as it is to the *Wisse* author.

Hugh's meditation on every aspect of a physical object—the ark—leads the contemplative to an understanding of the human heart, a psychological application of external reality that is also used by the author of the *Wisse*. It is in his discussion of the door of the ark that Hugh's exegesis most resembles that of the *Wisse* author, since both authors use a physical boundary as the starting point for inner meditation. Hugh writes:

> Ostium significat exitum per operationem, fenestra exitum qui fit per cogitationem ostium deorsum est, fenestra sursum quia actiones ad corpus pertinent cogitationes ad animam. Hinc est quod per fenestram aves exierunt, per ostium bestiae et homines. Quod autem per avem anima significetur, et per hominem corpus. . . . Quod vero ostium in latere positum dicitur hoc significat quod nunquam a secreto cordis nostri per operationem exire debemus ex proposito intentionis sed ex accidenti occasione necessitatis. (PL, 636)
> (The door denotes the way out through action, the window the way out through thought. The door is below the window because action pertains to the body, and thought to the soul. That is why the birds went out through the window and the beasts through the door. The bird denotes the soul and the man the body. But the fact that the door is situated in the side denotes that we must never leave the secret chamber of the heart through our own deliberate choice, but only as necessity demands it.)

Like Bernard and the *Wisse* author, Hugh employs the example of Dinah in discussing going out:

> Hunc igitur exitum caveamus, ne egrediamur temere. Nemo de conscientia sua confidat. Dina intus virgo, intus casta, intus columba fuit, sed quia columba seducta fuit non habens cor, egressa foras colorem pariter cum nomine mutavit. (PL, 639) (Let us beware then of our going out. Let none be too sure of his own moral sense. Dina was a virgin within, she was pure within, she was a dove within. But because the dove being heartless was seduced, when once it had gone out, it altered both its color and its name.)

Like the *Wisse* author, but unlike Bernard, Hugh refers to Dinah in the context of a discussion of a physical boundary. While Hugh discusses the dangers of going out through a door, the *Wisse* author treats those of going out through a window—in his case, through the window of the anchorhold. But although the *Wisse* author, like Hugh, considers the window a boundary crucial for the contemplative, he deliberately combines the function of the door and the window, so that the window represents the boundary across which both soul and body can escape.

What this conflation suggests is that, for women, the soul and the body are inextricably bound. While a man can purify his meditation by concentrating on his mind, a woman must always consider the body as well. Moreover, because Hugh's discussion is based on a sacred and historical object, his interest in the outside world is at some remove from the *Wisse*'s emphasis on objects common to contemporary experience. Ultimately, the idea of a door and a window in Hugh's account is a metaphorical and biblical one. The male contemplative is taken in meditation from a theological precept to a biblical context that reinforces an abstract meditative ideal. The female contemplative is given access to that biblical context only insofar as it relates to her body—that is, to the dangers that could follow if she should put her hands outside, not a sacred and metaphorical window, but the very real window of her anchorhold.

We have seen that the *Ancrene Wisse* is permeated with references to biblical commentaries of the day. We also have seen that, as a guide for women, it differs from those commentaries in its continual emphasis on the integration of the pressures of everyday life with spiritual goals. I propose that the English work's distinctive spirituality is primarily the result of the male author's very different interpretations of the places of men and women in religion. The comparison of the *Wisse* to its sources suggests that male contemplatives in the Middle Ages were trained to see themselves as part of an abstract hierarchy through which they progressed in stages to God, whereas female contemplatives were expected to perceive and participate in that hierarchy only insofar as it related to their everyday experience and their bodies. Whereas the texts written for men use biblical or sacramental objects or events to direct the attention of the contemplative to God's order, this work written for women introduces sacred exempla to direct their attention to daily experience as it should be ordered. Male contemplatives are encouraged to leave earthly experience behind, whereas female contemplatives are made always conscious of their rootedness in inherently sinful bodies. The very examples that have given the *Wisse* author a reputation for psychological realism and acumen also can be seen as misogynist, for through these images women are taught that they can never maintain the mystical heights available to men. Instead, as women, they are constantly reminded of their inferior status, in their present bodies and historically as well. In the end, a man writing for women, and responding to his tradition's construction of them, alters literary precedents to emphasize the concrete, personal, and contemporary, rather than the abstract and historical.

The English author's attitude toward women influences not merely his discussion of curiosity, but indeed the entire theme, structure, and imagery of the work. The stated theme of the *Wisse* is the need to control the unruly heart. This theme is meaningful for both men and women; but because women are presumed to be by nature willful, they have to give special consideration to controlling their unruly hearts. In women, the heart is governed finally by sexual desire. Women should beware of behaving like Eve, the first woman who let her heart "leap out" (Tolkien, 31), much less like Dinah, Bathsheba, and other women who sinned sexually. It scarcely matters that the sexual sin is not even their own; they are blamed for the sin they inspire in men. The face of a woman, writes the author, is the pit into which falls the animal, that part of man that is not controlled by reason (from the Nero text; see Salu, 25). Yet the woman is not urged to control this unruly heart through reason. Rather she is to control it through her heart again—this time, by redirecting her heart to a more appropriate object, Christ. The work as a whole reflects notions of the female body. As the work progresses, the author develops the idea of the anchorhold as a nest or a womb which must be prepared for the entry of Christ. A female recluse must mimic Mary by opening the nest of her heart to Christ. Paradoxically, it is only by becoming fully conscious of her body that the anchoress can overcome its potential for sin.

The anchoress's need to use her body as a guide to contemplation governs the structure of the entire *Wisse*, which is divided into eight parts, named by Salu: 1) "Devotions," 2) "The Custody of the Senses," 3) "the Regulation of Inward Feelings," 4) "Temptations," 5) "Confession," 6) "Penance," 7) "Love," and 8) "External Rules." Parts 2–7 follow an apparently conventional meditative plan, leading the anchoress from contemplation of earthly things to love of God. Underlying this progression, however, is the anchoress's inescapable attachment to her sinful body. Thus, parts 2 and 3 teach the anchoress to control those senses that lead specifically to sexual sin. She can overcome this sinfulness only through her body. Inherently "wounded" as a biologically incomplete man, she especially can identify with Christ's wounded body. Because the Bible defines woman as a handmaiden to men, it is natural that she meditate on comforting Christ in his passion and caring for his wounds. After overcoming the rule of her senses, the anchoress can progress through parts 4, 5, and 6— "Temptations," "Confession," and "Penance." While some early critics of the *Wisse* viewed temptation as an inappropriate subject for a devout audience, when the author's view of women is taken into consideration, failure is inherent in women, and temptation, therefore, is a necessary part of the work.[15] Thus the experience of the work is not one of gradual progress to union with God, but rather is one that elucidates a transformation of earthly desire into desire for Christ. The experiences of the senses are not overcome, but rather are redirected. As Georgianna has pointed out, the outer-inner frame of the work is a structure which is not simply convenient, but indeed mimics the whole idea of the work. It conveys the essential idea that the woman reader is one who must prepare her inner self as a nest for Christ while remaining continually aware of the desires of the outside world to violate that nest. Femininity—the idea of the woman's virginity—thus dictates the structure of the work.

Although the work culminates in the Christ-Knight allegory and assumes a movement towards union with God, the *Wisse* deliberately frustrates the development of an idea of ascent. The author's avoidance of the ascent affects the structure of the individual sections of his work. Shepherd comments on the "curious spiral quality to the structure of the *Ancrene Wisse*"—an idea that Grayson develops in her discussion of the work.[16] She describes the work's pattern:

> The conventional pattern of the Rule has been to establish one or more dominant metaphors surrounded and supported by related motifs, all of which grow organically in the course of the chapter and mature rapidly into allegorical 'themes.' As one distinction gives way to another, so the image-spirals rise and fall, and rise again.[17]

She writes also of the author's "habit of developing a theme, putting it aside temporarily, then reviving it in a slightly different context. The effect of this technique is a sense of movement and continuity, in which themes and motifs remain individualized even while they accrete to new arguments."[18] What Shepherd and Grayson have failed to consider in their description of the work's structure is that the distinctive fluidity of the work was viewed as peculiarly well suited to female readers. Ultimately, the lack of logical, progressive development in the work reflects the idea that a woman is forever caught in her body. She must recognize the ways in which she is governed by a random sensuality that may erupt at any moment. The author's habit of breaking down logic can be seen, for example, in part 3, "The Regulation of Inward Feelings." Grayson summarizes the author's eight reasons (for example, chastity) why the anchoress must flee the world; these reasons

> stand as a self-sustaining unit, organized into a graduated raising of the soul from the time it seeks refuge from the raging lion of hell (first reason) to the seventh reason (or step) when the soul finds refuge in heaven. Oddly, the author does not carry the spiritual progress into the eighth reason, but shows by means of extended exegesis and etymology how good may be turned back upon the world by the anchoress who is true.[19]

The author's avoidance of the eighth step is not an oddity, but rather is characteristic of his refusal to allow the reader to chart an ascent that takes her out of the body. While adopting some of the conventions of the graduated steps so common to male mysticism, this author ultimately abandons that idea of an ascending structure in favor of an emphasis on the reader's inevitable return to earth—a return that ultimately may await all mystics, but especially women, who this author feels do not by nature possess souls that allow them to escape the senses.

The necessity of continuous contemplation of the body may also be behind the unusual reading plan of the work. The work interweaves inner and outer meditation; the one can never escape the other. The author's concern with will rather than wit leads him, as we have seen above, to abandon the conventional progressive structure. Initially he follows the standard scholastic technique of division, whereby the book is divided into eight parts and many subdivisions, and tells his reader that this structure has a cumulative design. Finally, however, he urges the anchoress to abandon this hierarchical structure and read at random instead. Each part of the work contains the whole. He tells the anchoress to read as little or as much as holds her attention, and to dip into the book whenever she needs to. The discipline of the heart is to be achieved whether the anchoress reads a single line or one from the beginning followed by one from the end or vice versa. As noted above, the author often abandons a logical progression. His discussion of the dangers of sight, for example, is filled with references to all the other senses. Underlying this random structure is the author's view that the anchoress needs a guide that will infuse her daily experience with religious meaning. Rather than focusing her mind on an abstract, hierarchical discussion, reading exists for her only in order to affect her responses through the day. Implied in this structure is the inherent willfulness of women; their thoughts are randomly dictated by willful impulse rather than by reason.

The theoretical view of women as associated with matter, will, and imperfection also affects the imagery of the text. Each section is governed by a controlling image, as Grayson has demonstrated. Yet, as we shall see, the pattern of imagery in each section ultimately reflects the perceived physiological condition of women. Because the imagery pattern of each section is related so integrally to ideas of femininity, I shall consider each section in turn.

The author's view that a woman is governed by her sexuality underlies even the most apparently conventional section of the *Wisse,* the opening list of prayers known as "Devotions." At the center of this section is the twin celebration of the five joys of Mary and of the Eucharist. Grayson outlines how the text moves from outer concerns to inner ones and back out again, mimicking the overt theme of the work. What Grayson has not remarked upon is that this movement depends upon and reflects the idea of a woman's sexual guilt. The center of the passage celebrates the Eucharist, which exemplifies the transcendence of sinful flesh through Christ, an idea that has meaning for both men and women. For the anchoress, however, this redemption occurs only through her recognition of her sinfulness, not as a soul in flesh, but rather as a soul in female flesh. By admitting her inherent sinfulness as Eve and then using Mary as a model for denying her sexuality, she, like Mary, can serve the function of a woman without sexuality. The image of Mary as woman, maid, and mother is central to the section. In the praise of Mary, her passivity is emphasized, reinforcing a passive role for the female recluse. The five joys of Mary specifically celebrate Mary's transcendence of her sexuality: for example, she conceives without intercourse and gives birth without breach. Although a denial of flesh is central to all Christianity, for the woman, it is specifically female sexuality that must be overcome. For a man, in contrast, a denial of his sexuality is part of a hierarchical set of denials including such other sins as pride. Furthermore, for a man, the process of overcoming sin does not mean denying his maleness; whereas, for a woman, the process involves overcoming what is considered to be her femaleness, her corporeality. For a woman, all sins, even pride, are associated with her body.

Through her experience of the host and through her transformation of herself from Eve to Mary, a woman's flesh is redeemed because her gender is denied. The *Wisse* teaches the anchoress to make herself ready to receive Christ in the form of the Eucharist. She must emulate Mary who received Christ in the womb. Even the receiving of the Eucharist is described in terms that are ultimately physical, if not erotic. As Grayson describes it: "Cleansed and receptive, the communicant responds when the sacramental eating of the Body infuses the soul with spirit and sensual fervor, interpreted here in the literal sense as a physical lover entering the bower of the beloved." [20] Even at the most abstract moment—the infusing of the spirit—the author depends on the physical and concrete:

> Efter þe measse cos hwen þe preost sacreð. þer forȝeoteð al þe world. þer beoð al ut of bodi þer i sperclinde luve bicluppeð ower leofmon þe in to ower breostes bur is iliht of heovene. ȝ haldeð him heteveste aþet he habbe iȝettet ow al þ ȝe eaver easkið. (Tolkien, 21) (After the kiss of peace in the Mass, when the priest communicates, forget the world, be completely out of the body, and with burning love embrace your Beloved who has come down from heaven to your heart's bower, and hold Him fast until He has granted you all that you ask. [Salu, 14])

Thus, an apparently mechanical list of prayers turns out in fact to introduce the overarching metaphor of the work—that an anchoress, as a virgin recluse, must mimic Mary and make her anchorhold, like her body, ready to receive Christ. At the end of the chapter, as Grayson points out, the "devotions become increasingly physical in the motor sense, with growing attention to bending, kneeling, prostrating the body, etc."[21] This emphasis reasserts the idea that a woman's union with God is realized physically rather than mentally. The central structuring device of this chapter, then, is an imagery pattern focused on the nature of the female body.

In our discussion of St. Bernard, Hugh of St. Victor, and the *Wisse,* we looked in detail at some of the major images of part 2 of the *Wisse,* "The Custody of the Senses." This chapter is one of the more important ones in the work, first, because it introduces the major imagery patterns used in the work as a whole, and, second, because it develops the idea that the senses are central to female meditative experience. It is thus longer and more developed than the other chapters. In this chapter the following images are allied: anchoress, anchorhold, eye, window, heart, body. Using Eve as a central model, the author here teaches the anchoress that as a woman she must learn to guard her senses. The work is dominated by its opening metaphor, in which the heart is compared to a wild beast. The bestiality of human beings is, of course, a Christian commonplace. In this work, however, the emphasis on the animal nature of the heart is deemed particularly apt, since women readers are assumed to be more easily tempted through the senses. Second in danger to female sensuality is a woman's talkativeness, a danger warned of in this chapter and reinforced in later chapters. The anchoress is warned continually about the dangers of reckless speech. These dangers are conveyed in such images as a woman's face, which is described as a pit into which men fall, whose center is a talking woman's mouth. The chapter thus begins with a series of images that define women as fundamentally sensual and willful and then turns to a series of prescriptive images warning women to be silent.

In the last half of the chapter, the author teaches the reader to transform her dangerous senses into watchmen of the heart, a male image that reinforces a woman's dependence on paternalistic control. The cluster of images that follows is again particularly tailored for women. The purpose of the guardianship of the soul is not simply to protect against sin but to prepare the soul specifically for union with Christ, who is described as a jealous lover. The senses must become guardians jealously attending the spouse, and the senses must serve Him. The anchoress is told to close the window of the anchorhold and to close her own eyes so that she can turn her inward eye on her heart. The author reiteratively redirects the senses, a redirection fundamental to the mystical experience made available to women in this work. For example, the pervasive imagery of rotting animals, linked to the idea of the inherently rotten female body, is transformed into a specific erotic image, the sweetness of Christ's kiss. Her own bodily experiences merge with those of Christ and are thereby transformed. What her body suffers, His body once suffered. Her eyes, mouth, and body can overcome unpleasantness partly because Christ experienced unpleasantness and also in part so that those senses can be prepared for the ultimate sensual experience of union with Christ. At the end of the chapter, images of Christ's sense experiences structurally enclose images of the anchoress's own sense experiences, a paternalistic structure reinforcing the male author's view that the anchoress is dependent on men.

Through Christ's suffering, the anchoress receives a model of endurance which offers her a future reward for the suffering and endurance viewed as inherent in female nature:

> for se ful of angosse was þ ilke ned swat þ lihte of his licome aȝein þe angoisuse deað þ he schulde þolien. þ hit þuhte read blod. . . . swa swiðe fleaw þ ilke blodi swat. of his blisfule bodi. þ te streames urnen dun to þer eorde. . . . þus lo þe hale half ȝ te cwike dale droh þ uvele blod ut. frommard te unhale. ȝ healde swa þe seke." (Tolkien, 60–61) (For so full of anguish was that violent sweat which poured from His body at the thought of the agonizing death He was to die that it seemed like red blood. . . . And then, that bloody sweat flowed so freely and in such quantity from His blessed body that it ran in streams to the ground. . . . Thus, the living healthy part drew out the bad blood from that which was diseased, and so healed that which was sick. [Salu, 49–50])

Although the redemptive quality of Christ's blood is a Christian commonplace, the presumed association of women with excess moisture purged through menstruation makes this image particularly redemptive for women. Purgation, viewed as necessary to a woman's physical health, is here presented as necessary for spiritual health as well. The hyperbole of this image, as well as the conflation of blood and sweat, is typical in female mystical texts and reflects the perception that a woman's nature is essentially moist.

The rule moves inward in part 3, called "The Regulation of The Inward Feelings." The controlling images of this chapter, seemingly gender-neutral, again turn out to be seen as peculiarly apt for women readers. The chapter's central theme is the necessity of controlling anger. It is unusual that this sin should take such prominence in a contemplative guide. While it may be true, as Grayson suggests, that the author was responding to the quarreling and pettiness of small groups of contemplatives, the importance assigned to anger as a problem more than likely reflects an assumption that women especially should repress anger and instead cultivate the virtue of silence. Such a speculation receives support from the centrality of the problem of anger in the chapter as well as the authors' use of the twin models of Judith and Mary, where the violence and anger of Judith is offset by the passivity and complacency of Mary. Indeed, the suppression of female anger remains a pressing concern among women today.

Judith is presented in this chapter as the model anchoress. It is not surprising that Judith should be next in importance to Mary in this work, for Judith's central virtue was her ability to overcome lust, the one vice considered most dangerous for women. In the *Wisse* author's explication of Judith's significance, he not only associates her with lust, but also allies her more specifically with the flesh. He writes,

> On ebreische ledene oloferne is þe feond þe makeð feble ƺ unstrong feat kealf ƺ to wilde. Þ is Þ flesche þe awildgeð sone se hit eaver featteð þurh eise ƺ þurh este. . . . Ah ancre schal beo Judith . . . ƺ slean as dude Judith þes uvel oloferne. (Tolkien, 72) (In the Hebrew language, Holofernes is the devil who weakens the fat calf, which has grown too wild, that is, the flesh, which grows wild as ever it grows fat with ease and indulgence. . . . but an anchoress must be a Judith . . . and must slay, as Judith did, the evil Holofernes. [Salu, 61])

Because of a woman's association with matter, with fleshliness, it is a woman's central task to overcome that fleshliness. However, women can never win that battle.

That women can never fully succeed in transcending the flesh is further supported in the bird imagery of this section, where the author warns the anchoress that she is always vulnerable, no matter how high she flies:

> Alswa þe gode ancre. ne fleo ha neaver se hehe. ha mot lihten oðerwhiles dun to þer eorðe. of hire bodi. (Tolkien, 70) (So it is with the good anchoress. However high she flies, she must sometimes come down to the ground because of her body. [Salu, 59])

The ensuing bird images—images of the night-raven, the hen, and the sparrow—are described in especially feminine terms. The anchoress is warned, for example, not to be a chattering hen. And, most importantly, she is compared to a sparrow, a sparrow with falling sickness who inevitably returns to earth. The author writes:

> Spearewe haveð ƺet acunde Þ is biheve ancre þah me hit heatie. Þ is þe fallinde uvel for muche neod is Þ ancre of hali lif ƺ of heh habbe fallinde uvel. . . . ha walde awilgin elles oðer to wel leoten of. (Tolkien, 91) (The sparrow has an-

other characteristic which is becoming to an anchoress, though it is generally unpopular, and that is the falling sickness. For there is great need that an anchoress whose life is holy and exalted should have the falling sickness . . . Otherwise she would grow overconfident and think too highly of herself. [Salu, 76–77])

Although the author presents the sparrow's falling sickness as an image of humility and as a corrective to pride, the emphasis on the inevitability of that fall reinforces the idea that all women are inescapably rooted in the body. Furthermore, the author here alters conventional images of the soul as an eagle. Whereas the male contemplative is often imaged as an eagle, the female contemplative is presented here as a less ambitious and less transcendent bird, the domestic sparrow. Finally, as a bird, the anchoress must protect and prepare her nest. The nest is presented as a womb, and the author thus returns to his opening comparison of the anchoress to Mary, who prepares for Christ's entry into the womb.

In part 4, the section that follows, "Temptations," the author develops the image of blood, introduced in the previous sections, into an extended image of wounds. The image controlling the first half of this discussion is an image of a festering wound caused by the seven deadly sins. The author follows conventional descriptions of the sins, comparing them to animals, but the one sin described most fully is the scorpion of lechery, an animal significantly described as having a woman's face. Like all contemplatives, the anchoress is compared to the desert fathers, who confronted the seven deadly sins in the wilderness, but we should notice how the author of the *Wisse* subtly alters the terms of the confrontation in response to the femininity of his audience, emphasizing the anchoress's feminine spiritual dependence on Christ. Unlike the male contemplative, who overcomes the deadly sins in order to clear a path to God, the female contemplative is dependent on a male protector for success during that confrontation. This image of dependence is carried further in the author's depiction of the anchoress as a child chastised by her father, and in the comfort later found in the "gentle tolerance" of Christ as the bride's husband.[22]

Finally, the author instructs the anchoress to take refuge in Christ's wounds. This complex image has assumed central significance in recent feminist analyses of female mysticism. Many of these analyses make use of Freudian notions of the vagina as a wound. Whether or not the medieval reader identified the vagina as a wound is difficult to say. There is little evidence about how female genitalia were perceived in the Middle Ages. Although we might not be able to say that women perceived themselves as wounded because of their femininity, there was a late medieval male mystical tradition that associated the wounds of Christ with the female pudenda. As Riehle points out,

> Since the wound in Christ's side is given a new interpretation as an opening through which it is possible for the mystical lover to enter his beloved and thus become completely one with him, this gives rise in Franciscan mysticism, especially in such an eroticized text as the *Stimulis Amoris,* to a typical and quite consciously intended analogy between this wound of Christ and the female pudenda: the vulva, as the place of sexual ecstasy, has, so to speak, been transformed into the vulnus of Christ as the place of ecstatic union of the soul with its divine beloved. This is confirmed by the following statement of the Monk of Farne, whose fourteenth-century text represents the climax of Franciscan mysticism of the cross on the English soil: "latus meum aperio ut osculatum introducam ad cor meum, et simus duo in carne una."[23]

The image of hiding in Christ's wounds is present in both male and female contemplative texts, but, given the *Wisse's* emphasis on feminine dependency, the wounds here seem to be particularly evocative for women.

Christ's wounds are set against a woman's sinful flesh:

> I þe licome is fulðe z unstrengðe. Ne kimeð of þ vetles swuch þing as þer is in ?
> . . . Amid te menske of þi neb. þ is þe fehereste deal. bitweonen muðes smech. z neases smeal. ne berest tu as twa prive þurles? Nart tu icumen of ful slim? Nart tu fulðe fette. (Tolkien, 142–3) (In the body there is uncleanness and weakness. Does there not come out of a vessel such stuff as is in it? . . . In the middle of your face, which is a noble part of you and the fairest, between the mouth with its taste and the nose with its faculty of smelling, have you not as it were two privy holes? Have you not come from foul slime? Are you not a vessel of filth? [Salu, 123])

Although the denigration of the flesh is a homiletic commonplace, the author's attention to the fairness of the face suggests that he is directing his hatred of the flesh specifically toward female flesh. The anchoress is urged to recognize the sinfulness of her body and then to find refuge in Christ's wounds: "Creop in ham wið þi þoht. Ne beoð ha al opene? z wið his deorewurðe blod biblodde þin heorte" (Tolkien, 151) ("Creep into them, in thought. Are they not wide open? and with His precious blood cover your heart." [Salu, 130]). The wound of lechery is healed by the purity of virginity. The anchoress creeps into the clefts of Christ's wounds, the sanctuary of the dove. The *Wisse* author presents Christ's call to the anchoress in both paternalistic and romantic terms. She, like the dove of the Song of Songs, represents the beloved of Christ:

> Mi culure he seið cum hud te i mine limen þurles. i þe hole of mi side. Muche luve he cudde to his leove culure þ he swuch hudles makede. Loke nu þ tu þe he cleopeð culure. habbe culure cunde. (Tolkien, 151) ("My dove," He says,

"come and hide thyself in the holes in my limbs, in the hole in my side." Great love He showed to His dear dove in making such apertures. Now see that you whom He calls a dove, have the nature of a dove. [Salu, 130])

This image actually suggests an erotic union more suitable for male than for female readers. For a female audience, however, this image stresses both the protective, paternalistic attributes of Christ, as well as the prescriptive lesson to be learned.

Accompanying the hyperbolic images of blood and the wounds of Christ is the image of tears which further emphasizes a woman's essential capacity for compassion. The anchoress, compared to a castle, is told to fill her moat with tears and "as ofte as þe feond asaileð ower castel z te sawle burh. wið inwarde bonen warpeð ut up on him scaldinde teares" (Tolkien, 125) ("Whenever the devil attacks your castle, the city of your soul, dash scalding tears out on him as you make your heart-felt prayers." [Salu, 108]). The image of the tower or castle of the body is commonplace, but here and in its later developments, the castle is strongly associated with female virginity and seen as a fortress which ultimately can be protected from continual sexual assault only by the champion Christ-Knight. The *Wisse* author emphasizes that, by resistance, the anchoress can prevent herself from being mounted and ridden by the devil. The devil mounts her when she bows down through lack of faith. This image reasserts a woman's fundamental sexual nature and the extreme danger she faces from the temptation of lust. The remedy is the Eucharist—the body and blood of Christ, her champion. In a series of images with erotic overtones, Christ enters the maiden to protect her from the devil:

> Hardiliche ileveð þ al þe deofles strengðe mealteð þurh þe grace of þ hali sacrement hest over oþre. þ ʒe seoð as ofte as þe preost measseð. þe meidene bearn iesu godd godes sune þe licomliche lihteð oðerhwiles to ower in. z inwið ow eadmodliche nimeð his herbearhe. (Tolkien, 138) (Believe firmly that all the strength of the devil will melt away through the grace of the holy Sacrament which is above all the rest, and which you see as often as the priest says Mass, the child of the Maiden, Jesus God, the Son of God, who descends in bodily manner to your hostelry and humbly takes up His abode with you. [Salu, 119])

The replacement of the devil's mounting with the physical descent of Christ underscores the fact that for women the experience of Christ is not a transcendence of the desires of the flesh, but rather a transference of those desires to Christ.

The purpose of part 5, "Confession," is to emphasize the end point of sin. Having sinned so terribly, and having suffered such deep wounds, all the anchoress can do is nakedly confess her weakness. Carrying forward the imagery of Judith, here standing for confession, and the imagery of the battlefield, seen in earlier chapters, this chapter celebrates the power of confession to vanquish the devil. Although this chapter, compared to the previous one, is less densely packed with images, nonetheless an imagery pattern of family loosely holds the discussion of confession together. This imagery pattern ultimately reinforces the idea that a woman defines herself relationally, in terms of family and friends rather than in terms of an abstract hierarchy. For example, we are told that through sin, the anchoress has lost her spiritual family. The text compares her to a child who slays her parents and siblings and then to a mother who has lost a child.

The payment for such sin is one appropriate to woman's moist nature, blood and tears:

> We ahen him blod for blod. ant ure blod þah aʒein his blod þ he schedde for us. were ful unefne change . . . ant ure lauerd nimeð ed us ure teares aʒein his blod. z is wilcweme (Tolkien, 161) (We owe Him blood for blood, and even so, our blood for His blood, which He shed for us, would be a very unequal exchange. . . . And our Lord accepts our tears from us in exchange for His blood, and is well pleased. [Salu, 139]

It is typical of a work written for women that the actual nature of sinfulness should be described in homely and domestic terms. Thus the discussion moves from lost kingdoms to an image of a poor widow anchoress sweeping up the dust in her house. That the author is concerned specifically with female sinfulness—a sinfulness most likely, in his view, to be sexual—is emphasized in the hypothetical confession he suggests:

> Spec hit scheome schendfulliche ant tuk hit al towundre. alswa as þu wult schende þen schucke. Sire ha seið þe wummon ich habbe ihaved leofmon. oðer ich habbe ibeon ha seið fol of me seolven. þis nis nawt naket schrifte. Biclute þu hit nawt. do awei þe totagges. Uwrih þe z sei. Sire godes are ich am a ful stod meare. a stinkinde hore. (Tolkien, 163) (Speak of its [sin's] shame with obloquy and strike it violently just as you would want wholeheartedly to injure the devil. "Sir," a woman will say, "I have had a lover," or she will say, "I have been foolish about myself." This is not naked confession. Do not wrap it up. Take off the trimmings. Make yourself clear and say: "Sir, God's Mercy! I am a foul stud mare, a stinking whore." [Salu, 140–41])

Here the author betrays his view of women's essentially whorish nature. His disgust with the sinful body is further emphasized when he next presents a vivid series of images of the body as covered with stinking, fetid wounds. Given the author's obsession with sexual sin, this focus on the stinking body reflects his disgust not only with the body in general, but with the female body in particular.

The penultimate chapter, "Penance," paves the way for the anchoress's romantic union with Christ. The key themes of this chapter are identification with Christ's suffering and the laments of the three Maries at the cross. The author introduces three images: the spiritual ladder, the fiery wheel, and the flaming sword. While the ladder and chariot suggest a progressive ascent common in works written for male contemplatives, the images that follow stress aspects of the spiritual ascent that have special significance for women—that is, aspects suggestive of erotic, sexual union. Redemption is viewed as possible not only through the purgation of excess feminine moisture, but also through heat, the heat brought about through sexual union with Christ. While heat, or the fire of love—the *incendium amoris*— is a motif that pervades twelfth-century affective works, the centrality of heat here reinforces the notion that a woman by nature seeks heat. Erotic burning—what Irigaray would call *jouissance*—is emphasized in discussions of Elijah's wheel made of fire: "Fur is hat ʒ read. Iþe heate is understonden euch wa þ eileð flesch. Scheome bi ðe reade" (Tolkien, 181) ("Fire is hot and red. By the heat is signified every pain that afflicts the body; by the redness, dishonour." [Salu, 157]). The wheel is then transformed into a flaming sword which stands for both the sun and the cross: "Ne kimeð nan in to parais. bute þurh þis leitinde sweord þe wes hat ʒ read" (Tolkien, 181) ("No-one enters Paradise but by this flaming sword which was hot and red." [Salu, 157]). God will win the anchoress with his explicitly erotic flaming sword.

Rather than end on an image of ascent and/or union, the author returns to the everyday world of the anchoress, emphasizing the metaphorical and literal meaning of her enclosure in the anchorhold, where she is meant to become dead to the world. Here, as throughout the work, the author emphasizes not the joys of mystical union, but rather the mundane suffering of everyday life. After teaching the anchoress to identify with Christ's suffering, the author then urges her to identify as a woman with the three Maries. The first, Mary Magdalene, represents repentance; the second represents the bitterness of confrontation with sin. The last, however, Mary Salome, is of most importance to the development of a particularly feminine spiritual goal, for she signifies longing for God. This aspect of desire is central for women here, for it sets the stage for the arrival of the Christ-Knight lover. All three Maries further emphasize the centrality of the physical in female spirituality, because of the history of their physical proximity to Christ; not only can the anchoress model herself on the three Maries by mimicking the compassion and comfort they offered to Christ, but also she can mimic their experience of physical proximity to Christ. The anchoress must prepare herself for the entry of Christ as both her lover and her child. Her womb is particularly suited for the entry of Christ, for "Ant nes he him seolf reclus i maries womb" (Tolkien, 192) ("And was not He himself a recluse in Mary's womb." [Salu, 167]). Such images reinforce the idea of the anchorhold as a womb. Not only has the restrictive world of the anchorhold been transformed and redeemed, but the woman's body itself, the sinful, bloody, female body, has been redeemed in the anchoress's imitation of Mary. Thus, for a woman, penance is conditional upon a metaphorical childbirth, a specifically feminine image.

Cleansed by penance, the anchoress is then ready to contemplate her love of Christ. Even this love, however, in this work is ultimately defined in terms of her body. The Bernardine marriage of the soul to Christ is here literalized, whereas for a male audience it is allegorized.[24] The work culminates in a Christ-Knight allegory in which the female contemplative's relationship is defined as if she were literally Christ's wife. For example, Christ addresses the anchoress as a suitor in this passage:

> Nam ich þinge feherest. nam ich kinge richest. nam ich hest icunnet. nam ich weolie wisest. nam ich monne hendest . . . Wult tu castles. kinedomes. wult tu wealden al þe world? Ich chulle do þe betere. makie þe wið al þis. cwen of heoveriche. (Tolkien, 202–203) (Am I not fairer than any other? Am I not the richest of kings? Am I not of the noblest kindred? . . . Would you have castles, kingdoms? Would you have the whole world in your power? I will provide more for you, make you queen of the kingdom of heaven. [Salu, 175–76])

Even at the height of contemplation, a woman is assumed to be rooted in earthly, bodily, and domestic desires.

Given the significance of the Christ-Knight allegory as it is developed, the passage is worth quoting here at length:

> Herto falleð a tale. a wrihe forbisne. A leafdi wes mid hire fan. biset al abuten. hire lond al destruet. z heo al poure inwið an eorðene castel. A mihti kinges luve wes þah biturnd up on hire swa unimete swiðe. Þ he for wohlech sende hire his sonden. an efter oðer. ofte somet monie. sende hire beawbelez baðe feole z feire. sucurs of liveneð. help of his hehe hird to halden hire castle. Heo underfeng al as on unrecheles. z swa wes heard iheortet. Þ hire luve ne mahte he neaver beo þe neorre. hwet wult tu mare he com him seolf on ende. schawde hire his feire neb. as þe þe wes of alle men feherest to bihalden. spec se swiðe swoteliche. z wordes se murie þet ha mahten deade arearen to live. wrahte feole wundres z dude muchele meistries bivoren hire ehsidðe. schawde hire his mihte. talde hire of his kinedom. bead to makien hire cwen of al Þ he ahte. al þis ne heold nawt. nes þis hoker wunder? for heo nes neaver wurðe forte beon his þuften. ah swa þurh his deboneirte luve hefde overcumen him. Þ he seide on

ende. Dame þu art iweorret. ʒ þine van beoð se stronge. Þ tu ne maht nanesweis wið ute mi sucurs edfleon hare honden. Þ ha ne don þe to scheome deað efter al þi weane. Ich chulle for þe luve of þe. neome Þ fehte up o me. ʒ arudde þe of ham þe þi deað secheð. Ich wat þah to soðe Þ ich schal bituhen ham neomen deaðes wunde. ʒ ich hit wulle heorteliche forte ofgan þin heorte. Nu þenne biseche ich þe for þe luve Þ ich cuðe þe. Þ tu luvie me lanhure efter þe ilke dede dead. hwen þu naldest lives. þis king dude al þus. arudde hire of alle hire van. ʒ wes him seolf to wundre ituket ʒ islein on ende. þurh miracle aras þah from deaðe to live. Nere þeos ilke leafdi of uveles cunnes cunde. ʒef ha over alle þing ne luvede him her efter? þes king is iesu godes sune. Þ al o þisse wise wohede ure sawle þe deoflen hefden biset. Ant he as noble wohere efter monie messagers ʒ feole goddeden. com to pruvien his luve. ʒ schawde þurh cnihtschipe Þ he wes luve wurðe. as weren sumwhile cnihtes iwunet to donne. dude him i turneiment. ʒ hefde for his leoves luve his scheld i feht as kene cniht on euch half iþurlet. (Tolkien, 198–99)

(There was once a lady who was completely surrounded by her enemies, her land all laid waste, and she herself destitute in an earthen castle. But a king of great power loved her so much that he sent messengers to her one after another, and often several together, with many fair jewels, and with food to sustain her, and he sent his noble army to help in the holding of her castle. She accepted it all as if unthinkingly, and was so hard-hearted that he could never come any nearer to her love. What more would you? At last he went himself. He let her see the beauty of his face, the face of one who of all men was fairest to behold. He spoke so tenderly and spoke words of such delight that they might have raised the dead to life. He worked many wonders and brought great marvels before her eyes, revealed to her the power that he had, told her of his kingdom and asked that he might make her queen of all he possessed. All this availed nothing. Was it not strange, this disdain? For she herself was not worthy to be his handmaid. But love had so vanquished his tender heart, that at last he said, "Lady, thou art assailed, and thine enemies are so strong that thou canst by no means escape their hands without my help, which can prevent their putting thee to a shameful death after all thy misery. For love of thee I will take this fight upon myself and deliver thee from those who seek thy death. I know without any doubt that among them I must receive my death wound but I will meet it gladly in order to win thy heart. Now I beseech thee, for the love I show thee, that thou shouldst love me, at least after my death has been accomplished, who wouldst not while I lived." The king carried out all this, delivered her from all her enemies, and was himself outrageously tortured and finally slain. But by a miracle he rose from death to life. Would not this lady be of an evil nature had she not loved him thereafter beyond everything else. This king is Jesus, the son of God, who in just this way sought our soul's love when it was besieged by devils. And He, like a noble lover, after having sent many messengers and good gifts, came to give proof of His love, and showed by knightly deeds that He was worthy of love, as knights at one time were accustomed to do. He entered the tournament, and like a brave knight had His shield pierced through and through for love of His lady. [Salu, 172–73])

The allegory is not original to the *Wisse* author. Elaborated from the third century by Origen and other eastern writers, the original story tells of a king who woos a beggar maid, not of a knight wooing a lady. The story was not common in the West until the twelfth century, and the *Wisse* author was the first to add new chivalric conventions to the original. As I have argued elsewhere, one of the unusual features of this allegory is its assumption that its female audience of anchoresses would have been familiar with courtly romances.[25] Most importantly, however, the author uses romance imagery specifically to manipulate the anchoress's responses, so as to reinforce an emotional rather than an intellectual commitment to Christ. The courtly story has a literal as well as a metaphorical purpose. The male author apparently assumed that women were better able to understand their relationship to God through a concrete version of the *sponsa christi* motif than through the abstract terms of theology. The idea that women read romances led to the further idea that women could define their relationship to Christ as literally that of a lady and her knight. Through these images, the anchoress could be taught to redirect the desires of the flesh positively into love for Christ, a romantic dedication that rooted her in the body and defined her literally as the bride of Christ. The *Wisse* argument, therefore, focuses on emotions rather than logic, and theology is subordinated to relationships within a traditional female sphere—that is, marriage.

The courtly details of the Christ-Knight allegory simply underscore the dependence and passivity assigned to women in Christianity. Like many courtly lyrics, this romance seems peculiarly male-oriented. We learn more about the man's desire than about the nature of the woman he adores. What we do learn about her is negative—she is haughty, disdainful, and unworthy of the worthiest of knights. Since the audience was female, readers evidently were forced into identification with the disdainful lady, an identification designed to provoke guilt. While guilt and a sense of obligation may be attributes essential to Christians, this allegory conveys its themes by casting the anchoress in the role of the lady of conventional love lyrics. As the allegory progresses, the author reverses the terms of the lyric by giving all the active verbs to Christ and all the passive verbs to the beloved lady, reinforcing the sustained image of the work as a whole: the anchoress as Mary awaiting the entrance of Christ. Unlike her male counterpart, the anchoress can never escape her body by climbing an allegorical ladder to God; rather, she, like the lady in the castle, can only wait passively to be rescued from the castle of her body or wait for that body to be redeemed through Christ's entry into it.

Following the Christ-Knight allegory is an unusual catachretic image
that has never been adequately accounted for, the image of God's love as
Greek fire. After discussing the need to kindle sticks to promote desire, the
author writes,

> Grickisch fur is imaket of reades monnes blod, z þ ne mei na þing. bute Migge.
> ant Sond. z eisil. as me seið acwenchen. þis grickisch fur is þe luve of iesu ure
> lauerd. z ʒe hit schule makien of reade monnes blod. þ is iesu crist ireadet wið
> his ahne blod o þe deore rode." (Tolkien, 205) (Greek fire is made from the
> blood of a red man and cannot be quenched, it is said, except with urine, sand,
> and vinegar. This "Greek fire" is the love of Jesus our Lord and you shall make
> it from the blood of a red man, that is, Jesus Christ, reddened with His own
> blood on the precious cross. [Salu, 178])

Grayson writes of this passage:

> The uncontrollable wildfire, the bloodied Christ . . . the specifics of urine and
> vinegar that threaten to smother the consuming Greek fire—all converge here
> into the emotional, highly concentrated repetitions and refinements of the power
> of the sacrifice. And the pervasiveness of redness (initially the color of fire)
> provides a definite focus for the Passion, the *memoria Christi,* the affective in-
> fluence of Christ crossed that kindles the *incendium amoris* between anchoress
> and Christ, between lady and Christ-Knight . . . the kindling of love . . . sets
> the heart aglow. The heart fired with love becomes the dominant image into
> which all the other figures and emotional qualities flow.[26]

Although Grayson's description of this image alludes to the erotic implications of the passage, she does not emphasize the centrality of such eroticism to the model of female contemplative experience here presented. This
image particularly brings together received biological views of a woman's
innate desire for completion through union with the male, her need for
heat, and her natural condition of containing excess moisture. Ian Bishop
points out that the *Wisse* author here departs from his sources, including a
work closely associated with the *Wisse,* the *Moralia Super Evangelia.*[27]
Whereas in the sources, Greek fire is associated with lust, here it is equated
with its opposite, Christ's love. Underpinning this change is the author's
assumption that his female audience cannot escape its essentially lustful
female nature. Rather than being transcended, that lust must be redirected
to an appropriate object, Christ. This unusual image reflects biological
views of women, in that different kinds of moisture are interchangeable,
just as in medieval medical accounts of excessive fluid: the bad blood of
the earlier passages becomes the urine or vinegar which threatens the redemptive blood of Christ. Urine was the focus of diagnosis in medieval
medicine; here the ill moisture of the body is redeemed by the moisture of

Christ.[28] While the burning love, the *incendium amoris,* is a theme in male and female contemplative texts, it is of particular significance to female readers, especially in association with other images of moisture. It also emphasizes the emotional and erotic experience of Christ so particularly available to the female contemplative.

Rather than end the work with an image of the anchoress's union with Christ, the *Wisse* author returns the reader firmly to the earth in the last section of the work, "External Rules." Grayson and Georgianna have both explained the importance of this return as part of the interweaving of inner and outer concerns that permeates the work as a whole. This pedestrian list, focusing on issues such as the number of times the anchoress should take confession and warnings against having visitors or engaging in business, also reinforces the idea of the female reader as one particularly rooted in the body.

The idea of a female audience guides the author's choice of structure, theme, and imagery. Furthermore, although the *Ancrene Wisse* is psychologically innovative, it is actually just as prescriptive as the Benedictine rule. Women are taught to control their bodies. They are to be silent, repress anger, and, most of all, control their senses. The cackling Eve must be transformed into the passive, silent Mary rather than into an active, abstract thinker. If women have a voice, it is the constructed querulous female voice the author uses in his text. More often, because of their sexuality, women are denied any voice at all.

In examining the male author's representation of female spirituality in the *Ancrene Wisse,* I am also raising questions about the legitimacy of the female mystic's voice celebrated by Luce Irigaray and to some extent by Simone de Beauvoir.[29] At the basis of feminist analyses of female mysticism is a recognition of the centrality of a woman's sexuality to her mystical vision. Blood and tears, for example, considered to be physiologically prominent in women's experience, occur frequently in female mystical visions. The possible physiological basis of female mystical imagery raises a fundamental interpretive problem for feminists: Is the focus on the body redemptive for women or not? Simone de Beauvoir, for one, suggested that a mystical vision, as the logical expression of a woman's sociological condition "on her knees," redeems her body, but ultimately denies her a sphere of action in the world. Irigaray, taking this point to an opposite conclusion, argues that a woman associates her vagina with Christ's wounds. This association allows her access to a distinctively feminine voice unavailable to men: the lips of her vagina, Christ's wounds, and her mouth are all linked symbolically. I suggest that the elements that Irigaray and de Beauvoir identify as distinctively feminine features occur in women's texts—at least in medieval texts both for and by women—because male theories about women encourage women to think in such terms. Irigaray and de Beauvoir have not focused enough attention on the ways in which women's own images of themselves have been encouraged, if not defined, by men's views of women. Caroline Bynum's recent book, *Holy Feast and Holy Fast,* has done much to enhance our appreciation of the historical circumstances that shape female spirituality. Yet her study does not consider works written by men for women; some of her suggestions about the positive implications for humanity evoked by women's symbols may need to be qualified in the light of issues raised by texts such as the *Ancrene Wisse.*

An examination of the role gender played in the creation of the *Ancrene Wisse* is fundamental to an understanding of that text. The distinctive emphases of that text—on the heart rather than the mind, on the concrete rather than the abstract, on the practical rather than the theoretical—result from the interaction of historical circumstances, those that denied women access to other modes of thinking, with theories that reinforced that denial. The *Wisse's* method is double-edged. A failure to universalize and abstract unwittingly undermines the conservative male ideological position and method. Of course, the focus on the concrete and experiential rests on a basic abstract equation: the concrete equals women's bodies, and women's bodies equal sin. Even though women may not have been conscious of this abstraction, doubtless they often had absorbed, as self-contempt, the prevailing male attitudes. The equation of women's bodies with sin could be maintained psychologically if not theologically. However, a method which avoids abstraction itself entails risks; if the abstract equation is abandoned (and the work's method unwittingly encourages readers to abandon it), what remains is a celebration of the immediate, the physical; and the coordination of body and soul, God and the world. Such subversion gives women confidence. However, although a direct address to a woman's experience does give a woman's voice legitimacy and potential power, that reach of voice finally is restricted by categories that define woman as mindless. The female anchorhold therefore ultimately has the limitations and strengths of "a room of one's own," a room one recent critic has defined ultimately as the grave.[30]

The *Ancrene Wisse* is a work specifically tailored to the perceived needs not only of anchoresses, but of female contemplatives in general. The work defines a woman's relationship to Christ in terms of her body; indeed, it can be said to be a rule of the body. Closely related to the *Ancrene Wisse* in dialect and theme are the works known as the Katherine Group: "Sawles

Warde"; the lives of Saints Margaret, Katherine, and Juliana; and *Hali Mei-denhad*. While we have no assurance of their intended audience, their themes and images suggest that they, like the *Wisse*, were intended to be read, if not by these three anchoresses, then at least by female contemplatives. It might be argued that they act as a practical demonstration, a handbook, to be read in conjunction with the guidebook, the *Wisse*. Indeed, the *Wisse* recommends that the anchoresses should at least read saints' lives. In the following chapters, we shall consider the ways in which the works of the Katherine Group, like the *Ancrene Wisse*, elucidate male versions of what they perceive to be a specifically feminine spiritual experience.

CHAPTER 5

The Perfect Marriage:
Hali Meidenhad

Critical reaction to *Hali Meidenhad* has been harsh. Critics have called it "crude, earthy and prejudiced," and it has been compared unfavorably to the *Ancrene Wisse* as "less intelligent" and "less sensitive."[1] An early editor of some of the AB texts states that the text has "little elevation or spirituality."[2] Although a few critics praise what one commentator has called the "uncompromising realism" of the work, most object to its "deliberately shocking descriptions of the unpleasantness and trials of married life."[3] The text's most recent editor concludes that the text is merely conventional, "a skillful rehandling of commonplaces, rather than an independent contribution to its subject."[4]

These narrow views of the work spring from the failure of critics to see this work as designed specifically for women in the religious life. *Hali Meidenhad* shares the psychological sophistication of the *Ancrene Wisse,* and confronts the following problems specific to the female recluse: the centrality of virginity to the female recluse's experience; the isolation and sense of abandonment of the anchoress; the temptation facing women to lose their virginity; and the attraction of marriage, home, and children for women. The work scrutinizes these fears and desires and seeks to overcome them directly by substituting an image of a more emotionally fulfilling relationship to Christ.

Hali Meidenhad reflects both a positive and negative view of women: on the one hand, it celebrates the special opportunities available to women in the religious life as literal brides of Christ, and, on the other hand, it assumes that a woman's experience of Christianity is limited to this relational mode of experience. The relationship to Christ, which is one of general concern in the other AB texts, is the sole controlling theme of this work.

Previous commentators have viewed the work as essentially conventional, arising as it does from a variety of male sources. It is true that, as the most recent editor of the work, Bella Millet, has shown, *Hali Meiden-had* draws on a variety of standard texts ranging from the works of Jerome to the commentaries of Bernard. Millet has identified even some of the more unusual features of the work, such as the vivid descriptions of a pregnant woman's nausea and the psychologically realistic descriptions of the anxieties of a loveless marriage, as originating in previously unrecognized sources: Alan de Lille's "Summa de Arte Praedicatoria" and Hildebert of Lavardin's letter to the recluse Athalisa.[5] Seen in this way, the English work is a simple patchwork of conventional sources. The work opens with a discussion of the life of the prototypical virgin, based on the two conventional interpretations of her life, as an exile and as an angel (*vita angelica*), themes previously developed in the works of Augustine, Ambrose, and Jerome. *Hali Meidenhad* then delivers a scathing denunciation of the secular life the virgin has chosen to leave behind. (The woes of marriage (*molestiae nuptiarum*) had been a common theme, from Jerome to the more contemporary Hildebert.) *Hali Meidenhad* then celebrates the virgin's more fulfilling marriage to Christ, clearly drawing on the bride-of-Christ (*sponsa christi*) motif common in the twelfth-century works of Anselm, Bernard, Alan de Lille, and others. Finally the text analyzes the virtues and vices as spiritual offspring, a metaphor developed by Origen.

Although *Hali Meidenhad* is based on a number of sources, the arrangement of derived portions results in a completely new work. Like many medieval works, including the Wife of Bath's prologue, this text achieves its originality not through the invention of new images or allegories, but rather through the arrangement of old sources to express a new idea. The English author chose sources that reflect his concern for the specific pressures felt by the female recluse, and then arranged these sources to create a psychologically effective program to overcome these pressures. Critics, overlooking the thorough feminization of the work, have also missed its originality. Although conventional treatises on the celibate life include one or two of such standard motifs as the *vita angelica* or the *molestiae nuptiarum,* no source includes them all. In its comprehensive use of these conventions, *Hali Meidenhad* breaks with tradition by offering women the opportunity to experience the emotional fulfillments of marriage not in its usual secular context but through a spiritual alliance with Christ.

It is not only the choice of material that makes this work distinctive. The author's arrangement of his sources results in an emotional process different from that evoked by any previous work. Each motif in *Hali Meidenhad* elaborates the motifs that precede it, whereas in the sources each motif concerning virginity exists as an independent contribution to the subject. For example, when Origen discusses spiritual children as the vices and the virtues, he does not develop this subject within the context of the *molestiae nuptiarum* motif. In his work, although the virtues are meant to be loved and protected as children are, the metaphorical children are not meant to replace literal children. In *Hali Meidenhad,* on the other hand, the juxtaposition of the *molestiae nuptiarum* motif with the metaphor of spiritual children creates an additional meaning missing in the source. In this text, the emotions inspired by the desire for literal children are redirected to a spiritual goal. The arrangement of conventional sources thus not only presents a new argument but also evokes a series of emotional experiences in the reader, which in themselves exemplify the process the anchoress must go through in order to maintain her commitment to Christ.

One might argue that the rhetorical design I have outlined above is also conventional. As Millett points out, the invocation of a terrestrial thing in order to show the beauty of a spiritual one is a rhetorical convention that dates back to St. Paul and Gregory of Nyssa. But, while the convention may be the same, the purposes in *Hali Meidenhad* are different. The author examines the secular life not simply to dismiss it, but rather to utilize it as a step toward a fuller spiritual life. While the text *seems* to work through a series of negatives, showing the anchoress what she must not have, in fact it offers her a confirmation of spiritual marriage by showing how such a marriage fulfills as well as transcends the possibilities available in secular life. The author deliberately carries the reader from a generalized spiritual model through the harrowing details of earthly experience and forward to a much more resonant sense of spiritual reality. The author's rhetorical design succeeds because of his address to and manipulation of the variety of emotions that a woman was likely to experience in the anchoritic life.

Before discussing the work in detail, let me summarize *Hali Meidenhad*'s tripartite structure. In the first section, the author explains and praises the life of the female virgin. In the second part, the author examines the conventional states of women: the highest state is maidenhood; the second state is occupied by widows; and finally, married women occupy the lowest condition. The author concentrates his attention on a discussion of married life in order to demonstrate the undesirability of the married state. In the third section, the author returns to his discussion of virginity and offers Christ as a more suitable and more fulfilling partner than a secular husband.

In the three parts of the work, then, the author first establishes a spiritual model, then contrasts it with the alternatives available in the secular world, and finally redefines the spiritual model in terms of the desires and needs of the secular world. The author transforms a woman's desire for an earthly marriage into the fulfillment of a spiritual marriage to Christ that transcends the emotional needs of an earthly marriage, and the reader of this work experiences the metaphorical marriage of the soul to Christ as though it were a literal marriage.

PART ONE

The author begins his work with an allegorization of the opening lines of David's Psalms 14:11: "Audi, filia, et vide et inclina aurem tuam; et obliviscere populum tuum et domum patris tui" (p. 1) ("Listen, daughter, and see and incline your ears; and forget your people and your father's house.") This passage in itself is a convention in treatises on virginity. However, whereas other writers, such as Jerome, use this text as an allegory of the soul's relationship to God and to the devil, this author expresses his concern for the temptations that are of special concern to women—lust and marriage. He explains that the "people" represent temptations that distract the contemplative from her chosen life:

þe gederunge inwið þe of fleschliche þonkes þe leaðieð þe ant dreaieð wið har procunges to fleschliche fulðen, to lichomliche lustes, ant eggið þe to brudlac ant to weres cluppunge. (p. 1) (The assembly within thee of fleshly thoughts, that invite and draw thee with their prickings to fleshly corruption and to carnal lusts, and entice thee to marriage and a husband's embrace.)

The "people" described here reflect external and internal pressures on women: the external pressures of family and friends to marry and the internal pressure of her inherently lustful nature.

The author's address to a daughter emphasizes his fatherly concern:

"Dohter" he cleopeð hire, forþi þet ha understonde þet he hire lueveliche lives luve leareð, as feader ah his dohter, ant heo him as hire feader, þe blideluker lustni. (p. 1) (He calls her "Daughter" in order that she may understand that he is teaching her affectionately the love of spiritual life as a father should his daughter, and that she may the more cheerfully listen to him as a father.)

To capture the reader's attention, *Hali Meidenhad* focuses on an issue likely to distress the novice, the emotional isolation of the female contemplative. The author suggests that the protection of a family can be found in the spiritual life as well as in secular life. Emphasizing the anchoress's need for paternal guidance, the author investigates the contemplative's emotional needs throughout the text and closes the work with a reminder of his initial protective image by urging the virgin to *"wrist te under Godes wengen"* (p. 24) ("hide yourself under God's wings").

The opening of the last third of the text celebrates the special role of the virgin available to women in the religious life. The author emphasizes the singularity and honor of the position that the female recluse holds, by describing virginity as a tower. The elevation of the tower suggests the superiority of the virgin's life to the lives of the widowed or married: "bitacneð þis tur þe hehnesse of meiðhad, þe bihald as of heh alle widewen under hire ant weddede baðe" (p. 2) ("this tower typifies the elevated state of virginity, that beholds as from on high, all widows and wedded women both"). The central paradox of the tower, and thus the conflict facing the virgin, is that this tower, despite its closeness to heaven, nevertheless is on earth:

> Of þet Syon ha bihalt al þe worlt under hire; ant þurh englene liflade ant heovenlich þet ha lead, þah ha licomliche wunie upon eorðe, ha stiheð gasteliche, ant is as i Syon, þe hehe tur of heovene, freo over alle from worldliche weanen (p. 2) (From that Sion, she beholds all the world below her; and by the life of angels, the heavenly one, that she leads, though in the body she dwell on earth, she is as it were in Sion, the highest tower in heaven, free beyond them all from all worldly vexations.)

The virgin, like a tower, is part of the earth, but reaches towards heaven. By maintaining herself in the heights of the tower, she can recreate a part of heaven on earth. This image asserts the author's conception of women as fundamentally rooted in the body despite their spiritual aspirations.

The author of *Hali Meidenhad* suggests an approach to the virgin's dilemma that breaks with tradition by arguing that one way for women to overcome the temptations of the earth is to recognize that a spiritual marriage to Christ not only earns heavenly rewards, but also has advantages on earth. The author here draws on another convention, the metaphor of the soul's marriage to Christ, but he suggests a literal as well as a metaphorical meaning for marriage. The virgin is God's spouse, Jesus Christ's spouse, before whom all kings bow. She therefore is not only a bride in heaven, but also "of al þe worlt leafdi, as he is of al lauerd" (p. 2) ("a lady of all the world, as he is Lord of all"). The author commends the virgin's intellectual and physical freedom: she is "se freo of hireseolven þet ha nawiht ne þearf of oðer þing þenchen bute ane of hire leofmon" (p. 2) ("so free of herself that she need think nought of any other thing but only of her lover"). If she marries, she will lose everything:

> Nis ha þenne sariliche (as ich seide ear) akeast ant into þeowdom idrahen, þe of se muchel hehschipe ant se seli freodom, schal lihte se lahe into a monnes þeowdom, swa þet ha naveð nawt freo of hireseolven. (p. 2) (Is she not (as I said before) sorely cast down and drawn into servitude, that, from so high an eleva-

tion and so happy freedom, shall descend so low into a man's thralldom, so that she shall have nothing free of herself.)

An earthly husband, as opposed to Christ, has fewer possessions, "leasse haveð" (p. 3), and married to a man, she will have "to carien for se feole þing, teonen, þolien, ant gromen ant scheomen" (p. 3) ("care for so many things, endure vexations and anger and shame"). The author clearly establishes that a virgin on earth, let alone in heaven, is infinitely freer from cares than is a married woman. If the virgin turns to God, all will turn to good, even on this earth "for he wule carie for hire þet ha haveð itake to of al þet hire bihouveð hwil ha riht luveð him wið sode bileave" (p. 2) ("for he will care for her, unto whom she has committed herself, in all that she wants, while she rightly loves him with true faith"). The author here describes the celibate life solely in terms of what are taken to be feminine concerns.

The choice to marry Christ not only provides freedom from care but also brings with it emotional fulfillment. The author emphasizes the joys of the virgin's intimate relationship to Christ:

> Swuch swettnesse þu schalt ifinden in his luve ant in his service ant habbe se muche murhðe þrof . . . se muchel confort is in his grace þet al ham sit þet ha seoð, ant þah hit þunche oþre men þet ha drehen hearde, hit ne derveð ham nawt, ah þunched ham softe, ant habbeð mare delit þrin þen ei oðre habbe i licunge of þe worlt . . . þus habbeð Godes freond al þe frut of þis worlt þet ha forsaken habbeð, o wunderliche wise, ant heovene ed ten ende (p. 3). (And such sweetness shall thou find in his love and in his service, and have so much enjoyment thereof . . . and there is so much comfort in his grace, that all that they see, suits them well; and though to other men it may seem that they suffer hardships, it grieves them not, but seems to them soft, and they have more delight therein than any others in the satisfactions of the world. . . . Thus God's friends have, in a wonderful manner, all the enjoyment of this world, which they have forsaken, and heaven at the end.)

Although an emphasis on the personal relationship of the virgin to Christ is not new to devotional writing, the relationship posited here goes beyond the traditional in being not only intensely personal, but also in transforming the traditional roles of women both as daughters cared for by fathers, and as wives who both serve and are cared for by husbands. Christ plays the double role of father and husband.

Clearly stressing the immediate earthly rather than heavenly rewards of maidenhood, the author praises maidenhood as the best of all earthly conditions: "Hwet is lufsumre þing ant mare to herien bimong eorðliche þing þen þe mihte of meiðhad" (p. 5) ("What is a more lovesome thing, and more to be extolled among earthly things than the virtue of maidenhood?"). Maidenhood is "Heovene cwen, ant worldes alesendnesse" (p. 5) ("Queen of heaven, and redemption of the world"). Through maidenhood, earthly men and women become like angels, even on earth: "Engel ant meiden beoð evening i vertu i meiðhades mihte, þah eadinesse han twinni ȝetten" (p. 6) ("An angel and a maiden are equal in virtue of maidenhood's excellence, though in blessedness they are yet separated"). Purity is the only heavenly virtue that can exist on earth:

> þis mihte is þet an þet i þis deadliche lif schaweð in hire an estat of þe blisse undeadliche . . . ant teacheð her on eorðe in hire liflade þe liflade of heovene; ant i þis worlt þet is icleopet "lond of unlicnesse," edhalt hire burde in licnesse of heovenlich cunde, þah ha beo utlahe þrof ant i licome of lam; ant i bestes bodi neh liveð heovene engel. (p. 6) (This virtue is the only one that in this mortal life shows in its estate of the bliss immortal and which teaches here on earth, in its mode of life, the life-leading of heaven; and in this world which is called a land of unlikeness, maintains her birthright in the purity of the heavenly nature, though she be an outlaw therefrom, and in a frame of clay and in a body of a beast, almost lives as a heavenly angel.)

Although she must not suppress her erotic desire for Christ, a woman can find heaven on earth only by denying actual sexual experience.

After describing the exalted state of the virgin on earth, the author goes on to warn of the threat to the virgin which the secular world poses, in the form of the devil. The way in which the author describes the devil's techniques typifies the distinctive stylistic features of this text as a whole; that is, the author presents a detailed, psychologically immediate portrait of the devil that recalls the particular circumstances of the female recluse. The devil is particularly vengeful against woman. He is *ontfule* (p. 7) ("spiteful") of the high station of virgins because it was "þurh ure leafdi meiðhad þe hit bigon earst, þe meiden Marie, he forleas þe lauerdom on moncun on eorðe" (p. 7) ("through our Lady's maidenhood, who began it first, the maiden Mary, he lost the dominion over mankind on earth"). This reference to Mary compliments women, stresses that even the seemingly weak can overcome the devil, and explains the particular danger that maidens represent for the devil. The devil is anguished that he was overcome by a maiden: "For swa muche þe hoherluker him þuncheð to beon overcumen, þet þing se feble as flesch is, ant nomeliche of wummon, schal him overstihen" (p. 7) ("for the more ignominious it seems to be overcome; that a thing so feeble as flesh is, and especially that of women, shall overpass him").

In order to emphasize the constant threat that the secular world poses for the female recluse, the author presents a relentless picture of the devil's temptations in his description of a hypothetical meeting between a man and a woman. Because the devil's target is female, his most powerful weapon is lust: "Euch fleschlich wil ant lust of leccherie þe ariseð i þe heorte, is þes feondes fla" (p. 7) ("Every will of the flesh and lust of lechery that ariseth in thy heart is the fiend's arrow"). Lechery begins with sight: "ʒef þu bihaldest ofte ant stikelunge on ei mon, leccherie ananriht greiðeð hire wið þet to weorrin o þi meidhad" (p. 8) (if you gaze often intently upon any man, lechery anon prepares herself to make war on your virginity"). Speech follows sight, then a kiss, and finally *unhende felunge* (p. 8) ("improper handling"). The author warns the reader of the precariousness of a virgin's life and insists that the maiden be self-conscious and analytical about every possible situation that might lead to sin. Although this description of the stages of sin echoes Augustine, the author's emphasis reflects his particular anxiety about a woman's naturally lustful desires.

PART TWO

The author of *Hali Meidenhad* includes the second section of the work, an analysis of the problems and rewards of secular marriage, not simply to reinforce the virgin's spiritual commitment, but also to show her how to put into practice the new kind of feminine spirituality the text advocates. The author first analyzes the motives for marriage and childbearing, and then shows that the desires underlying these motivations can be more perfectly realized in the spiritual life. He recognizes the temptation to marry that a maiden might feel and posits her hypothetical thoughts:

> Ah monnes elne is muche wurð, ant me bihoveð his help to fluttunge ant te fode. Of wif ant weres gederunge worldes weole awakeneð, ant streon of feire children, þe gleadieð muchel þe ealdren. (p. 13) (But a man's vigour is worth much, and I need his help for maintenance and food; of a woman's and man's copulation, worldly weal arises, and a progeny of fair children, that give much joy to their parents).

While the author apparently reinforces the maiden's unworldliness by showing her that her idealized notions of a happy marriage, secure property, and the joys of children are rarely realized, paradoxically his detailed, realistic descriptions of these events actually draw the reader into a world she has supposedly denied. The author's description of married life, though drawn from a variety of sources, is notable for its wealth of realistic detail. Such detail encourages her to imagine vividly her own hypothetical marriage. Unlike Jerome and Ambrose, who urge the choice of virginity solely on account of the rewards in heaven, the author of *Hali Meidenhad* sets out to prove the preferability of the life of a maiden with reference first to this life alone, and then to its spiritual context.

The author first addresses the maiden's image of a happy marriage. He argues that the love of husband and wife is "seltscene on eorðe" (p. 13) ("seldom seen on earth") and continues to argue that even when love is found in a marriage, the marriage will by no means be free from troubles. Minor anxieties, sighs, and sorrows will separate the couple; even their happiness, in the unlikely event of its coming about, ends in death: "Ant eauer, se hare murhðe wes mare togederes, se þe sorhe is sarre ed te twin-nunge" (p. 14) ("and the greater was their satisfaction together, the sorer is the sorrow at parting"). What appears to the maiden as enviable security is pictured as often an inevitably fragile alliance. The author then shifts from his somewhat sympathetic account of the trials of a loving couple to a more general Christian precept:

Wa is him forþi, as Seint Austin seið, þet is wið to muche luue to ei eorðliche þing iteiet; for eauer bið þet swete aboht wið twa dale of bittre. (p. 14) (Woe is to him, as Saint Austin says, that is tied with excess of affection to any earthly object, for the sweet is bought ever with a double dole of bitterness.)

Tension is created here by the juxtaposition of a conventional Christian ascetic precept with a realistic portrait of an anxious, loving couple. The author's shift of perspective is typical of his methods. Assuming that women cannot escape their dependence on men, he sympathizes with the natural desire for love, shows that the fulfillment of this natural instinct is only imperfectly realizable in the world, and then shows that such a psychological need can be fulfilled in this world only by shifting the object of desire from the human dimension to the divine. The author argues that God is a better husband than a man because when a maiden is betrothed to God, she will never experience the loss that he has detailed: "for him ne mei ha nanes weis . . . neauer mare leosen, ah schal ifinden him aa swetture ant savurure from worlde into worlde, aa on ecnesse" (p. 14) ("For she can never lose him any wise . . . But she will find him ever sweeter and more savoury from age to age, for ever and ever"). The author dispels the maiden's envy of a wife's worldly possessions by reminding her that it is difficult to enjoy worldly goods because of the anxiety that surrounds them:

Al þe este ant al þe eise is þer, as þe oþre beoð godlese ant ignahene, nabben ha neauer se muchel wiðuten i þe worlde, for þet ha beoð offearet eauer forte leo-sen. (p. 14) (All the delicacy and all the ease is here on earth as the other things

of the earth void of good and corroded—have their possessors never so much of
those external worldly advantages—because they are always alarmed about losing them.)

Thieves may steal a couple's possessions, rievers may rob them, superior
lords may harass them about their possessions, and "mohðe fret to claðes
ant cwalm sleað þet ahte" (p. 15) ("the moth fretts the clothes, and plague
slays the cattle"). The author shifts perspective again from the worldly to
the heavenly by praising the riches the maiden has in her heart: "Ne mei na
worldlich unhap bireavin ham hare weole, for ha beoð riche ant weolefule
inwið i þe heorte" (p. 14) ("Nor may any worldly mishap bereave them of
their wealth, for they are rich and wealthy within the heart"). The author
emphasizes the anxieties of the housewife: she must "wakien i moni care,
nawt ane for þe seolf . . . ah schalt for monie oþre . . . ant mare beon
idrechet þen ei drivel i þe hus" (p. 14) ("lie awake in many a care, not only
for yourself . . . but for many others . . . and be more worried than any
drudge in the house"). Although a description of the anxieties that worldly
possessions bring with them is conventional in Christian writing, the description in *Hali Meidenhad* is particularly forceful because it is cast in
terms appropriate to women's experience: wives in the Middle Ages often
took considerable responsibility for the care of a household and its property.

Even if a woman has worldly goods, the author continues, they may be
meaningless when considered in the context of her relationship to her husband:

> ti were beo þe wrad, oðer iwurðe þe lað, swa þet inker eiðer heasci wið oþer,
> hwet worltlich weole mei beo þe wunne? Hwen he bið ute, hauest aȝein his ham
> cume sar care ant eie. Hwil he bið at hame, alle þine wide wanes þuncheð þe to
> nearewe. His lokunge on ageasteð þe; his ladliche nurð ant his untohe bere
> makeð þe to agrisen. Chit te ant cheoweð þe ant scheomeliche schent te, tukeð
> þe to bismere as huler his hore, beateð þe ant busteð þe as his ibohte þrel ant his
> eðele þeowe. (p. 15) (If your husband were angry with you, and should be
> hateful to you, so that each of you two shall be exasperated against the other,
> what worldly good can joy be to you? When he is out, you shalt have against his
> homecoming, all sorrow, care, and dread. While he is at home, all your wide
> dwellings seem too narrow for you: his looking on you makes you aghast; his
> loathsome mirth and his rude behaviour fill you with horror. He chides and jaws
> you, and he insults you shamefully; he makes mock at you, as a lecher does his
> whore; he beats you and mawls you as his bought thrall and patrimonial slave.

Such a situation is particularly difficult because the wife cannot escape the
marriage: "Beo þe cnotte icnut eanes of wedlac, beo he cangun oðer cru-
pel, beo he hwuch se he eaver beo, þu most to him halden" (p. 16) ("If the

knot of wedlock be once knotted, let the man be an idiot or a cripple, be he whatever he may be, you must keep to him"). It is difficult to assess how accurate a picture of medieval marriage this is, but because women at this time were expected to play a subordinate role in marriage and because they had little opportunity for divorce, the situation is not unlikely.[6] The author goes on to describe the difficulties of maintaining equal love in a relationship: "ȝef þu iwurðest him unwurð ant he as unwurð þe, oðer ȝef þu him muche luvest ant he let lutel to þe, hit greveð þe se swiðe." (p. 16) ("If you become of small esteem to him, and he of as little to you, or if you love him much and he regards you little, it will grieve you so strongly.")

The author's account of the difficulties of childbirth and childraising shows broad knowledge of the physical and psychological pressures of raising children. Although many of the details of the author's description of these activities can be traced to Hildebert of Lavardin's letter on virginity, the author's use of the source's details is particularly effective because he contrasts the difficult but rewarding life of the virgin with a legitimate desire to marry and bear children. The author first discusses the pain of childbirth, with its threat of death for both mother and child. In addition, the mother fears that her child may be deformed:

> Sone se hit lihteð i þis lif, mare hit bringeð wið him care þen blisse, nomeliche to þe moder. For ȝef hit is mis-boren . . . hit is sorhe to hire. (p. 17) (As soon as it appears in this life, it brings with it more care than joy, specially to its mother; for if it is a misshapen birth . . . it is a sorrow to her.)

Even if the child is perfect at birth, the mother is anxious because "fearlac of his lure is anan wið him iboren, for his ha neaver bute care leste hit misfeare" (p. 17) ("a fear of the loss of it is instantly born along with it; for she is never without fear lest it go wrong"). Although the author chooses to emphasize the most negative aspects of childbearing, the fears he describes were quite justified. As Emily Coleman points out, "Infant mortality at birth and among the first few months of life was notoriously and astoundingly high."[7] The author continues to argue that even the most loved child sorrows its parents in the end:

> þe haveð of þet forschuppet bearn sar ant scheome baðe, ant fearlac of þet forðlich aþet ha hit leose? For gode þah hit nere neaver for Godes luve, ne for hope of heovene, ne for dred of helle. (p. 17) (She has from this misshapen child, sad care and shame and both; and for the thriving one, fear, till she loses it for good, though it were never for the love of God, nor for the hope of heaven, nor for the dread of hell.)

Shifting perspective from the earthly to the heavenly again, the author first examines the intense hopes and fears that a mother experiences, and he then reminds us suddenly that we should avoid such excesses in any context, and especially when the experiences do not even have the virtues of spiritual lessons. It is typical of this author to stir up emotional responses and to relocate them in a spiritual context.

Emphasizing the difficulties of pregnancy in particular, the author describes the physical changes that the pregnant mother will experience. First, "þi rudie neb schal leanin ant ase gras grenin" (p. 17) ("your ruddy face shall turn lean and turn green as grass"). The pregnant woman will be dizzy, swollen, with pain in her bowels and in her breasts from the burden of milk; her "muð is bitter" (p. 18) ("mouth is bitter"); she will vomit, will be unable to sleep, and then at the end of the pregnancy will experience the great pain of childbirth. Such a forceful description is discouraging to a reader who anticipates only the joys of pregnancy. The baby commences "wanunge ant wepunge þe schal abute midniht makie þe to wakien" (p. 18) ("a crying and a weeping, that must about midnight make you to waken"), and the mother must take care of "cader fulðen, ant bearmes umbe stunde" (p. 18) ("cradle foulness and the constant giving the breast"). The author shows surprising interest in one of the minor anxieties a mother feels, how much to feed the child: "hu muchel ha schule ed eanes in his muþ famplin" (p. 19) ("how much she must at once put into its mouth"). The author speaks of these anxieties to demonstrate "i hwuch þeowdom wifes beoð, þe þullich mote drehen, ant meidnes i hwuch freodom, þe freo beoð from ham alle" (p. 19) ("in what slavery wives be, that must endure the like, and in what freedom maidens be, that are free from them all"). This is not the statement of a misogynist. He concludes with an almost Dickensian portrait of the harassed housewife:

> þet wif stonde . . . hire bearn schreamen sið þe cat et te fliche ant ed te hud þe hund . . . hire cake bearnen o þe stan ant hire kelk suken; þe crohe eornen i þe fur ant te cheorl chideð. (p. 19) (the wife stands . . . her child screams . . . the cat is at the flitch and the hound at the hide. Her cake is burning on the stone and her calf is sucking the milk up, the pot is running into the fire, and the churl is scolding.)

The author concludes this passage by observing that this is what St. Paul meant by the tribulations of the flesh.

Thus, in the second section, the author demonstrates to the female recluse that the security and rewards she imagines are to be found in a secular marriage are illusory. The author, addressing the female recluse's potential desire for a husband, a household and children, presents a portrait of a typical wife and mother to show that secular marriage, far from providing a life of emotional fulfillment, is most often a life of frustration and harassment. The author's opening biblical text, "Forget thy people"—here those people that deceive a woman about the joys of marriage—has gained extra force through his contrasting of secular marriage with the life of the virgin.

PART THREE

In the third and final section of *Hali Meidenhad*, the author reconsiders the ideal of virginity posited in the first section of the work in the light of the secular alternatives discussed in the second section. The author has shown that the desires of the female recluse are only imperfectly realizable in the secular world. He does not, however, conclude that these desires therefore should be shunned or forgotten; rather, he suggests that the desire to marry and have children is both legitimate and reasonable. Moreover, available to the recluse is a perfect marriage to the best husband, Christ. The author demonstrates his notion of feminine psychology first by trying to dispel the recluse's image of the joys of marriage and then by displacing the desire that was invested in these images to a heavenly object. The heavenly husband has the special advantage of giving women children without pain: "Eadi is his spuse, hwas meiðhad is unwemmet hwen he on hire streoneð, ant hwen ha temeð of him, he swinkeð ne ne pineð" (pp. 19–20) ("Blessed is his spouse of Him, whose maidenhood is untouched, when He begets on her; and when she gives birth by Him she neither labours nor suffers"). The children she bears are the virtues. According to this author, the maiden's choice of a heavenly spouse over an earthly one satisfies her emotional need for both husband and children. The author has shifted from the level of everyday physical experience, realistically described, to a spiritual and allegorical level, but the echo of his realistic account resonates as an emotional backdrop to the heavenly marriage he describes. Even a woman's everyday needs will be fulfilled in a heavenly marriage. If the maiden desires a beautiful husband, "nim him of hwas wlite beoð awundret of þe sunne ant te mone" (p. 20) ("take Him at whose beauty the sun and the moon are astonished"). If the maiden desires offspring, she should "temen dehtren ant sunen of gasteliche teames, þe neaver deie ne mahen ah schulen aa bivore þe pleien in heovene, þet beoð þe vertuz" (p. 20) ("bring forth daughters and sons of spiritual teemings, that never can die, but shall ever before thee play in heaven"). The most important virtues the recluse can foster are "rihtwisnesse ant warschipe, . . . mesure ant mete ant gastelich strengðe" (p. 20) ("righteousness, prudence, temperance, and spiritual strength").

Like a marriage in the everyday world, spiritual marriage to Christ has its worries and difficulties. Although a heavenly union escapes the problems of secular marriage, it is especially susceptible to the emnity of the devil. The spiritual marriage carries with it responsibilities and loyalties, and it can be violated by adultery. If she fornicates with the devil, a maiden commits the worst kind of adultery, and Christ will abandon her. Moreover, such an infernal alliance also produces offspring—the depravities of the heart. The author emphasizes that the maiden, in spite of physical purity, can give birth to vices:

> Ah þa þu, meiden, beo wið unbruche of þi bodi, ant tu habbe prude, onde, oþer wreaððe, ȝisceunge, oðer wac wil inwið i þin heorte, þu forhorest te wið þe unwiht of helle ant he streoneð on þe þe team þet tu temest. (p. 20) (But though you, maiden, be intact of body, if you have pride, spite or wrath, covetousness, or weakness of will, within in thy heart, you fornicate with the evil one of hell, and he begets on you the offspring that you bear.)

Thus, the author uses the emotions of his reader and the attributes of a literal secular marriage to illuminate the nature of a marriage to Christ. In this way he creates a portrait of a heavenly union with Christ that has both literal and allegorical dimensions.

The recluse's profession is not unprecedented, and the author urges the virgin to follow the examples of Mary and the saints. He recommends that they

> þench o Seinte Katerine, o Seinte Margarete, Seinte Enneis, Seinte Iuliene, Seinte Lucie, ant Seinte Cecille . . . hu ha nawt ane ne forsoken kinges sunes ant eorles, wið alle worldliche weolen ant eorðliche wunnen, ah þoleden stronge pinen ear ha walden neomen ham, ant derf deað on ende. (p. 23) (think of Saint Katherine, St. Margaret, St. Agnes, St. Juliana, St. Lucy, St. Cecilia . . . how they not only refused kings' sons and earls, with all worldly wealth and earthly joys, but endured strong pains rather than accept them, and a sorrowful death at last.)

Mary is the supreme model of virtue for a maiden, but the saints are models whose temptations are most closely related to those faced by an anchoress.

Atlhough the author has displaced the desire to marry to an appropriate heavenly object, he realizes that emotions are not fixed and that the desire for a secular marriage may return. The devil is to blame for the vacillating emotions of the recluse, and she is urged to withstand his temptation. Just as the *Ancrene Wisse* discusses temptation at length because the author assumes it to be a common experience of the female contemplative, *Hali Meidenhad* warns the maiden about the devil's persistence and urges her not to despair if desire for earthly satisfactions returns:

> Ant ȝef he alles efter þis inohreaðe etstonde, ant halt on to eili þi flesch ant prokie þin heorte, þi Lauerd Godd hit þeaveð ant þoleð him to muchli þi mede.

(p. 23) (And if he still after this, soon enough, persists and continues to torment your flesh and prick your heart, your Lord God permits this to enlarge your reward),

for "ne schalt beon icrunet bute þu beo asailet" (pp. 23–24) ("you shalt not be crowned, unless you are assailed"). The maiden's most dangerous enemy is herself: "Ne bið nan icrunet bute hwa se treoweliche i þulli feht fehte, ant wið strong cokkunge overcume hire seolf" (p. 23) ("None is crowned except whosoever fights faithfully in that fight, and with strong combating overcomes herself"). The author's concern with emotional fluctuation reflects his conception of a woman's essential willfulness. Unlike men, who can ascend a ladder to God, women, because of their feminine willfulness, cannot experience a progressive ascent to heaven.

Stressing a woman's natural and continual temptation by lust, the author gives her an example of how to cast off the devil:

ȝef hit eaver timeð þet ti licomes lust, þurh þe false feont, leaðie þe towart flesliche fulðen, ontswere i þi þoht þus: "Ne geineð þe nawt, sweoke! þullich ich chulle beon in meidenes liflade, ilich heovene engel . . . ne nulle ich nawt for a lust of ane lutle hwile, þah hit þunche delit, awei warpe þet þing hwas lure ich schal biremen wiðuten coverunge." (p. 23) (And if it ever happens that thy body's lust, through the false fiend, invites you towards carnal filth, answer in your thought "You make no progress, deceiver! Such will I be in a maiden's life as is an angel in heaven. . . . Nor will I, for the lust of a little while, though it seems a delight, cast away that thing, the loss of which I shall bewail without recovery.)

The final prayer of the work emphasizes that lust can be overcome only by replacing the desires of the body with desires for Christ, and reasserts a maiden's choice of Christ over an earthly love:

Ant Iesu Crist leve hire þe þurh his blescede nome, ant alle þeo þe leaveð luve of lami mon forte beon his leofmon . . . ant helpe ham swa in him to hehin towart heovene . . . as hare brudlac schal . . . wið þene seli brudgume þet siheð alle selhðe of sitten bute ende. (p. 24) (And may Jesus Christ grant you, through His blessed name, and all them that quit the love of man of clay, to be his lover . . . and help them so in Him to hasten to heaven where their bridal shall . . . endure without end with the blessed bridegroom from whom all happiness is derived.)

A woman achieves success in the religious life not through abstract recognition of the virtues of heaven, but rather through a relationship, a marriage to Christ.

Before concluding, I would like to address briefly the problem of the misogyny of *Hali Meidenhad*. The Middle English text draws on a patristic tradition that most commentators view as misogynistic. In tone, *Hali Meidenhad* is closest to the writing of Jerome on virginity, and Jerome's invectives against the female body as the source of sin are certainly misogynistic.[8] Because of its criticisms of secular marriage, *Hali Meidenhad* perhaps is more appropriately labeled misogamistic rather than misogynistic.[9] The author is prejudiced only against secular marriage. As we have seen, he recommends and praises marriage to Christ. It may be a mistake to see the author solely as misogynistic, since he consistently analyzes experience from what he perceives to be a woman's point of view. Although the author chooses to emphasize only the negative aspects of marriage, childbirth, and the cares of the household, his work is one of the earliest extant English pieces that describes the emotional and physical demands of such responsibilities. The author addresses the difficulties inherent in such disparate occurrences as the physical trauma of childbirth, the tragedy of mental illness in children, and the emotional stress of a marriage without love. Furthermore, the author celebrates the ascetic life as liberating for women, that is, as a life that can satisfy their personal ambitions and desires. The term "liberation," in the modern sense of freeing a woman from the bonds of motherhood, marriage, and male definitions of the self, perhaps is an inappropriate one to use in this context, because the liberation celebrated in the medieval text is one that frees a woman from earthly concerns so that she can communicate with Christ—that is, she is spiritually liberated. The text is not misogynistic, however, in its insistence that a woman's social role inhibits her personal development, either spiritual or social. Finally, we must see the harsh realism of the work within the context of the work's purposes. Its realism is not simply a gratuitous attack on secular marriage, but is part of a sophisticated structure which affirms a woman's choice of what is, in the author's view, a more fulfilling life.

Finally, the originality of *Hali Meidenhad* does not lie in its individual details; as Millett has shown, many, if not all, of its details can be traced to Latin sources. The originality of this work lies, rather, in the author's development of a spirituality based on insight into the peculiar and particular pressures likely to oppress a woman pursuing the reclusive life. Unlike Jerome, who saw marriage as an unhealthy although sometimes necessary state, the author of *Hali Meidenhad* views the desire for marriage as natural and healthy, but insists that it is important to make the best possible marriage, a marriage to Christ. The author examines many facets of secular, worldly marriage and demonstrates its imperfections through a detailed description that makes the hypothetical marriage come alive. The recluse, moreover, can fulfill her desire for marriage by marrying Christ, a union that has rewards both on earth and in heaven. In this text, the world is not a stumbling block to the pursuit of a religious vocation, but rather reinforces the choice of that life. The author's originality is seen in the way he structures his work in order to reinforce his theme: in his tripartite structure, the author establishes an ideal, examines an alternative to the ideal, and then reexamines the ideal in the light of the alternative. He demonstrates that the desire for marriage and for children is appropriate not only for secular women, but also for the recluse whose desires can be met perfectly through a spiritual marriage to Christ. Thus, although *Hali Meidenhad* appears to resemble the conventional tracts on virginity produced by so many of the Church Fathers, in actuality it breaks with that tradition. Its Middle English author appropriates these conventions for an innovative purpose: he establishes a spiritual model for women that is rooted in an understanding of the pressures and attractions of everyday life and then uses these insights as a guide to transcendence.

The Triumph of Female Spirituality: The Lives of St. Katherine, St. Margaret, and St. Juliana

The story of the successful subjugation of a vicious yet seductive devil by an apparently weak and defenseless woman whose only weapon is her faith in Christ obviously would be of interest to the female recluse. Within the confines of the anchorhold, despite her domestic surroundings, she reenacted the desert fathers' more epic confrontations with the devil. The three saints' lives of the AB texts, the lives of Katherine, Margaret, and Juliana, gave the anchoress models with which she could identify. That it was correct for an anchoress to take such female saints as models was indicated in the other AB texts, where the reader was encouraged to read saints' lives. The *Ancrene Wisse*, for example, urged the anchoress to read saints' lives and specifically recommended "ower englische boc of seinte margarete" (Tolkien, 25) ("our English book of St. Margaret"). *Hali Meidenhad* advised its readers to "þench o Seinte Katerine, o Seinte Margarete, Seinte Enneis, Seinte Iuliene, . . . ant Seinte Cecille" ("think of Saint Katherine, Saint Margaret, Saint Juliana, and Saint Cecilia").[1]

That the works were intended for female readers in particular is suggested by the works' direct address to women. For example, Margaret's life opens, "Hercneð alle þe earen + herunge habbeð: widewen wið þa iweddede, + te meidnes nomeliche" ("Hearken all you who have hearing and ears, widows and the married, and especially maidens").[2] Later, Margaret asks God that she may overcome the devil specifically so that the faith of women will be confirmed: "Ich him overcume mahe, swa þet alle meidnes eaver mare þurh me þe mare trusten on þe" (16) ("May I overcome him so that all maidens evermore because of me will trust in you the more"). Margaret's life emphasizes the importance of reading a saint's life or even simply having such a book in one's possession; Teochimus, the supposed author, prays to Christ to save anyone who reads the life or who even holds the book in her hand. More indirectly, both St. Katherine and

St. Juliana address female experience in particular by stressing their own roles as Christ's maidens.

At the center of each of these lives, as in most female saints' lives, is the sexual temptation of the saint.[3] As I have argued earlier, male contemplatives were also subject to sexual temptation, but such a lure was seen as one of many that beckoned, and was usually subordinated to more serious and more abstract temptations such as pride. The centrality of sexual temptation in female saints' lives reflects the prevalent view of women as bound by their fundamentally guilty sexual natures. Although women and men commonly shared the experience of the three temptations of the World, the Flesh, and the Devil, a woman's experience of the temptation of the World and the Devil was depicted as conditioned by her continual experience of the temptation of the Flesh, one that could be overcome only through the body.[4] As we shall see, in these three lives, the saint redirects the desires of the flesh to a more appropriate object, Christ.

That these three lives celebrate a woman's betrothal to Christ has not gone unnoticed. Indeed, critics such as Margaret Hurley and Cecily Clark have argued that the major distinction between the Middle English lives and their Anglo-Saxon and Latin predecessors is the addition of alliterative, lyrical phrases describing such a marriage.[5] These critics have pointed to recurrent phrases such as the following: St. Katherine prays to Christ as "mi lif ant mi leofmon, mi wunne ant min iweddet, mi murhðe ant mi mede" ("my life and my love, my joy and my betrothed, my mirth and my reward."); at her death Margaret hears Christ's voice say, "Cum, leof, to þi lif, for ich copni þi cume" (48) ("Come, beloved, to your life, for I await lovingly your arrival"); Juliana celebrates her love of Christ, "luvie as leoflukest ant lufsumest lauerd" ("I love him as the most lovely and the most gracious lord.")[6] As Hurley points out, the alliterative style of these phrases springs from the Anglo-Saxon alliterative tradition, while their substance clearly echoes St. Bernard's popular commentary on the Song of Songs. Most critics have simply attributed these phrases to St. Bernard. They have failed to recognize that the frequency of these phrases reflects a larger conception of a specifically female experience of Christianity. John Bugge, on the other hand, in an important but neglected analysis of the three lives, has argued that these works, as opposed to Latin and Anglo-Saxon works, literalize the *sponsa christi* motif.[7]

Such literalization, as a crucial aspect of the feminine spirituality of these works, raises some fundamental questions about the way in which women were perceived to experience the Christian life. In the three lives discussed here, sexual temptation is transformed into commitment to Christ. Simone de Beauvoir has discussed the particular suitability of Christian mysticism for women. She begins her essay, "Love has been assigned to woman as her supreme vocation, and when she directs it toward a man, she is seeking God in him; but if human love is denied her by circumstances . . . she may choose to adore divinity in the person of God himself."[8] This statement may be anachronistic for the medieval female mystic, since love, in a modern sense, is not clearly a woman's vocation in the Middle Ages. Yet the centrality of a literalized *sponsa christi* motif in the saints' lives reveals that a woman's relationship to Christ was perceived as fundamental to her experience of Christianity.

The relationship between Christ and the virgin posited in these lives allowed a woman both to identify with Christ and to replace her perceived necessary attachment and dependence on men with a more appropriate paternal figure. These three saints' lives explore the special power available to women through identification with and dependence on Christ. A crucial element of this shared masculine conception of feminine spirituality is the assumption that a woman is by nature dependent. All three lives assume that a woman's place in the religious life is fundamentally relational rather than hierarchical; that is, the female saint defines herself primarily through her relationships to others, rather than through her commitment to abstract ideals. Thus, each author adds passages that illustrate the female saint's anxiety about her isolation from family and friends. Such concern surely reflects the very real isolation and sense of abandonment felt by the anchoresses. Yet rather than being encouraged, as men are, to abandon such a preoccupation in favor of a higher, more abstract commitment to Christianity, the anchoress is shown how the female saint substitutes for her dependence on family and friends a more fulfilling and protective relationship with Christ. The saint's fundamentally feminine dependence on others is resolved through her relationship to Christ, who acts, with regard to her, as father, mother, lover, and friend.

The saints' lives' almost obsessive interest in physical torture raises further questions about the vision of female spirituality presented in the works. Because women especially are identified with the flesh, physicality is depicted as the central impediment to their spiritual self-realization. For these texts, however, physicality is not only a woman's problem, it is also her solution. Physical suffering has often been viewed as the primary corrective to female sexual temptation. As Marina Warner writes, "The particular focus on a woman's torn and broken flesh reveals the psychological obsession of the religious with sexual sin."[9] In these lives, what we see is not just the obsession of the religious with sexual sin, but specifically the obsession of male religious writers with female sexual sin. Their portrayal of torture is excessive if not sexually perverse. In the saints' lives, the female saints must overcome their inherent feminine weakness through the twin processes of physical identification with Christ's suffering and the endurance of extreme physical torture.

A woman's assumed identification with the flesh further qualifies the nature of her experience of temptation. Hurley has observed that the three lives of Katherine, Margaret, and Juliana explore the three temptations of the world, the flesh, and the devil, respectively. I would add that these accounts explore these temptations in specifically female terms. The life of St. Katherine shows women how to overcome the temptation of worldly power gained through theological education and to substitute a new intellectual power gained from her relationship with Christ and her knowledge of Christ's words alone. The English author recasts the Latin life of St. Margaret to emphasize matters of the flesh. Through physical suffering, as well as through physical confrontation with the devil, Margaret overcomes the temptations of the flesh through the flesh. Juliana's life emphasizes the saint's triumph over the temptations of the devil. Her spiritual strength allows her to unmask the devil even in the most domestic of settings. Yet that strength emerges from her dependence on Christ. All three texts together illustrate the triumph of a specifically feminine spirituality. That triumph is double-edged, however, for while the lives demonstrate the unique power available to women in the religious life, they also represent a triumph entirely determined by male assumptions about female limitations within that sphere.

The three authors also adapt their presentations of the devil to highlight problems assumed to be of primary concern to women. Indeed, the centrality of the virgin's temptation by a devil or by devils whose primary weapon is sexual temptation reinforces a concept of feminine spirituality that assumes women's inherent sexual guilt. As in the *Ancrene Wisse,* in which a long chapter is devoted to the nature of temptation, temptation by the devil or by devils is central to each of these lives. The lives act as practical demonstrations of the theory of temptation set forth in the *Ancrene Wisse.* While confrontation with a devil is often an issue in male lives, in these three lives the devil takes a form with particular resonance for women. First, the devils represent themselves as harbingers of lust. Second, they are domesticated. Finally, they are presented in a wealth of concrete quotidian detail, reinforcing the idea that women experience temptation through their senses and within the most domestic surroundings. Thus the female reader is assumed to be susceptible, not to abstract temptations of the mind such as pride, but to concrete, physical temptation.

The stories of these three saints, in both Latin and English versions, provide specifically feminine models of spiritual triumph over the devil. The Middle English versions of the stories, however, highlight these female concerns: feminine weakness and dependence; the female contemplative's presumed fear of isolation; the disadvantages of the uneducated woman in the face of temptation; the devil's interest in women; and the existence of the temptations of the devil even in the most domestic of settings. These specifically feminine aspects of temptation are dealt with in all three lives by the female protagonist's dependent, romantic relationship to Christ. Each life explores feminine spirituality from a different viewpoint; therefore, I shall now consider each life in turn.

THE LIFE OF ST. KATHERINE

Throughout section 2 of the *Ancrene Wisse,* which deals with guarding the heart, the author warns the anchoress to be especially wary of the advances of priests. However holy the man may be, his presence may easily lead the anchoress into many sins. When the anchoress asks by what authority she can dismiss a priest, she is told she need only cite the Bible. If she wishes to leave the room, she should quote the Canticles: "Listen," she says, "I hear my beloved speaking. He calls and I must go." [10] Clearly it would be difficult for a young anchoress, dependent on her parish for food and clothing, and dependent on priests who knew Latin for explanations of doctrine, to dismiss the authority of a priest. *The Life of St. Katherine* directly confronts this problem of authority. The female saint outdoes the arguments of fifty philosophers, simply by her reliance on the authority of Christ's words alone. Her power emanates from more than her knowledge of the Bible, however; both by depending on Christ as her lover and protector and by identifying with Christ, the saint finds a power that is distinctively feminine. Christ acts both as her literal betrothed and as a model of the redemptive power of endurance, a quality believed to be a special attribute of women. Crucial to the realization of this redemptive power is the saint's articulation of the Anselmian explanation of the importance of Christ's humanity. As Caroline Bynum has argued, this doctrine was of particular significance for women, because the celebration of the flesh that results from the consideration of Christ's humanity also redeems that quality most associated with women, her essential physicality. The saint's life exemplifies, then, not just saintly power, but a specifically feminine spiritual power to be found by women through their exploration of their special relationship to Christ.

It is possible to argue that the Middle English translator chose the story of St. Katherine because of its general popularity alone. In all its versions, the apocryphal story tells of a woman who, through her knowledge of scripture, wins a debate with fifty renowned philosophers. After converting these men and many other people, she is tortured and finally executed. The story had been popular since early times, perhaps having its origins in the story of the brilliant Greek scholar, Hypatia. Latin versions proliferated throughout Europe from about the year 1000 A.D. The well-publicized presence of the saint's relics in Rouen in the first half of the eleventh century probably inspired several of these versions.[11] Her cult spread throughout Europe, and many churches and chapels were named after her. There is reason to believe that her life was translated into several vernaculars, since at least one Anglo-Norman life was written in the twelfth century. The rise of the schools might well explain the multiplication of Latin versions: a work that demonstrates the triumph of theological discussion over pagan philosophy certainly would have been a favorite of struggling scholars. The saint's popularity spread to England and even to Herefordshire, that corner of England where the AB texts most likely originated. At least one church in Ledbury was named after St. Katherine, and later in the period, in the fourteenth century, a well-known recluse, Katherine Audley, was named after the saint. *The Life of St. Katherine* certainly would have been suitable and appealing reading for female contemplatives.

However, the alterations that the English author made in the Latin source of the life suggest that he chose it not only for its general appeal, but also because it allowed him opportunity to reinforce his conception of a woman's place in the religious life. His version stresses two aspects of the religious life that particularly concerned women. First, the work shows a woman that feminine "intelligence"—that is, woman's knowledge of scripture—is sufficiently powerful to counteract the authority of the more learned men around her. Second, the work shows her that her intellectual power both originates in and leads to her relationship to Christ.

That the Middle English versions of *The Life of St. Katherine* are particularly concerned with the significance of the saint's intellectual powers is emphasized by this life's presentation of a saint who is notable more for her mind than her appearance—an issue of importance in the Latin version, but especially stressed in the English alterations.

Nearly everything we are told about Katherine concerns her mind. Passing references to the loveliness of her body are given to heighten the pathos of her torture, but these details are far fewer than those in the Latin source, and finally are subordinated to her commitment to Christ. She is "feier ant freolich o wlite ant o westum ah ʒet þet is mare wurð—steaðelvest wiðinnen of treowe bileave" (pp. 4–6) ("beautiful and noble in face and figure, but what is more worthy, steadfast within of true belief").[12] Maxence's initial exchange with Katherine emphasizes his fascination with her intelligence. He is taken with her looks, but entranced by her words: "þi leor is, meiden, lufsum ant ti muð murie, ant witti ant wise wordes hit weren ʒef ha neren false" (p. 18) ("Thy face, O maiden, is lovely and thy mouth delightful, and the words would be witty and wise if they were not false"). Whereas the Latin version says, "Speciosa quidem hec ista forent, o virgo, que asseris si rationis munimento fulcirentur" ("What you have said would be beautiful indeed, Oh maiden, if it had the proper support"), the English version first emphasizes her beauty and then focuses immediately on her mouth.[13] Her true beauty lies in the words she speaks, words directed by the Holy Spirit. Most saints cross themselves on the upper torso when asking for God's help, but Katherine crosses herself on the mouth in particular. Christ, speaking through Katherine, conquers her enemies: she "wrat on hire breoste ant biforen hire teð ant te tunge of hire muð þe hali rode-taken" and became "itent of þe lei of þe hali gast" (p. 12) ("wrote on her breast and in front of the teeth and tongue and her mouth the holy rood token and became kindled with the flame of the Holy Ghost").

These passages illustrate the potential effectiveness of the *Wisse*'s advice to the anchoress that, when a visitor comes to her cell, she should "crossið ful ʒeome muð. ehnen z earen. z te breoste mid al. z gað forð mid godes dred" (Tolkien, 35) ("make the sign of the cross on your mouth, ears, and eyes, and also on your breast . . . and then go forward in the fear of God" [Salu, 28]). By interweaving images of her beauty with a focus on her mouth, the author suggests the ability of women, through their dependence on Christ, to transform the evil mouth of the talkative Eve, with her related sinful seductive power, into a redemptive orifice. The emphasis on the mouth in these passages asserts the feminine voice available to the female ascetic through her dependence on Christ.

Katherine's life further explains the kind of training an anchoress should seek. Katherine is well read and skilled in argument. She knows the popular word play of the day, but dismisses it:

Ne luvede ha nane lihte plohen ne nane sotte songes; nalde ha nane ronnes ne nane luve-runes leornin ne lustnin, ah ever ha hefde on hali writ ehnen oðer heorte, oftest ba togederes. (p. 8) (She loved no light plays nor foolish songs;

she would learn no love songs, nor listen to love secrets, but she had her eyes and her heart together ever on Holy Writ.)

Proud masters, like devils, try to trick her and to best her in argument, but "mid alle his crefti crokes" ("with all his crafty tricks"), no-one could turn her "ut of þe weie" (p. 8) ("out of the way"). Maxence objects to her learning and when she blasphemes his pagan gods, he calls her a "motild," a babbler (p. 22). He is determined to show that she is a fool and that her words "beoð al witlese ant windi of wisdom" (p. 20) ("are all completely mindless and empty of wisdom"). Maxence stands for every man of authority who minimizes the words of women. He does, however, recognize the power of her words, though he considers them misguided. He says, "ti sputi speche walde of wisdom ant of wit beoren þe witnesse ȝef þu ne misnome onont ure maumeȝ" (p. 24) ("thy contentious speech would bear witness of thy wisdom and understanding if you did not make a mistake about our idols"). Here, again, the persuasive potential of women's persuasive speech, so dangerous in Eve, is transformed into a Christian force.

The text shows an anchoress, moreover, that knowledge of popular literature is insignificant. Even though she is well trained, Katherine is not interested in the conventional learning of the world. When she argues with the philosophers, she states that she has cast away their religion and the "glistinde wordes" (p. 44) ("glistening words") in their books, and given up the "witlese leie" (p. 44) ("senseless religion") for a "liffule leave" (p. 44) ("life-giving" belief). To her, the philosophers' books, "beoð wiðuten godleic ant empti wiðinnen" (p. 44) ("are empty within and devoid of goodness"). She tells them: "ȝe beoð wið toswollen nawt wið wit ah wið wint of ane wlonke wordes" (p. 46) ("you are swollen not with wit but with the wind of proud words"). To Katherine, the words she has found in the works of classical writers are not even worthy of the status of words, but instead are empty tricks; "Homers motes, Aristotles turnes, Esculapies creftes, ant Galienes grapes, Filistiones flites ant Platunes bokes" (p. 46) ("Homer's arguments, Aristotle's wiles, Euscalapius' craft, Galen's tricks, Philistiones' arguments, and Plato's books") are not "evening" (p. 46) ("equal") to Katherine's arguments because they are full of "idel ȝelp (p. 46) ("vain boasts").

Finally, it is only the Bible that an anchoress should study. Katherine's knowledge, instead of being acquired through education, comes from Christ, and she is fearless in confrontation with the philosophers because she relies on Christ's help. She remembers the words of I Cor. 1:19: "Ich chulle fordon þe wisdom of þeos wise worldmen ant awarpen þe witte of þeose world-witti" (p. 46–48) ("I shall destroy the wisdom of the wise worldly men and cast down the wit of the prudent of the world"). The fifty philosophers chosen to argue with Katherine are "in alle wittes of world-liche wisdomes wisest o worldes" (p. 28) ("in all knowledge of worldly wisdom wisest in the world"). She prays to Christ before meeting the philosophers, and she trusts that Christ will speak through her. She again refers to the Bible, Matt. 10:18–19: "Hwene ȝe stondeð bivore kinges ant eorles, ne þenche ȝe neaver hwet ne hu ȝe schulen seggen" (p. 34) ("When you stand before kings and earls do not think ever of what you shall say"). The female saint is urged to abandon her own intellectual powers in favor of the power of Christ speaking within her—advice suggesting a solution to the limitations of female education in thirteenth-century England. Like the saint, the anchoress must trust in Christ as a source of strength when she confronts men who are of greater ecclesiastical authority or higher rank than she.

The text suggests the power and importance of this kind of intelligence in other ways as well. In this work, the essence of sinfulness seems to be lack of the right kind of intelligence or, as it is called in the text, "wit." Maxence becomes a devil in the later part of the work because he goes "out of his wits" ("ut of his witte"). At the beginning he is not described as a cruel tormentor, but rather as a man who is intellectually perplexed by Katherine's argument. "Wod" ("mad") is one of the most common words used to describe Maxence. When Katherine overwhelms the philosophers, Maxence is unable to comprehend Katherine's arguments and asks them, "Hwider is ower wit?" (p. 68) ("Where is your wit?"). In addition, Maxence misuses words. When he sees that the philosophers have failed him, he tries to win Katherine over with flattery. He offers to have a gold statue made of her to be revered by all, and he promises to make her chief philosopher in the court. Katherine sees through the false speech of Maxence: "Feire uleð þi muð ant murie þu makest hit. Ah ich drede þet tis dream me dreaie towart deaðe" (p. 78) ("Your mouth speaks fair and you make it seem delightful, but I dread that this music may draw me to my death"). This emphasis on Maxence's fair speech and flattery, absent in the Latin, reinforces the idea that words are only powerful when guided by Christ, an emphasis that ultimately underscores female dependence. Finding his words lacking in persuasive power, Maxence abandons his attempts to understand Katherine and finally goes mad: "þe king ne cuðe na wit ah bigon to cwakien" (p. 80) ("The king did not know what to do and began to quake"). From then on, he is described in increasingly animalistic imagery as "þe þurs Maxence, þe wedde wulf, þe heaðene hunt" (p. 96) ("the devil Maxence, the mad wolf, the heathen hound"). This interaction between Maxence and Katherine demonstrates the emptiness of worldly wit. Given the age's association of men with wit and women with will, this deconstruction of worldly wit is especially powerful for the female reader. The pagans also are sinful particularly because they are "witless." Katherine explains that the worship of idols is especially offensive to God because it violates the "wit" given by God to men:

> Ne nis na þing . . . wreaðeð him wið mare þen þet te schafte of mon, þet he schop ant ȝef schad ba of god ant of ufel þurh wit ant þurh wisdom, schal wurðe se vorð ut of his witte þurh þe awariede gast þet he ȝelt þe wurðemunt to unwitelese þing þet . . . he ahte to godd. (p. 14) (Nothing angers him more than that the creature man, to whom He gave the gift of distinguishing good and evil through wit and wisdom, should lose his wit so far through the influence of the accursed spirit that he pays to witless things the worship which he ought to pay to God.)

The witlessness of worshipping idols is compounded by the fact that the idols themselves are witless: "blodles ant banles ant leomen bute live" (p. 14) ("bloodless and boneless and limbs without life"). Thus, sinfulness is a deliberate denial of true wit, and the fiend tries to draw men to sin by disrupting knowledge and obscuring the true wit of men who "ahten to wite wel þet ha beoð biȝetene . . . þurh þe heovenliche feader" (p. 16) ("who ought to know well that they are begotten by the true father"). Men, partly because of their "wit," have forgotten their dependence on God, a dependence that women, by nature, never forget.

At the center of Katherine's life lies her debate with the fifty philosophers during which she elucidates the fundamental paradox of Christianity—Christ's dual nature as both human and divine—a subject hotly debated in the century preceding the composition of this version. Katherine uses her "wit" to explain this paradox, which is indeed difficult to explain, since "alle wise witen wel" (p. 52) ("all wise men know well") that God cannot die. Katherine explains that "þes is al þe lare þet ich nu leorni [that] beon isehen soð mon Godd þah unsehelich in his ahne cunde" (p. 50–54) ("this is all the learning that I now learn: that God who is invisible in his own kind is seen as true man"). It is in the paradox of God's humanity that truth lies: "Of his feader soð Godd, of his moder soð mon—in anhad ba somet soð mon ant soð Godd" (p. 50) ("From his father, true God, and from his mother, true man; in unity both together true God and true man").

The philosophers object that Christ could not die because God cannot suffer. In an argument resembling Anselm's *Cur Deus Homo*, Katherine explains that God chose to suffer as man, because such suffering was the only way to foil the devil and make amends for man's sins.[14] God "bi-

chearde þene feont" (p. 62) ("outwitted the fiend") and, although he could
have done this "wið an anlepi word, ȝe, wið his an wil" (p. 64) ("with a
single word, even with his will alone"), "þe witti wealdent" (p. 64) ("the
wise ruler") planned that he who overcame man should be overcome
by man.

This debate serves two important functions for female readers. First, it
emphasizes the power women have to influence more learned men, for the
philosophers, who had scorned to "motin wið a meiden" (p. 32) ("argue
with a maiden") immediately recognize the inadequacy of their worldly
wit. Katherine, they say, "schawde seoððen suteliche þe deopschipe ant te
derne run of his deað on rode, al wat awei ure worldliche wit" (p. 70)
("showed manifestly the depths and hidden mysteries of his death on the
rood so that our worldly wit fled"). Acknowledging the power of the spirit
within her, they immediately convert to Christianity and become martyrs.

Second and more important, the Anselmian doctrine itself has special
significance for women. Through Christ's adoption of flesh, female flesh is
redeemed. Furthermore, in Katherine's version, it is Christ's will, rather
than his wit, that has power, an idea that further reinforces a woman's
power to utilize her essential willfulness as a source of power. In addition,
Christ's suffering legitimates that quality of endurance and suffering especially which, in Aristotelian philosophy, had been associated with women.
Finally, Katherine's intimate knowledge of Christ's experience suggests her
special relationship to Christ, a relationship to be developed as the life
progresses. Like the anchoress who is urged to contemplate daily every
aspect of Christ's life and passion, and to anticipate with joy her union with
Christ, her betrothed, this life demonstrates the power to be gained from
an intimate knowledge of Christ, available only in undistracted contemplation. Thus, the account of the saint's life shifts in interest from the nature
of right and wrong knowledge to the rewards to be found in right knowledge, which is a function of a mystical union with Christ—rewards gained
by study and prayer.

Katherine's intellectual knowledge gives her mystical power that takes
her beyond the pleasures of debate alone. This fact is illustrated by the
vision of the heavenly city, which she describes. Her speech differs from
her earlier arguments in that she uses images that appeal to the senses rather
than to the intellect. Her words, based on the apocalyptic vision of the
heavenly city, are in keeping with the sensual appeal already established by
the presence of the angels. Katherine's emphasis on knowledge gained
through the senses rather than through the intellect further reinforces her

particularly feminine powers, for, from Philo on, women especially were associated with sense perception. That association, considered by commentators on Genesis as a sign of a woman's inferior ability to perceive God, here is turned to a woman's advantage. Katherine says:

> Constu bulden a burh inwið i þin heorte, al abuten bitrumet wið a deorewurðe wal, schininde ant schene, of ȝimstanes steapre þen is ei steorre? Ant euch bolt þrinwið briht as hit bearnde ant leitinde al on leie, ant al þet terin is glistinde ant gleaminde as hit were seolver oðer gold smeate, isteanet euch strete wið deorewurðe stanes of misliche heowes imenget togederes, isliket ant ismaket as eni glas smeðest bute sloh ant slec, eaver iliche sumerlich. (P. 86) (Can you build in your heart a city enclosed all around with a precious wall, shining and bright with gems more brilliant than any star; and burning and blazing in flame, and all that is therein glittering and gleaming as if it were silver or gold: every street paved with precious stones of various colors mingled together and polished and smooth as the smoothest glass; without slough or mud, always summerlike?)

Katherine's vision is a compressed version of Revelations 21 and 22. The hierarchy of John's account is omitted in favor of a generalized, impressionistic account in which light predominates. Katherine does, however, include a reminder of daily life in this mystical vision, in her mention of the absence of mud. She also adds the word "summerlich," emphasizing the general pervasiveness of light. Her account gains momentum by the accumulation of paratactic clauses, and she supports the sensual appeal of the vision by the use of alliteration. Katherine ends her account with a passage drawn from 1 Cor. 2:9: "Monie ma murhðen þen alle men mahten wið hare muð munien" (p. 88) ("And many more pleasures than men might with their mouths mention"). Katherine's use of Corinthians is particularly effective, because she breaks the passage in half, interpolates suggestions of other pleasures she could cite, and then returns to the passage, creating the impression that she easily could go on forever listing the pleasures of heaven.

The virgin's special love relationship with Christ is demonstrated in this earthly life by the concern Christ shows for her suffering. Unlike several other saints' lives, in which the saint is aided indirectly by Christ, here Christ himself visits Katherine to comfort her. He comes "wið swuch dream ant drihtfeare" (p. 96) ("with such joy and such a glorious procession"). Christ, "ah wið fode of heovene, þurh his ahne engel i culurene iliche, fedde hire al þe tweolf dahes, as he dude Daniel" (p. 94) ("with food of heaven through his own angel in the likeness of a dove fed her all the twelve days as he did Daniel"). Later on, Christ sends an angel, seen by all, to comfort Katherine: "An engel com wið ferliche afluhte fleoninde adunewart, ant draf þerto dunriht as a þunres dune" (p. 104) ("An angel came with a wonderful flight, flying downward, and drove straight down towards it like a thunderclap"). Throughout, these passages contain spirited alliterative phrases which are not found in the Latin version, phrases which are distinguishing features of all the texts of the AB dialect. Notably, these phrases—such as "mi leave leofmon" ("my dear love") or "min deorewurðe lauerd" ("my most dear Lord")—celebrate the virgin's romantic tie with Christ.

Katherine's last prayers bear witness to the fulfillment of the mystical union toward which every contemplative strives, but she uses a romantic language presumed to be of particular relevance to a female reader. Katherine prays to "mi lauerd ant mi luve, mi lif ant mi leofmon, mi wunne ant min iweddet, mi murhðe ant mi mede ant meidene crune . . . milde Jesu þe art te seolf meidene mede" (p. 122–24) ("my lord and my love, my life and my lover, my joy and my betrothed, my mirth and my reward and maiden's crown, mild Jesus, thou art thyself a maiden's reward"). In passages added to the Latin version, a voice comes from heaven speaking the words of the Song of Songs: "Cum, mi leove leofmon, cum nu min iweddet, leovest an wummon! Low, þe ȝete of eche lif abit te al iopenet" (p. 126) ("Come my dearly beloved, come my spouse, most beloved of women, and behold the gift of eternal life awaits thee fully opened"). This voice confirms Katherine's vision of Christ, and Katherine says, "Iesu Crist mi lauerd haveþ nu icleopet me" (p. 128) ("Jesus Christ my lord has now embraced me"). When, at the end of her life, Katherine is beheaded, the milk which mingles with blood flowing from her wounds confirms her purity. This final image confirms the specifically feminine concerns of the work as a whole, for through this image, the Aristotelian physiology of women that had defined women as containing interchangeable excess fluids, blood and milk, is redeemed. The life thus ends with especially feminine images that reassert the saint's mystical union with Christ through the body.

THE LIFE OF ST. MARGARET

Of the three major foes of the contemplative, the weakness of the flesh is the one emphasized in *The Life of St. Margaret*. The author of the *Ancrene Wisse* recommends to his anchoresses "ower englishche boc of seinte margarete" (Tolkien, 125) ("our English book of St. Margaret") in a passage which discusses the nature of temptation, particularly emphasizing the temptation of the flesh. *The Life of St. Margaret* opens by praising the martyrs who, after Christ's resurrection, overcame three foes: "þe veont + teos wake worlde + hare licomes lustes" (2:8–9) ("the fiend, the wicked world, and the lust of the body"). In this life, however, the temptations of the flesh take thematic precedence over the other two. Although Margaret, like Katherine and Juliana, overcomes all three of these temptations, the narrative of her life especially emphasizes her battle against the weaknesses of the flesh. Like the other lives, the work makes sexual temptation its central focus. It particularly explores, however, the ways in which women can overcome sexual temptation through the body—that is, through the endurance of extreme physical torture. In addition, the work's concrete imagery seems linked with the work's representation of femininity; as in *The Life of St. Katherine,* the female saint is portrayed as perceiving her relationship to God and the devil primarily through the senses rather than through the mind. The images in this work, which are both domestic and concrete, reinforce a circumscribed view of female spiritual potential. Here, as in the other lives, a woman can achieve redemption only by recognizing her essential physicality, by identifying with Christ's suffering, and, most importantly, not by transcending earthly desire, but by transfering that desire to Christ.

The author's alterations of the Latin version, in which he expands and emphasizes physical suffering, suggests that the Middle English version's exploration of the temptation of the flesh was deliberate. That the fiend tempts women primarily through the flesh is stressed by the Middle English version's emphasis, not prominent in the Latin original, on the lust of Margaret's tormentor, Olibrius. Unlike Maxence, who is particularly interested in Katherine's intelligence, Olibrius, "þe veondes an foster" (6:6) ("the fiend's own foster child"), is particularly attracted to Margaret's body, which "schimede + schan al of wlite + of westume" (6:11) ("shimmered and shone in face and form"). Because of her beauty alone, he tempts her with worldly goods: "hire wule freohin wið gersum + wið golde + wel schal hire iwurðen for hire lufsume leor" (6:15–16) ("wishes to liberate her with treasure and gold, and good shall come to her because of her lovely face"). When Margaret refuses to submit to Olibrius, he urges her to consider her threatened beauty: "nim ȝeme of þi ȝuheþe + of þi semliche schape" (10:9–10) ("take heed of your youth and your seemly shape"). In a passage which, in response to her verbal resistance, threatens implicitly sexual physical torture, he emphasizes the physical suffering she will undergo if she refuses to submit: "Bute ȝif þu swike ham mi swerd schal forswelten + forswolhen þi flesc + þerefter þine ban schulen beon forbernde o berninde gleden" (10:30; 12:1–2) ("Unless you cease them [words of refusal] my sword shall destroy and devour thy flesh, and afterwards your bones shall be burned with burning coals").

Margaret herself fears her vulnerability in the face of others' lust. Yet, in this work, lust is overcome specifically by her alliance with Christ; indeed, the work suggests that rather than overcome lust, the female saint substitute for it a prior spiritual and bodily commitment to Christ. She asks Christ to "biwite mi bodi, þet is al bitaht to þe, from ulche fulþen; þet neaver mi sawle ne isuled beo in sunne, þurh þet licomes lust" (6:25–27) ("protect my body *that is completely committed to you* from all defilements, so that my soul never be soiled in sin because of the body's lust" [my emphasis]). Margaret requests aid specifically in maintaining her virginity:

> Send me þi sonde i culurene heowe, þe cume me to helpe, þet ich mi meiðhad mote wite to þe unwemmet + lef me ȝet i-seon, lauerd, ȝef þi wil is, þe awariede wiht þe weorreþ aȝein me. (16:15–18) (Send me your messenger in the appearance of a dove who will come to me to help me keep my maidenhood for you unspotted and allow me to see, if that is your will, the accursed being who wars against me.)

Thus, the work stresses the centrality of sexual temptation for women and offers a solution to that temptation in betrothal to Christ. The Aristotelian problem of female nature, viewed as conditioned by desire for a male mate, is here answered by transferring that inherent and inescapable feminine desire from an earthly male to Christ.

The author casts Margaret's own weakness, and the weakness of sinners generally, in especially physical terms. The heroine comments on the weak flesh of those who are born of sin and on the physical suffering of birth. She describes the wicked as "al blodi biblodeget of sunne" (6:22) ("completely bloody and made bloody by sin"). Here sinfulness is associated with birth, whose blood and pain are linked with femininity itself in that they arose from the gender-specific punishment of Eve to bear children in pain. Further, Margaret describes herself as "lomb wið wedde wulves, + ase þe fuhel þe is ivon in þes fuheleres grune, as fisc a-hon on hoke, ase ra inumen i nette" (8:8–10) ("a lamb among mad wolves, as a bird in the fowler's snare, as a fish hung on a hook, as a roe caught in a net"). These images both reinforce woman's sense of her own physical vulnerability and reflect the history of female victimization.

The centrality of sexual temptation in the female saint's experience is further emphasized in Margaret's encounter with the devil. From the description of this incident we learn, through the author's addition to the Latin original, that the primary concern of the devil is to overcome a woman's resistance to sexual temptation. The English author's portrait of the devil betrays the author's assumption that women are particularly vulnerable to lust. The Latin version says simply:

> Ego enim pugno cum iustis, incendens renes eorum, et obceco sensus et oculos eorum, et facio eos oblivisci sapientiam celestem. Et cum dormierint, venio et excito eos a somno . . . quos vero movere de somno non potuero facio eos somno peccare. (136:23–28) ("For I fight against the just, enkindling their innards and blinding their senses and eyes, and I make them forget the wisdom of heaven. And when they are sleeping, I come and excite them from sleep . . . those indeed who I am not able to move from sleep, I make them sin in sleep.)

The English version expands this passage and adds a hypothetical meeting between a man and a woman who are both pure. The subsequent description of the stages of temptation which the couple undergoes follows the three stages of sin described by St. Augustine: *suggestio* (suggestion), *delectatio* (delectation), and *consentio* (consent). It also illustrates the utility of warnings given by the author of the *Ancrene Wisse,* that anchoresses should avoid meetings with men even when the men appear holy.[15] Like the passages of the *Ancrene Wisse,* this passage is striking for its psychological realism. At first, the devil explains, he leaves his couple alone so that the two may feel secure. Such false security is one of the great dangers that both the *Wisse* author and the author of *Sawles Warde* warn against. The devil explains:

> Ich leote ham talkin of Godd + tevelin of godlec . . . þet eiþer of his ahne + of þe oðres ba treowliche beo trusti + te sikerure . . . þenne ich scheote swiðe dearnliche + wundi . . . hare unwarre heorte. (32:8–16) (I leave them talking of God and arguing about goodness . . . so that each of himself and of the other becomes trusting and secure . . . then I shoot quickly and secretly and wound their unwary hearts.)

Appropriate to the overall theme of the work, the devil particularly tempts through lust. As he says, he desires to "in ham sparken of lustes se luðere, þet ha forberneð inwið + þurh þet brune ablindeð . . . hare heorte mealteð þurh þe heate" (36:6–9) ("spark in them lusts so fierce that they burn inwardly and are blinded through that burning . . . their hearts melt through that heat"). He leads maidens "lutlen + lutlen into se deope dung þet ha druncnið" (36:5–6) ("little by little into the deep dung in which they are swallowed up"). Finally, "falleð fule + fenniliche i flescliche fulðen . . . for a lust þet alið in an hondhwile, leoseð ba þe luve of Godd + te worldes wurdschipe" (36:15–17) ("she falls foully and filthily into fleshly filth . . . for the lust that perishes in a moment, loses both the love of God and the worship of the world"). Although in these passages the man and woman are equally susceptible to sexual sin, the author's association of the concrete images of flesh, filth, and dung solely with the woman's fall reinforces the impression that his picture of female sexuality is negative.

The idea that a woman's temptation is in the main realized corporeally is conveyed once again by the description of the other devil that Margaret confronts, one who appears in the form of a dragon. The English author's representation of the dragon is significant both for the density of its detail and for the way these details emphasize the sensual and the quotidian. The Latin version says:

> Et ecce subito draco exiuit de angulo carceris, totus horribilis, variis coloribus, deauratis capillis, et barba aurea, et ferrei dentes; et oculi eius splendebant sicut margarite, et de naribus eius ignis et fumus exiebat, et lingua eius ignem anhelabat, et fetorem faciebat in carcere; et erexit se in medio carceris, et fortiter sibillavit, et lumen factus est in carcere ab igne qui exiebat de ore draconis. (133:21–28) (And behold at once a dragon came out of a corner of the prison, completely horrible, of various colors, with gold hair and a gold beard, and with teeth of iron, and his eyes were shining like pearls, and from his nostrils came fumes and fire and his tongue exhaled fire, and he made a stench in the prison and raised himself in the middle of the prison and the prison was lit up with the light which came out of the mouth of the dragon.)

The English version is considerably longer:

> Com ut of an hurne hihendliche towart hire an unwiht of helle on ane drakes liche, se grislich þet ham gras wið þet sehen: þet unseldhðe glistinde as þah he al overguld were. His lockes + his longe berd blikeden al of gold + his grisliche teð semden of swart irn. His twa ehnen steareden steappre þen þe steoren + ten ʒimstanes, brade ase bascins, in his ihurnde heaved on eiðer half on his hehe hokede nease. Of his speatewile muð sperclede fur ut, + of his nease þurles þreste smorþrinde smoke, smecche forcuðest; + lahte ut his tunge, se long þet he swong hire abuten his swire; + semde as þah a scharp sweord of his muð scheate, þe glistnede ase gleam deð + leitede al o leie + al warð þet stude ful of strong + stearc stench, + of þes schucke schadewe schimmede + schan al. He strahte him + sturede toward tis meoke meiden, + geapede wið his genow upon hire ungeinliche ant bigon to crahien + crenge wið swire, as þe þe hire walde forswolhe mid alle. (20:20–35; 22:1–3)
> (There came out of a corner hastening toward her a devil of hell in the likeness of a dragon so grisly that she was terrified of the sight: that evil creature glistened as though he were covered with gold. His locks and his terrible teeth seemed made of black iron. His two eyes stared brighter than the stars and ten gemstones and were as broad as washbasins, in his horned head on either side of his high hooked nose. Fire sparkled out of his horrible mouth and out of his nostrils issued smothering smoke most hateful; and his tongue darted out so long that he swung it about his neck; and it seemed as if a sharp sword shot out of his

mouth, glistening as a gleam and setting everything aflame; and the place became filled with a strong stench and from the devil's shadow everything glittered
and shone. He made his way toward her, and moved toward the meek maiden.
He gaped with his mouth wide open toward her threateningly and began to
stretch his neck and draw it in against the neck, gulping as if he would swallow
her whole.)

The dragon of the Latin version is colorful and resplendent with jewels and
gold. Although the English version retains these wondrous elements, the
English dragon is much more threatening. The English version includes
many more adjectives such as *grislich* and *swart,* creating a more textured
description. The dragon is more directly threatening to the maiden: in the
Latin version, the dragon simply raises himself; whereas, in the English
version, the dragon is clearly interested in Margaret as a victim. The accumulation of adjectives combine with devices such as the comparison of his
tongue to a sword, not only to render the passage more vivid, but also to
place the dragon firmly within the physical world. Comparing his eyes to
the quotidian "basins" reminds the reader that such a creature may be found
even in the most domestic settings. Such a description is typical of the three
saints' lives, in that it exploits both the literal and the metaphorical meaning of the devil: the devil may appear directly as a peculiarly thirteenth-
century dragon, or it may appear in disguise, hidden in the basins resented
by the anchoress during her routine tasks. The author warns the female
contemplative reader to beware the devil, whether disguised by the piety of
a visiting counselor or lurking in routine everyday tasks. That the dragon
poses a direct physical, if not a particularly sexual, threat to the maiden is
conveyed by the hyperbolic image of the dragon's tongue. The additions to
the English version intensify the physical horror of the dragon; thus the
description emphasizes the main theme of the saint's life—that is, the
saint's battle with the physical world.

In the face of a visible physical threat, God may seem remote, but Margaret wisely recognizes God's presence in the physical world. Even her
understanding of God is cast in physical terms. She reminds the reader that
God controls all animals, "þe fisches" (22.16) ("the fish") and "þe fuheles"
(22:17) ("the fowl"), as well as all natural processes: "þe sunne . . . þe
mon + te steorren . . . þe sea-strem, . . . þe windes, þe wederes, þe
wudes + te weattres" (22:19–25) ("the sun, the moon, and the stars, the
seas, the winds, the weather, the woods, and the waters"). While the celebration of God's presence in the physical world was, by the thirteenth century, almost a commonplace due to the influence of the Chartrians and the

Victorines, Margaret's emphasis on God's physical immanence, here added to the Latin original, suggests the author's concern to elucidate the female saint's relationship to the physical world.

In both the Latin and English versions, the dragon swallows Margaret. Additional physical details are added to the English, however. The rood saves Margaret, and she bursts from the belly of the dragon unharmed. Thus the Rood, or Christ, can save the contemplative from the most intimate contact with the physical world. Later versions of the Margaret legend shy away from Margaret's encounter with the dragon. Several versions simply say that she waved her cross and the dragon went away, while others say that her encounter was purely metaphorical. However, the swallowing of Margaret by the dragon is central to this AB text. The author's major concern is to illustrate the conquest of the flesh, and Margaret's success against the dragon is a triumph over the physical world, achieved through a complete realization of the physical. In addition, this image feminizes Christ's temptations in the desert by transforming a woman's central confrontation with the devil into an image of birth; here, in this male appropriation and transformation of an image of childbirth, a woman could be said to give birth to her own spirituality.

Furthermore, a woman's dependence on Christ affords her specifically physical powers. Through physical strength, combined with the power of prayer to weaken her opponent, Margaret overcomes this devil also:

> þet milde meiden Margaret grap þet grisliche þing þet hire ne agras nawiht + heteveste toc him bi þet eateliche top + hef him up + duste him dunriht to þer eorðe ant sette hir riht-fot on his ruhe swire. (28:9–13) (The mild maiden Margaret seized the grisly being which did not terrify her at all and securely took him by the horrible hair of his head and raised him up and dashed him down to the earth and set her right foot on his rough neck.)

The physical power Margaret finds through dependence on Christ has sufficient strength to blind the devil. Even a woman's salvation is cast in physical terms.

Despite the power women can exhibit, in this text they nonetheless are fundamentally weak. The devil says that he is particularly anguished that he has been overcome by a maiden. He laments, "alre wundre meast, þet tu þe ane havest overgan . . . wake beo we nu ant noht wurð mid alle hwen a meiden ure muchele overgart þut avealleð" (36:30–36) ("the greatest wonder of all is that you alone have overcome . . . weak are we now and not worth anything when a maiden can cast down our great arrogance"). Some might suggest that Margaret's display of strength, as well as the devil's recognition of that power, here reverses the accepted gender roles.

However, the devil's comment does not dispel the view that women are by nature weak, for it is not that he has misperceived women's strength, but only that his own strength is that much the weaker if he can be overcome by a woman. Further, he adds that devils choose to war against maidens above all because "Iesu Crist godes bern, wes of meiden iboren; + ðurh þe mihte of meiðhad wes moncun iborhen; binumen + bireavet us al þet we ahten" (38:30–33) ("Jesus Christ, God's son, was born of a maiden, and through the might of maidenhood was mankind redeemed and was taken away from us and bereft all that we were owed"). This passage again reinforces women's essential corporeality, for even Mary is praised primarily for her physical power in bearing Christ.

Female saints not only experience temptation through the body, but also triumph over temptation through the body. Not only was Margaret swallowed by a dragon, but also she underwent extreme physical torture. In this work, she herself views physical suffering as a corrective to Olibrius's temptations. She says,

> Hwen mi sawle bið bivoren godes sihðe in heovene lutel me is hwet me do mid mi bodi on eorðe . . . ȝef ich wrahte þe wil of þe flesc þet tu fearest as þu wilt wið, mi sawle schulde sinken . . . to sorhen in helle. (18:6–14) (When my soul is before God's sight in heaven, little will I care what was done to my body on earth . . . if I wrought the will of the flesh with which you do what you wish, my soul would sink to the torments of hell.)

The Middle English author emphasizes the redemption found through physical torture by expanding the details of Margaret's torture found in the Latin original. Her tormentors "beteð hire bere bodi wið bittere besmen . . . leiden se luðerliche on hire leofliche lich, þet hit brec overal + liðerede o blode" (12:16–19) ("beat her bare body with cruel rods, labored so fiercely that her lovely body broke all over and lathered with blood"). Those witnessing the event pity her willingness to lose her beauty: "Wa is us þet we seoð þi softe leofliche lich to-luken se ladliche . . . hwuch wlite þu leosest + forletest for þi mis-bileave" (14:14–16) ("Woe are we that we see your soft lovely body torn apart so cruelly. . . . What beauty you lose and give up because of your misbelief"). Such a statement might well remind an anchoress of her own choice to sacrifice her beauty for the sake of her faith, a sacrifice commended in the *Ancrene Wisse*.[16] Although this statement may address a literal anxiety of the anchoress, it also assumes that a woman is bound to her body. The addition of adjectives such as "softe" and "leofliche" in these passages associates a woman's sexual attractiveness with a male need to abuse that beauty. Furthermore, these passages assume that a woman's transcendence of that essential sensuality is achieved through the body. Unlike Katherine, who asks God both to salve her wounds and to give her mental strength, Margaret only asks for help to overcome her physical suffering: "Softe me mi sar swa, + salve min wunden, þet hit ne seme nohwer, ne suteli o mi samblant, þet ich derf drehe" (14:2–4) ("Alleviate my pain and salve my wounds so that it will nowhere appear in my appearance that I suffer grievously"). This passage is striking in its assumption that a woman in these circumstances would be concerned about her appearance. Margaret, however, asserts that such suffering will guarantee her salvation: "ȝef mi lich is toloken, mi sawle schal resten wið þe rihtwise: sorhe + licomes sar is sawulene heale" (14:20–21) ("If my body is torn apart, my soul shall rest with the righteous; pain and bodily wounds are the salvation of the soul").

As Margaret's final passion approaches, her physical suffering is emphasized again. Because she refuses to worship the idols, her body is burned with torches, and the snow-white skin blackens as it is scorched. She prays David's prayer that the holy fire of the Holy Ghost may comfort her and that the flame of God's love may light up her limbs. She is then thrown into water, and she asks that the Holy Ghost come in the likeness of a dove to bless the waters: "Festne wið fulluht mi sawle to þe seolven, + wið þes ilke weattres wesch me wiðinnen + warp fram me awei eavereuch sunne" (44:6–8) ("Fasten my soul with baptism to yourself and with these same waters wash me within and cast away from me every sin"). Margaret's physical power extends even to the inanimate world. She is able to transform potentially dangerous elements, fire and water, into spiritual experiences; she transforms fire into the fire of the love of God, and water into the water of baptism.

Margaret is able to endure torture in part because of her identification with Christ's own experience of physical tortuure. The above images are often applied to Christ, and in this work references to Christ emphasize the physical suffering that he endured for mankind. For example, Olibrius is perplexed that Margaret could love one who suffered so much, who "reufilliche deide + reuliche on rode" (8:28–29) ("died pitiably and miserably on the rood"). She is willing to suffer extreme torments because of the suffering Christ endured for her: "Drihten deide for us, þe deorwurðe laured + ne drede ich na deð for to drehen for him" (12:10–12) ("The Lord died for us, the dear lord, and I fear no death to suffer for him"). Notice how her attachment to her betrothed is associated with physical torment through the alliteration of "deorwurðe" and "deð" Even her apprehension of Christ is realized physically. Although she dwells on his past physical suffering, she also emphasizes his present physical appeal: "he is leoflukest to lokin upon + swotest to smellen" (10:25–26) ("he is loveliest to look upon and sweetest to smell"). In these passages, the saint merges with Christ, whose physical suffering mirrors her own inherently physical wounds.

Not only does Margaret identify with Christ, but also she depends upon Christ, who is presented as her literal betrothed. At her death, her beloved calls to her, echoing the Song of Songs: "Cum, leof, to þi lif, for ich copni þi cume" (48:29) ("Come beloved, to your life, for I await longingly your arrival"). This literalization of the *sponsa christi* motif is important not only because it defines a woman's relationship to Christ as emotional—a level of relationship also open to the male contemplative—but also because Christ is presented here as the answer to sexual temptation. That is, the female saint transcends sexual temptation by transferring her physical desires to a more suitable object, Christ.

The female saint is defined not only by her romantic dependence on Christ, but also by her dependence on others in general. The male writer assumes that a woman's place in the religious life is fundamentally relational rather than hierarchical; that is, the female saint is defined first and foremost through her relationship to others rather than through her commitment to abstract ideals. In the Latin version, for example, the saint calls Christ "spes despatorum, pater orfanorum, et iudex verus" ("hope of the desperate, father of orphans, and true judge.") The English version personalizes these attributes, heightening the pathos of the virgin's sense of isolation and enhancing the especially emotional comfort Christ provides. Margaret laments, "Min ahne flesliche feader dude + draf me awei, his anlepi dohter, + mine freond aren me, for þi luve, lauerd, famen + feondes; ah þe ich halde, healent, ba for feader + for freond" ("My own fleshly father drove me away, his own daughter, and my friends are foes and fiends to me, but I have you, saviour, as both father and friend) (18:33–36). Earlier she claims, "þu art foster + feader to helplese children. þu art weddede weole + widewene warant, + meidenes mede" (You are foster parent and father to helpless children. You are the joy of the wedded, protector of the widowed and maiden's reward) (18:28–29). The saint's fundamentally feminine dependence on others is resolved through her relationship to Christ, who acts for her as father, mother, friend, and lover.

In keeping with the overall theme of the work—physical suffering—Margaret's life ends with her prayers for women in childbirth. In a long passage on childbirth added to the Latin version, Margaret comments on the physical suffering not only of women in childbirth, but also of the new-born:

> i þet hus þer wummon pineð o childe, sone se ha munneð þi nome + mi pine, lauerd; lauerd, hihendliche help hire + her hire bene; ne i þe hus ne beo iboren na mislemet bearn, nowðer halt ne houeret, nowðer dumbe ne deaf ne idervet of deofle (46:34; 48:1–4). (In that house where women suffer in childbirth as soon as they remember your name or my passion, Lord, Lord, quickly help them and hear their prayers; let there not be born in that house neither a deformed child, nor lame, nor hump-backed, nor dumb, nor deaf, nor injured by the devil.)

Such fears, also elaborated in *Hali Meidenhad,* are a warning to female contemplatives considering marriage rather than the life of a virgin. It may seem odd that a chaste saint should be the patron saint of childbirth, but given this life's exploration of the particularly physical aspects of female spirituality, such a link is quite appropriate.

The Life of St. Margaret provides the reader with a model of a woman successful in her battle against the temptation of the flesh, a model that is meaningful for any contemplative but particularly significant for a woman pursuing the anchoritic life. Central to the conception of sanctity presented in this work is an assumption that a woman's essentially corporeal nature determines both the nature of her confrontation with temptation and the means of her salvation. This life offers a distinctive paradigm of female sanctity. In contrast to male models of sanctity, according to which the male saint follows a progressive ascent away from the flesh towards spiritual union with God, in this model the female saint inevitably is rooted in the body. The desires of the body are both a danger to her and the way in which her relationship to God is defined. The feminine power celebrated in this work is double-edged; although it offers women an avenue of identification less fully available to men, the possibility of identification is limited to that physical sphere alone. A woman's essentially sensual nature requires that she come to understand God through the physical world, a requirement emphasized in this work through use of concrete details that underscore the association of a woman's spirituality with her essential sensuality. She realizes the wondrous spiritual world through the physical world, through the objects of her daily life that surround her—including even that most domestic of all mundane objects, the washbasin.

THE LIFE OF ST. JULIANA

The Life of St. Katherine and *The Life of St. Margaret* provided their readers with models of women successful in their battles against the temptations of the world and the flesh. Juliana's life, while encompassing these two temptations, primarily concerns the temptations of the devil. Although at first glance Margaret's battle with the devil seems more memorable, Juliana's battle with a devil disguised as an angel is more significant for two reasons. First, the devil's disguise shows the reader the danger of feeling secure, even when apparently successful in the battle against temptation. The struggle thus reminds the reader of the moral of "Sawles Warde," the need for constant vigilance. Second, it is through Juliana's struggle with the devil that the reader learns the spiritual history of the world. That such an emphasis was intentional is suggested by the author's alteration of the Latin version to play down deliberately the torments of the flesh which Juliana experiences, and to expand her discussions with the devil. Thus, *The Life of St. Juliana* has a wider spiritual range than the other two saints' lives, although, as in the other lives, the scope is determined above all by the saint's special romantic dependence on Christ.

Central to this life is the contrast between Juliana's tormentor, Eleusius, and Christ. Unlike the other two lives, in which the tormentor is from the beginning presented as unattractive and evil, this life presents Eleusius as an attractive suitor. This emphasis dramatizes the choice facing the anchoress between commitment to a worldly lover and commitment to Christ. After rejecting Eleusius and proclaiming her commitment to Christ, Juliana next faces a confrontation with the devil. While resembling devils in the other accounts in his psychological acuity, this devil nonetheless differs from the previous ones in that he, like Eleusius, is presented as another seducer competing for Juliana's hand. Disguised as an angel, he is another reminder of those men who wish to tempt women away from their spiritual pursuits. After overcoming this devil, Juliana learns from him the history of salvation. Although conventional in many respects, this account of salvation history explains to the female reader the devil and Christ's contrasting roles in the temptation and redemption of women in particular. Like Eleusius and Christ, the devil and Christ fought and continue to fight for the possession of the female soul. The history of redemption, in which Eve's fault is corrected by Mary, reinforces Juliana's—and ultimately the female contemplative reader's—choice of Christ over any earthly lover. The life as a whole provides the reader with insights into the difficulties and dangers awaiting the female contemplative in her chosen profession, sets forth a model of a woman who gains both physical and spiritual strength from her adherence to her spiritual goal, and outlines the rewards to be expected both on earth and in heaven by those who pursue the religious life.

A central opposition of the Middle English version of Juliana's life is the comparison of Christ and Eleusius as lovers. Unlike the Latin version of Juliana's life and Cynewulf's Anglo-Saxon version, in which Eleusius is simply a villainous persecutor of Juliana, the Middle English version initially presents Eleusius as a suitor who resembles lovers of courtly romance.[17] Only later does he become a villain. The Middle English author also embellishes the Latin description of Eleusius with conventional figures drawn from courtly romance. In this version, Eleusius suffers from the conventional wounds of love: when he first sees Juliana, he "felde him iwundet in wið in his heorte wið þe flan of luve" (35–36) ("he felt himself wounded inwardly in his heart with the arrows of love"). He cannot live without the "lechnunge" (38) ("medicine") of Juliana's love. Juliana is described as a conventional lady of romance with "hire lufsume leor lilies ilicnesse ant rudi as rose" (196–97) ("her lovely face, the likeness of a lily and blushing like a rose"). Eleusius experiences the conventional symptoms of "love sickness." He

> weorp a sic as a wiht þet sare were iwundet. His heorte feng to heaten ant his meari mealten þe rawen rahten of luve þurh euch lið of his limes ant inwið bearnde of brune swa ant cwakede, as of calde. (198–202) (Gave a sigh as if he were being sorely wounded; his heart became hot and his marrow began to melt; the rays of love penetrated every limb of his body, and inwardly he burned with the flame and shivered as if with cold.)

As an earthly lord, Eleusius offers Juliana the best of the world's goods. He tempts her with wealth as he rides through town in a triumphal chariot covered with rich robes. The sumptuousness of the clothes are detailed in the Middle English version. Affrican, Juliana's father, urges her to accept such wealth:

> Sei me hwi þu forsakest þi sy ant ti selhðe? þe weolen ant te wunnen. þe wulden awakenen ant waxen of þe wedlac . . . hit nis nan eðeliche þing. þe refschipe of Rome. ant tu maht beon burhene leafdi. ant of alle þe londes þe þer to liggeð. (96–102) (Tell me why you forsake the triumph and happiness, the wealth and the joy that would awake and grow from your marriage . . . it is no inconsiderable thing, the prefect of Rome, and you could be the lady of the city and of all the lands that belong to it.)

Juliana recognizes the worldly worth of her suitor, but explains to her father that his attractions are worthless unless he converts to Christianity: "ʒef he wule luvien. ant leven godd almihti. þenne mei he speoken þrof ant speden inohreaðe; for ʒef he þet nule . . . ne schal he wiven on me" (103–106) ("if he will love and believe in God almighty, then may he speak of this and succeed readily enough . . . but if he will not, then he will not marry me"). To choose a godless man is to choose eternal death, whatever his wealth on earth:

> Schulde ich do me to him þet alle deoflen is bitaht ant to eche deað fordemet to forwurðe wið him worlt buten ende i þe putte of helle? for his wedlakes weole oðer for ei wunne. (123–27) (Should I join myself to him that is committed to devils and doomed to eternal death to perish with him, world without end, in the pit of hell, for the good fortune of marrying him or for any joy?)

Juliana has chosen a better lover, one who can offer her far more than even the considerable wealth and the dignified position offered by Eleusius. She explains to her father that she is betrothed to Christ:

> Ich am to an iweddet þet ich chulle treowliche to halden ant wiðute leas luvien. þet is unlich him ant all wortliche men. Ne nulle ich neaver mare him lihen ne leaven. for weole ne for wunne. for wa na for wontreaðe. (129–33) (I am betrothed to one and I will truly keep on loving him truly, one who is unlike him and all men of the world. I will never more be false to or abandon him for wealth or joy, for woe nor for misery.)

Her lover, Christ, is the best of courtly lovers: "Ich luvie as leoflukest ant lufsumest lauerd" (114–15) ("I love him as the most lovely and the most gracious lord"). Her "leofsume leofmon" (162) ("lovely beloved") is "luvewurðe" (162–63) ("worthy of love") and "deorwurðe" (80) ("precious"). In these passages, the author of the life recasts the *sponsa christi* motif with romance imagery to create a figure of Christ as an emotionally fulfilling alternative to a human suitor.

Juliana emphasizes her personal relationship to Christ in such addresses as "þi meiden an þet ich am. ant luvie þe to leofmon luvewende lauerd.þet havest se muche for me iwraht.wið ute mine wurðes" (617–19) ("your maiden alone that I am who I love as a lover, lovable Lord, who has done so much for me despite my unworthiness"). She often addresses intimate requests to Christ, such as

> Mild heortfule godd milce me, þi meiden. ant mid ti softe grace salve mine sunnen. Ihesu mi selhðe ne warp þu me nawt ut of þin ehsihðe. bihald me ant help me. (653–55) (Merciful God, comfort me, thy maiden, and with thy soft grace salve my wounds, Jesus, my joy, do not cast me away from thy eyesight, behold me and help me.)

The choice of Christ as a lover, the author suggests, is suitable not only emotionally, but also intellectually. Christ is not only more attractive than mortals but also more powerful, because he overcame the devil and saved mankind. Juliana urges her father to consider the debt all mankind owes to

Christ, who, "forte alesen moncun . . . lette lif o rode" (142–43) ("to redeem mankind, lost his life on the rood"). Eleusius is afraid to convert to Christianity because he fears his Kaiser will put him to death. Juliana explains how much more powerful Christ is:

> ȝef þu dredest se muchel an dedlich mon þe liveð al aȝein lay ant leneð al his luve in liflese schaften . . . schuldich þenne for saken ihesu Crist, godes sune, þe is ort ant ende of al þet eaver god is þe wule hefter þis lif þet ich lete lutel of for his lufsume luve leve þet ich livie wið him seolf i þe sy ant te selhðe of heovenriches wunnen. (Royal 17 A XXVII:173–80 Corrupt in Bodley 34) (If you fear so much a mortal man who lives completely against law and bestows all his love on lifeless creatures . . . should I then forsake Jesus Christ, God's son, who is the beginning and end of all goodness, with whom I believe I will live after this life that I care for little? Because of his gracious love I will live with Himself in the triumph and happiness of the joys of heaven.)

This passage, present only in the English account, emphasizes the inferiority of the worldly lover in comparison to Christ, and it also indicates the intensity of Juliana's personal devotion to Christ.

After Eleusius fails to win Juliana's love, his true nature emerges. As the life proceeds, he changes from an unenlightened lover to a beast driven by devils, and finally to a devil himself. Juliana warns him that he is surrounded by devils: "for þe cwike deoflen doð ham þrin on hwet ȝe bileveð" (Royal 17A XXVII; 162–63 Corrupt in Bodley 34) ("for live devils drive those in which you believe"). Juliana names the men who follow Eleusius' order "deofles limen" (223) ("devil's limbs"). Juliana calls Eleusius by animal names such as "heaðene hund" (521) ("heathen hound") and "colt of swuch cunde" (530) ("colt of such a sire"). At the conversion of his men, Eleusius acts like a beast: he "gromede þet he gristbetede" (640) (grew so angry that he ground his teeth"). And when the angel delivers Juliana, he becomes completely bestial:

> Se grundliche him gromede, ant set te balefule beast. as eaver ei iburst bar þet grunde his tuskes ant fen on to feamin ant gristbeatien grisliche up o þis meoke meiden. (669–72) (So deeply was he angered and the sorrowful beast, as any bristly boar, ground his tusks and began to foam and grind his teeth horribly at the maiden.)

In accord with his bestial nature, at his death Eleusius is torn apart by wild beasts. The bestial imagery in which Eleusius is described confirms the wisdom of Juliana's choice of a heavenly lover rather than an earthly one.

The Life of St. Juliana's extended investigation of the nature of Eleusius, as a courtly lover whose true nature is revealed as bestial, reveals the author's assumptions about his female readers. The author assumes that his

readers will be well acquainted with the commonplaces of courtly literature, and that they will be likely to respond to the courtly *accoutrements* of
a suitor. More importantly, he assumes that they will conceive of Christ as
a competing suitor. A woman's spiritual experience is thus limited to the
literal level of the *sponsa christi* motif. Furthermore, the author's portrayal
of Eleusius's bestial nature suggests the author's disgust with sexuality; the
female reader must learn that the real experiences offered by the seductive
figures of romance are in actuality bestial.

The presentation in this work of the devil who is disguised as an angel
further warns the reader to be wary of the intentions of apparently holy
men. The devil's disguise places him as yet another suitor competing with
Christ for the female contemplative's devotion. Just as Juliana unmasks
Eleusius's bestial nature, so she unmasks the devil's evil nature. As in the
other saints' lives, the devil is revealed to be a familiar if not domesticated
creature, remarkable particularly for his psychological perceptiveness. He
is also portrayed as essentially weak, a simpering servant of Beelzebub,
busy, officious, and terrified of his master. This picture contrasts sharply
with the courtly elegance of his original disguise as an angel. His unmask-
ing recalls warnings that run throughout the text, concerning the danger of
spiritual complacency. Juliana is constantly aware of the threatening potential of the devil, even when she is apparently secure. The implication is that
the reader also must be aware of the constant threat of the devil, especially
in the form of men.

In this work, the devil is particularly concerned to disrupt the devotion
of the saint to Christ. The devil describes how he "bisiliche" (412)
("busily") sets about tempting the devoted. The picture of the devil, busily
searching for any crack to penetrate the devotion of a good man or woman
(especially the latter), is reminiscent of the descriptions of the devil in
"Sawles Warde" and the *Ancrene Wisse*. The devil begins his temptations
in small ways, first simply by urging the religious to be bored with frequent
prayer:

> Hwer se we eaver iseoþ mon oðer wummon eani god biginnen.we wepnið us
> aȝein ham ant makieð iswiken al þet best mahte wenden hare heorte . . . makieð
> ham for te leose lust for to bidde ȝeorne. (400–406) (Wherever we see a man or
> a woman begin any good thing we arm ourselves against them and make them
> forsake all that might best turn their hearts and make them lose the desire to pray
> earnestly.)

The Middle English version adds "oðer wummon," emphasizing this
work's concern for women. The Middle English also states that this temptation will come when least expected: "ant we strenged þerwið on ham.

[e]ar ha lest wenen" (408–409) ("and we prevail therewith on them when they least expect it"). The English work especially emphasizes the devil's interest in the most holy person, an emphasis of particular significance to an anchoritic reader. The Latin version says that when the devils find someone who prays and listens to scripture, they have found those who have escaped the devil: "Si aliquis . . . ierit et oraverit et scr[i]pturas sanctas audierit et communicaverit divina misteria ille fugat nos" (160–162) ("if we find someone who goes to church and prays and listens to holy scripture and takes divine communion, that one we flee"). The Middle English version, on the other hand, like the other AB texts, emphasizes that it is the most religious whom the devils set out most earnestly to overcome. If the devils find persons "ʒeornliche sechen to chirche" (410) ("earnestly seeking church") and "swiðe bi ham seolf bireowsin hare sunnen ant leofliche lustnin hali chirche lare" (410–12) ("earnestly by themselves repenting their sins and lovingly listening to Holy Church"), these people are the devils' prime targets: "þer we beoð ʒetten bisiliche ham abuten ant mare þer þen elles hwer to letten ham ʒef we mahen ant wrenchen hare þonkes towart unnette þinges" (412–15) ("there we are even then busily about them and there more than elsewhere to prevent them if we can and to turn their thoughts to unprofitable things").

Juliana's interaction with the devil has particular relevance for a female audience, because Juliana shows women the strength inherent in reliance upon God. The English version's devil specifically praises the might of women: "O þe miht of meiðhad as þu art iwepnet to weorrin aʒein us!" (476–77) ("Oh the might of maidenhood as you are armed to war against us!"). The devil's comments in this text warn the reader of the particular hatred devils have for virgins:

> We wulleð meidenes aa mare heanen ant heatien ant þah monie esterten us summe schulen stutten. . . . O Ihesu godes sune! þe hevest þin hehe seotel o meiðhades mihte hire to muche menske. (481–84) (We will ever more oppress and hate maidens and although many shall escape us some shall not get away . . . Oh Jesus, God's son, you have too much honored women on thy high seat!)

The devil is surprised by the strength of a mere maiden: "Hu derst tu halde me ant hondlin se heterliche" (428–29) ("How dare you hold me and handle me so fiercely?"). He then, almost perversely, compliments her for the special place she will have in heaven, "evening wið apostel. patriarchen ilich. ant leof wið alle martyrs. englene feolahe.ant archanlene freond" (454–56) ("equal of apostles and patriarchs alike, and beloved with all martyrs, fellow of angels and friend of archangels"), reminding the female reader of the special place reserved for her also in heaven. The reader also witnesses Juliana's strength in action, as she binds, beats, and drags the devil and finally pushes him into a "put of fulþe" (513) ("a pit of filth"). She often asserts that her strength comes from God alone, emphasizing that such strength is available to even the weakest woman.

The Middle English version of the life is interspersed with speeches given by Juliana that are considerably longer than the corresponding passages in the Latin version. These speeches serve a number of purposes. First, unlike Katherine's speeches, Juliana's speeches are given not to argue, persuade, or explain, but rather to praise God as he helps Juliana and as he has helped humanity throughout history. Juliana's speeches are closer to liturgical celebration than to theological explanation. Second, her speeches place her sufferings within the context of spiritual salvation. The speeches provide the reader with historical precedents in the figures of the Old Testament patriarchs, the apostles, the early saints, and Christ. The reader also learns the history of the Old and New Testaments through Juliana's summaries. Finally, the history of woman's temptation by the devil is balanced with the history of woman's salvation.

In her first major speech, Juliana compares herself to Abraham: "þu fondedest Abraham ant fundest him treowe" (243–4) ("You tested Abraham and found him true"). After she is covered with molten brass, she compares herself to St. John:

Ah þe worldes wealdent þet wiste Sein Juhan his evangeliste unhurt i þe veat of wallinde eoli þer he wes idon in. þet ase hal com up þrof. as he was hal meiden. þe ilke lives lauerd.wiste him unwemmet.his brud of þe bres. (259–63) (Oh the world's ruler who kept St. John, his evangelist, unhurt in the vat of boiling oil in which he was put, so that he came out whole as if he were a pure virgin, that same Lord of life kept his bride unspotted from the brass.)

Juliana asks God to comfort her as he comforted Israel's people and Daniel. The devil, Belial, tells her that he has tempted her just as he tempted Adam, Eve, Cain, Nebuchadnezzar, and Isaiah, and that he tried to destroy her as he destroyed Jerusalem, Job, St. John, and, finally, Christ. In all these passages, Juliana is placed within the context of a long line of men tempted by the devil. This context is of particular significance for female readers, since it suggests that women are as capable of spiritual strength and triumph as men.

Juliana's most significant speech is one she gives after she is tortured on the Katherine wheel. In this speech she balances the devil's history of torment by summarizing the history of salvation in the Old and New Testaments. She praises God for making man of clay and for giving him a soul, and then summarizes the major events of the Old Testament. She speaks not only of God's comfort, but also of his wrath. By presenting the temptations Belial mentions within the context of God's overall plan, she minimizes the devil's power. The Old Testament references in the Latin versions are expanded in the Middle English versions, with Juliana giving detailed versions of the stories of Noah's flood, Abraham and Isaac, Joseph, and David. Most significant to our investigation of female sanctity is the English version's addition of a reference to Eve as the ultimate cause of the downfall of humankind. Eve is cited as the cause of Adam's fall: "Ah he forgulte him anan þurh þe eggunge of Eve" (577–78) ("and he sinned through the instigation of Eve"). Unlike the Latin version, the Middle English version includes a break to mark the end of the Old Testament version: "þus þe makest milde godd alle þeo muchel.þe makieð ham meoke.ant þeo þe heið ham her. leist swiðe lahe" (595–97) ("Thus you make, mild God, all those great who were made meek and raise up those who lie so low"). This passage emphasizes that even the meekest and lowest—a woman—can be raised up high through spiritual strength. The Old Testament has been recounted through a specifically feminine filter.

The history of the New Testament, similarly detailed, is carefully structured to begin with Christ's birth and baptism and end with the passion, the harrowing of hell, and Christ's ascension. The text ends with an anticipation of Judgement Day. In the Middle English version, Christ's humanity is emphasized: he "lihtest hiðer to us of heovenliche leomen. ant nome blode ant ban i þe meare meiden ant were in Beðleem iboren moncun to heale" (598–601) ("came down hither in heavenly rays and took on blood and bones in the noble maiden and was born in Bethlehem to save mankind"). The feminine sin of Eve is redeemed through Mary. Here the author emphasizes the paradox of the unification of the flesh and the spirit, seen in Christ's assumption of humanity. As I have argued earlier, this doctrine is of crucial significance for the female contemplative, because, through Christ's assumption of human flesh, all flesh—even women's flesh—is redeemed.

The Life of St. Juliana offers the anchoress a model of a woman successful in her battle against the temptation of the devil. This life examines, in more depth than the other two works, the choice which the anchoress has to make between an earthly lover and a heavenly lover, an issue that is central to the work previously examined, *Hali Meidenhad*. In Juliana's life, the heavenly lover, Christ, is shown to surpass the earthly lover, both in the conventional qualities of courtly love, such as graciousness and beauty, and in power. As a lover, Christ fulfills the needs of the anchoress not only for a husband but also for family and friends. Christ's power surpasses not

only the power of men, but also that of the devil. Because the temptation
of the devil lies at the center of this work, this text has a wider spiritual
frame than the other two. The history of the Old Testament and the New
Testament given by Juliana shows Christ's help to mankind throughout salvation history. Juliana's discussion diminishes the devil, who whimpers
under her control. The devil is forced to explain how he tempts; his description warns the anchoress that the devil particularly hates women, especially women who appear secure in their holiness. By observing Juliana's control of this devil, the reader learns that even a woman is capable
of the spiritual strength needed to overcome the devil. Through faith, a
woman can overcome the devil on earth and be rewarded both on earth and
in heaven.

CHAPTER 7

Allegory and the Emotions in "Sawles Warde"

It is not obvious that, when the unknown cleric who composed the homily known as "Sawles Warde" ("The Guardianship of the Soul") sat down to write his sermon, he had a female audience in mind. At first glance, the homily appears to be a conventional translation of a Latin sermon attributed to St. Anselm, "De Custodia Interioris Hominis."[1] Both the Latin and the English works are allegorical explications of Matthew 24:43: "Hoc scitote quoniam si sciret paterfamilias qua hora fur veniret, vigilaret utique et non sineret perfodi domum suam" ("Know this, if he knew what hour the thief would come, he would watch and would not allow his house to be penetrated"). Both versions describe a household of the soul, visited by two messengers in turn, one from heaven and one from hell, who describe the horrors of hell and the joys awaiting the saved in heaven. Such a discussion seems appropriate for a wide variety of Christian audiences ranging from laymen to the most rigorously ascetic group.

However, both internal and external features of the English work indicate not only that the Middle English author intended for his version of the Latin sermon to be read by women, but also that he changed the sermon deliberately in consideration of that audience. Paleographical evidence suggests, in fact, that "Sawles Warde" originally was intended not just for women as opposed to men, but for a particular group of female recluses. After all, the homily appears in a number of manuscripts (MS Bodley 34, Royal 17A27, etc.), all of which include one or more of the AB texts more obviously addressed to anchoresses.[2] For example, "Sawles Warde" is found bound with the *Ancrene Wisse* in Cotton Titus D18 and with the saints' lives and *Hali Meidenhad* in Bodley 34. Furthermore, its dialect is that of the other AB texts, a West Midlands dialect associated with the anchorhold of the Deerfold near Wigmore Abbey.[3] This last fact leads us to believe that "Sawles Warde" might have been translated specifically for the three anchoresses for whom the *Ancrene Wisse* was also written.

Thus we can reasonably say that the author chose this Anselmian homily with an audience of female contemplatives in mind. The general subject matter certainly was well suited to the needs of the solitary contemplative, whether male or female. As we have seen in the previous chapter, the anchoritic life was acknowledged to be stressful both emotionally and physically. In addition, such a life was considered to be fraught with spiritual danger. Confrontations with the devil were thought to be frequent and potentially more dangerous for the committed ascetic than for ordinary, active devotees. These dangers were particularly acute for women. As St. Bernard wrote discouraging a nun who wished to become a solitary, "When there is no fear of blame, the tempter approaches more boldly, and evil is committed with greater freedom. The wolf lurks in the wood. If you, a little sheep, penetrate the shadows of the wood alone, you are offering yourself as a prey to the wolf." [4] (Notice how Bernard presumes here a woman's fear of isolation and stresses her smallness and lack of protection. Like Little Red Riding Hood, she faces the dangers of sexual temptation and never should venture out in the world alone.) We have seen in the *Ancrene Wisse* that many such dangers are from without—the temptation to luxury or to sexual corruption, for example. But what of the dangers within? The anchoress, unlike the monk or nun, lacks both the support and the variation of monastic routine. She has neither superior to warn her about her excesses, either of indulgence or of asceticism, nor monastic duties to distract her from contemplation of heaven and hell. Thus the anchoress easily can be lured into the deadly sin of despair brought on by fear or the sin of pride brought on by excessive hope. "Sawles Warde" focuses on the two emotions central to contemplative solitary experience, fear of hell and hope of heaven, and on the two concomitant dangers facing the solitary, despair and pride. Like so many of these early Middle English texts, "Sawles Warde" attempts to educate the contemplative concerning the nature of these emotions and teach her how to regulate them. This work's particular interest in the regulation of the fluctuating emotions of a rigorous ascetic life seems clearly designed for an uneducated ascetic audience. The subject of the homily, while of concern to any Christian, is of acute concern to the solitary ascetic of both sexes and especially to the anchoress, whose propensity for reclusion, as we have seen, is starker and more extreme than that of the male anchorite.

It is not only the general subject matter that makes "Sawles Warde" a work particularly suitable for anchoresses. The work has been recast, to address not only the unusual problems of anchoritic life, but also the ways in which women in particular were perceived to experience those problems. To begin with, the English author's additions to and deletions from the Latin original indicate that he intended his version specifically for women. More importantly, the very idea of a female audience led the author to make subtle and far-reaching changes in tone, feeling, and emotional content of the narrative.

The English author first restructured the Latin text so that, rather than an abstract, hypothetical consideration of the emotions the anchoress must control, it became a pointed example of an emotional process she must repeat daily. Although based on conventional material such as biblical quotations and standard homiletic advice, the particular arrangement of the material forces the reader not only to learn the lesson of the text, but also to experience it directly. Through a descriptive sequence which solicits a particular reader response, the reader experiences fear of hell followed by hope of heaven, and then she is shown how to balance the two. Second, this evocative structure is reinforced by the dramatization of its parts: in each section, the author has added or heightened characterization, direct speech, and dialogue. Third, the drama is made more emotionally resonant through the addition of vivid, concrete details. All three techniques contribute to the work's sophisticated literary structure, one that seems designed to involve the reader in the text and make her, in effect, the protagonist of the work.

It might be argued that the psychological emphasis of the English work is simply a reflection of continental explorations of the nature of the self in relationship to Christian goals. However, by looking at the Latin version of the homily, we can see that continental texts, though interested in psychology, present that psychology within an abstract, hierarchical Christian frame. The experiential qualities of the English work indicate that the author viewed such a static hierarchy as inappropriate for his audience. The author's revision is more suitable for an uneducated audience assumed to be unfamiliar with intellectual debate. Furthermore, the nature of the revision reflects a deeper consideration not only of the anchoress's lack of education but also of the male author's view of her femininity. The highly personalized analysis of emotions, a technique characteristic of the English work, is appropriate for an audience considered to be highly emotional. The dramatic affective features of the English text can be taken as direct reflections of the author's assumption that his female readers are rooted in their bodies, incapable of theorizing, and capable of religious training only through the senses. Thus, while the psychological subtlety of the work does reflect the new twelfth-century interest in the self, common to both the Latin and the English versions, the particular psychology of the English work is shaped by attitudes about feminine psychology, including the prevailing view that a woman was fundamentally and inescapably willful.

That the Middle English author was writing for women is best shown by comparing the English version to its Latin source. Between the Middle English text and the Latin one, there are some minor but significant structural differences that heighten the appeal of "Sawles Warde" for women readers. The vision of heaven in the Latin version, for instance, includes a long passage describing the joys experienced by monks in heaven. The monks earn "pro claustris et cellis angustis immensa et sole clariora palatia possidentes, pro nigris et asperis tunicis nive candidiores; omnique suavitate molliores vestes induti, ab oculis quorum abstersit Deus omnem lacrimam" ("instead of prisons and narrow cells, immense palaces brighter than the sun; instead of rough, dark tunics, garments whiter than the snow; and dressed with all gentleness in softer clothes, and God wipes away all tears from their eyes") (359:5.8). The English version omits this passage entirely. R. M. Wilson suggests that the English author may have made this omission deliberately, or that he may have had a different Latin original before him which lacked this passage.[5] It seems most likely, however, that the English author omitted the passage in question because it had no relevance to his audience. A corollary to this exclusion is the English author's expansion of a passage on the joys that female virgins experience in heaven. The Latin version says:

> Postremo ad chorum virginum respexi, quarum gloria, species, ornatus et melodia qua cantabant canticum, quo nemo alius dicere poterat, nulla hominum eloquentia digne enarrari potest. Sed et odor in regione earum tam suavis exuberat, qui omnia aromatum genera exuperat. (359:8–12) (Last I looked at the choir of virgins whose countenance is radiant with glory, and they were singing a song in which meter no-one else could sing and which cannot worthily be recounted by any human eloquence. And even the odor in their area abounded so sweetly that it excelled all kinds of aromas.)

The English version is considerably longer, and it includes a complimentary comparison of maidens to angels:

> Ich iseh þet schene 7 þet brihte ferreden of þe eadi meidnes ilikest towart engles. ant feolohlukest wið ham blissin 7 gleadien.þe libbinde i flesche overgað flesches lahe ant overcumeð cunde þe leadeð heovenlich lif in eorðe as ha wunieð.hare murhðe.7 hare blisse. þe feierleac of hare wlite. þe swetnesse of hare song ne mei na tunge tellen. Alle ha singeð þe þer beoð. Ah hare song ne mahe nane buten heo singen. Se swote smeal ham folheð hwider se ha wendeð. þet me mahte libben aa bi þe swotnesse. (I saw that shining and bright company of blessed maidens most like angels, rejoicing and reveling with him in the most friendly manner. Those living in the flesh overcame flesh's law and overcame

nature and led a heavenly life while they dwelled on earth. No tongue may tell their mirth, their bliss, the fairness of their faces and the sweetness of their song. Whoever is there sings, and their song none but they may sing. Such a sweet smell follows them wherever they go that one might live forever by that sweetness.)[6]

Unlike the Latin, the English text also includes a digression explaining the life of the virgin on earth, stressing that her earthly role is a model for the possible creation of heaven on earth. This earthly model of the celibate contemplative, absent in the Latin, would be particularly relevant to an audience of anchoresses.

Some smaller differences between the Latin and the English texts add further support to the hypothesis that they were intended for different audiences. For instance, to the allegory of the figure or character, Will, the English version apparently gratuitously adds an unruly wife controlled only with difficulty by her husband, Wit. To the male author, this figure could seem to hold particular interest for women readers, since the unruly housewife is a personification of that quality of willfullness thought to be essential to women. Moreover, whereas in the Latin text the four guardians of the household are listed as the Four Virtues, in the English version they are called the Four Daughters of God. The Four Virtues were often presented as women, but emphasizing their femininity by designating them as daughters may have been a strategy employed by the English author to attract the attention of a specifically female audience. Two other indications of a female readership are that the English text includes a number of feminine pronouns and that there are frequent comments about women. Prudence, for example, tells how to distinguish between good and evil in order that "þurh unweotenesse ne mei ha nawt sunegin" (193–94) ("through ignorance she may not sin"). The feminine pronoun may be included simply because the Four Daughters are speaking to one another, but it is just as likely that the pronoun refers to the reader. Justice urges the audience to judge itself unmighty, "eðeliche 7 lahe" (208) ("lightly and humble") and praises Strength because "ha ne trust nawt on hire ahnen wepnen" (198–99) ("she does not trust in her own weapons"). If the readers deem themselves weak and trust in God, He will deem them worthy and "halt for his dehtren" ("hold them for his daughters") (209–10). Again, the feminine emphasis here may be attributed to the fact that the discussion takes place among women, but it is significant that the English version adds a discussion, absent in the Latin, of weakness, a quality ascribed particularly to women.

These changes do more than indicate a direct address to a female audience; further, they are part of a larger "feminine" conception of the work. The allegory has been feminized within a patriarchal framework. A woman, Will, the unruly wife of Wit, is blamed for the precarious balance of an allegorical household. Female nature thus is held responsible for the downfall of man's rational order. That order is controlled by Wit, the father of the household, but Wit's lessons are realized through an emotional experience processed by women, the Four Daughters of God.

The feminization of this allegory affects the overall structure of "Sawles Warde" as well as the details of its parts. The English work has been revised to emphasize an emotional, rather than an intellectual, realization of Christian truths. Such a design suggests the author's conviction that, because of their natures, women can experience Christian truths only in this way. The structural innovation of this text perhaps can be grasped best by comparing its outline with the outline of its Latin source:

The Latin Text	The English Text
1–3 Biblical quotation	1–3 Biblical quotation
3–13 Allegorical household	4–37 Allegorical household
13–24 Four Virtues introduced	37–57 Four Daughters introduced
24–57 Timor Mortis arrives and describes hell	58–152 Fearlac arrives and describes hell
58–69 Four Virtues respond to the vision	153–219 Four Daughters respond to the vision
70–160 Amor Vitae Aeternae arrives and describes heaven	220–356 Lives Luve arrives and describes heaven
161–175 Four Virtues celebrate heaven	357–79 Four Daughters respond to the vision
	379–85 Household responds to visions
	386–400 Return to opening quote
Author's prayer	Author's prayer (only in the royal text)

At first glance, the two texts appear to be similar. However, the different endings of the two, as well as the fact that the Latin text devotes over half its lines to the vision of heaven, result in two radically different works. Whereas the Latin text leads the reader through a progressively ascending hierarchy to heaven, the English text takes the reader from earth to heaven and back. The ascending order of the Latin text seems particularly appropriate for monastic readers. Like many of the continental theological works of the period, the Latin text presents and discusses the abstract, moral

Christian order in conventional terms. Through the personification of abstract concepts, the Latin illustrates how the soul, by maintaining the four virtues of prudence, moderation, strength, and justice, can protect itself in its quest for mystical union with God. It then celebrates this anticipated union in its final vision of heaven. The work thus traces the progress of the soul as it moves from fear of hell to mystical union with God. It both explains the nature of Judgment Day and celebrates heaven, the reward which the religious hope to achieve. In this way, the Latin homily might have fitted well into the celebration of the mass.

Changing the ending of the English work radically altered the meaning of the Latin original. Rather than emphasizing the celebration of heaven that awaits the saved, the English text directs the reader's attention back to the sublunary world. The reader experiences emotions which are not progressive, as they are in the Latin; instead of guiding the reader from fear of hell to hope and celebration of heaven, the English text takes the reader from earth to hell, back to earth, and then to heaven, returning in the end once more to earth. The English work thereby teaches the reader that fluctuation between fear and hope is a central, recurring problem of the ascetic life. Indeed, it is the precarious balance of hope and fear that constitutes the ascetic life. The structural alterations in the English text therefore suggest that women have a different place in the religious order than men do. Women, because of their earthbound, sensual natures, do not climb an allegorical ladder to God; rather, they perceive Christian truths piecemeal. Furthermore, women realize these truths emotionally rather than intellectually.

In addition, the text suggests that, despite their recognition of Christian truths, women are primarily earthbound. Although they may hear of the joys awaiting them in heaven, their natures will always draw them back to earth. Therefore, first and most importantly, the female religious must learn to regulate her emotions. The depiction of heaven and hell is important not in order to hold out hope of posthumous rewards, but to call attention to emotions central to the daily life of the contemplative. The Latin work celebrates transcendence; the English work focuses on everyday life; through its structure, it analyzes the complex emotions inspired by the pursuit of the religious life; and suggests methods of regulating them.

This structural focus is further emphasized by the development of each section. Notice that each section of "Sawles Warde" is considerably longer than its Latin counterpart and that the vision of hell is expanded in the English version to roughly the same length as the vision of heaven. Furthermore, the English author maintains the allegory of the household throughout the piece, emphasizing his concern for the present, rather than the future, state of the soul.

Furthermore, the arrangement of the sections of the English work reinforce the emotional lesson of the whole. These sections are arranged and developed in such a way that the action occurs in frames that function like plays within plays. As in Shakespeare, plays within plays permit both presentations of events and commentaries upon these events, all in the space of a single work. If we consider "Sawles Warde" to be a dramatic structure, we can describe it as follows:

Act 1:
   Scene 1: Presentation of the Household of the Soul
   Scene 2: Introduction of the Four Daughters
Act 2:
   Scene 1: The Vision of Hell
   Scene 2: The Four Daughters Discuss the Vision
Act 3:
   Scene 1: The Vision of Heaven
   Scene 2: The Four Daughters Discuss the Vision
Act 4: The Household Discusses the Entire Play

Going further and regarding the work as a *series* of plays within a play, however, we can say that the play of the household encloses the play of the Four Daughters, which in turn encloses the play of the visions. Thus, in this schematization, the soul occupies center stage, experiencing the twin visions of heaven and hell. The two visions are preceded and followed by commentary from the Four Daughters of God, who direct the responses evoked by the accounts of heaven and hell. The speeches of the Four Daughters are circumscribed by the responses of the household members, who in turn react to the visions and to the Four Daughters. In this interpretation of the structure, the female reader, who must synthesize all the responses, is the primary audience of all these plays.

In summary, the psychological movement of the English work proceeds as follows: the first step of the work explains the daily emotional state of the contemplative; the second step evokes the emotions of fear and hope that are central to the ascetic life; the third step analyzes these emotions within the context of conventional Christian precepts; and the final step returns the reader to the daily life of the contemplative, showing her how emotional responses and moral frameworks are to be integrated into that daily life. The work thus emphasizes, both structurally and thematically, not merely *what* one should do to protect the soul, but *how* one is to do it.

The author in fact explains the purpose of his allegory in the following way: "Ure lauerd . . . teacheð us þurh a bisne.hu we ahen wearliche to biwiten us seolven wið þe unwiht of helle 7 wið his wernches" (4–6) ("Our lord teaches us through a parable *how* we ought carefully to guard ourselves against the devil of hell and against his tricks"). This insistence on the experiential realization of Christian truths reflects the author's notion that a woman is unable to think abstractly.

Although it is above all through its structure that the English work recreates the emotional process that a female recluse undergoes when contemplating heaven and hell, this emotional structure is reinforced by the drama and detail of its parts. The way in which drama and detail redirect the reader's attention to emotional issues can be seen, once again, by comparing the English work to the Latin.

The homily opens with a descriptive allegory of the household of the soul. The contrast between the evocative dramatization achieved in the English version and the Latin work's more static allegory is readily apparent in the presentations of the household/soul at the beginnings of the two works. The Latin version opens:

> Sed pater iste familias animus rationalis potest intelligi, cuius multa familia sunt cogitationes et motus sui, sensus quoque et actiones tam exteriores quam interiores. Quae videlicet familia lasciva nimis et petulans erit, nisi eiusdem patris rigore coercita ac disposita fuerit. Si enim vel parum a sua sollicitudine torpeurit, quis potest dicere quomodo cogitationes, oculi, lingua, aures, et cetera omnia insolescant? Domus est conscientia in qua pater iste habitans thesauros virtutum congregat, propter quos ne domus eadem perfodiatur, summopere invigilat. (355:3–8; 356:1–4) (The father of the household can be understood as the soul, whose large family consists of the thoughts and the emotions, as well as the senses and the actions, both interior and exterior. It is clear that this family will be too wanton and petulant unless it is severely controlled and disciplined by this father. If indeed his care becomes sluggish, who would be able to say how the thoughts, eyes, tongues, ears, and all the rest would become haughty? The house is the conscience in which the father lives, assembling the treasury of the virtues, on whose account, lest the house be penetrated, he must watch above all.)

The more detailed and complex English version begins:

> þis hus þe ure lauerð spekeð of. is seolf þe mon inwið þe monnes wit. I þis hus.is þe huse lauerd.ant te fulitohe wif.mei beon wil ihaten. þet ga þe hus efter hire. ha diht hit al to wundre. bute wit ase lauerd chasti hire þe betere. 7 bineome hire muchel of þet ha walde.ant tah walde al hire hird folhin hire over al. gef wit ne forbude ham for alle hit beoð untohene.7 rechelese hinen. bute ȝef he ham rihte. Ant hwucche beoð þeos hinen: Summe beoð wið uten. 7 summe wið innen. þeo wið uten beoð.þe monnes fif wittes . . . Inwið beoð his hinen.in se

moni mislich þonc to cwemen wel þe husewif. . . . 7 ba wið eie. 7 wið luve [Wit] tuhte ham þe betere. (8–26) (The house our lord speaks of is the self, the man inside is man's wit. In this house is the lord of the house and his unruly wife, who can be called Will. All the household follows her. She would drive the household to ruin, unless Wit as lord chastised her and kept from her much of what she wished to have. All the household would follow her above all, unless Wit forbade them, for they are all undisciplined and careless servants. Some are without and some are within. Those without are man's five senses. Within are those servants who in many ways thought to please the household . . . and with both fear and love, Wit taught them a better way.)

The changes the English author has made result in a feminization of the allegory. In the English version, that quality perceived as the essence of woman, willfullness, is personified as the unruly wife of Wit. That wife is held responsible for the irresponsible and reckless behavior of the servants. Will's feminine irresponsibility is held in check by a patriarchal husband. In the English text, the head of the household is given both a name, Wit, and character traits. He is responsible and concerned, and he teaches with both firmness and love. This detail, not included in the Latin version, communicates the allegory's altered intention, for it is only through the experiences of fear and love, conveyed by the two messengers, that the household becomes vigilant. Furthermore, the fully realized characterization of Wit suggests that women finally must depend on men for their direction, rather than on internalized wit as a dimension of their own personalities. By the author's addition of the adjectives "untohene 7 rechelese" and "fulitohe," and the descriptive verbs, "chasti," "diht," and "cwemen," the reader of the English version sees a household in action, whereas the reader of the Latin version is merely told about the scheme (existence) of one. Whereas the Latin version confines itself to generalities, the English version supplies vivid and highly evocative details which reinforce a separation of masculine from feminine qualities. Women are associated with reckless, unruly behavior; men are associated with discipline and control. The English version's allegory of the household thus introduces the major problem of the female contemplative: governed by her willfulness, the female contemplative is subject to wildly fluctuating emotional states.

In the next section, the vision of Hell, the female reader experiences an emotional realization of the nature of hell. Fearlac's (Fear's) presentation of the vision of hell is the most fully realized "play" of the allegory, and it presents an emotionally charged, detailed vision of the daily life of the damned. In the Latin version, Timor Mortis (Fear of Death), is not described, and he is eclipsed by the description of hell he brings with him. A messenger by any other name could have told his tale. In the Middle English version, Fearlac is clearly described and provided with intense feelings. Fearlac's message is partly conveyed by his appearance: "for lonc he is. 7 leane. 7 his leor deaðlich.7 blac 7 elheowet" (63–64) ("for long he is and lean and his face deadly and pale and a strange color"). Here the congruence between the theme and the allegorical figure reinforces the larger dramatic purpose.[7] In the Latin version of the homily, the demons accompanying Timor Mortis are merely described: "Mille daemones veniunt cum ea ferentes secum libros grandes, et uncos igneos catenas" (356:27–28) ("one thousand demons come with that one carrying with them great books and iron hooks and fiery chains"). The significance of these objects is explained immediately: the books have the sins of men written in them and the hooks drag the guilty to hell. In the Latin, the explanation of the objects has more significance than the objects themselves. The sins enumerated in the English version, on the other hand, are written "wið swarte smeale leattres" ("with small dark letters"), and each devil carries "an unrude raketahe gledread of fure" (77–78) ("a cruel chain red-hot with fire"). The additional adjectives heighten the terror inspired by the devils. Thus, whereas the Latin version emphasizes the moral significance of the vision, the English version stresses the actual fear evoked by contemplation of hell as well as the moral to be drawn from contemplation.

The emotion of fear not only is evoked by the vision itself, but also is enhanced by Fearlac's dramatic description of his personal experience of hell, a feature also lacking in the Latin text. The Latin is composed of rhetorically balanced generalizations:

> Infernus latus est sine mensura, profundus sine fundo, plenus ardore intolerabili, plenus fetore incomparabili, plenus dolore innumerabili. Ibi miseria, ibi tenebrae, ibi ordo nullus, ibi horror sempiternus. (357:1–4) (Hell is wide without measure, deep without bottom, full of intolerable odors, full of incomparable decay, full of innumerable sorrows. Here is misery, darkness, no order, here is eternal horror.)

Some concrete particulars are given—snow, stench, ice, burning, worms—but these are conventional details. In the balance of phrases, the author seems to be striving more for elegance than for genuine horror. The English version, in contrast, focuses less on descriptive detail and more on the quality of Fearlac's experience: "se þicke is þrinne þe þosternesse þet me hire mei grapin" (94–95) ("so thick was the darkness therein that one could grab it"); the fire "blent ham þe ehnen" (95–96) ("blinded him"); and he is covered with "a smorþrinde smeke smeche" (96) ("smothering smoky fumes"). The alliteration of these latter phrases heightens the emotional effect. The English author's addition of such emotionally evocative details suggests his belief that his readers can grasp the concept of hell only through emotions.

The author's additions further suggest that women readers can realize the moral significance of hell only if it is personalized. The text goes on to elaborate Fearlac's reaction to his experiences. Fearlac says, for example, that even if some other sinner had killed his family, he himself would suffer a thousand deaths to release the offender from even the smallest of hell's pains:

> For þe leaste pine is se heard þet hefde a mon islein ba mi feader. 7 mi moder ant al þe ende of mi cun. 7 ido me seolven al þe scheome 7 te hearm þet cwic mon mahte þolien . . . ich walde ʒef hit mahte beon.þolien a þusent deaðes to arudden him ut þrof, swa is sidðe grislich 7 reowðful to bihalden. (126–31) (For the smallest pain there is so hard that, had a man slain both my father and my mother and all the end of my kin and done to me all the shame and harm that a live man might endure . . . I would, if it might be, suffer a thousand deaths to deliver him out thereof, so grisly and pitiable is the sight to behold.)

Fearlac would be unable to bring his catalogue of horrors to an end even if he had a thousand tongues of steel. He breaks into the vocative: "O helle deaðes hus.wununge of wanunge . . . Ich cwakie of grisle 7 of grure" (138–42) ("Oh hell, death's house, dwelling of woe . . . I quake with pain and terror"). He ends his account with a series of laments: "Wa is me.7 wa beo þe. wa he ʒeieð.7 wa ha habbeð ne of al þet eaver wa is" (144–45) ("Woe is me and woe is you. Woe she cries and woe she gets of all that is ever woe").

Not only are we focused in the English version upon Fearlac's horrific personal experience of hell, but also we are reminded of the horrible experiences people may expect in general. These terrors are enumerated in detail first in the introductory account of hell, which depicts sinners tormented by horrible creatures: "iteilede draken grisliche ase deoflen þe forswolheð ham ihal. 7 speoweð ham eft ut bivoren 7 bihinden" (99–100) ("tailed dragons who swallow them whole and spew them out before and behind"); worms, toads, and frogs eat out the sinners' eyes; ants, adders, and water frogs creep into their bodies. Then, again, the sinners' experiences are evoked: whereas the Latin version, for example, merely states that hell "transitus a frigore nivium ad calorem ignium" (357:7–8) ("passes from snowy cold to fiery heat"), the English version provides insights into the sinners' experience of psychological distress occasioned by changes of temperature: "Ferliche ha flutteð from þe heate into þe chele. Ne neaver nuten ha of þeos twa. hweðer ham þuncheð wurse" (109–11) ("Fearfully they flee from the hot to the cold, not knowing which of the two is worse"). Sinners suffer from this "ferliche mong" (112–13) ("fearful alternation") and live in "unhope" (115) ("despair"). The author's use of the rare word "unhope" calls attention to his interest in emotion. *Unhope*, in fact, is a key concept in the English author's vision of hell, for it is just this emotional state that the ascetic must avoid. With this image, the author links the sinner and the prospective reader who must moderate the "ferliche mong" of the contemplative life.

Act 4 of the "inner play" examines the second emotion of significance to the contemplative: hope of heaven. Like the vision of hell, the English version of the vision of heaven is more affective than the Latin. Lives Luve's appearance underscores the message he conveys, for he is "feier 7 freolich 7 leoflich aturnet" (224) ("fair and pretty and beautifully attired") and "al þet hus schineð 7 schimmeð of his leome" (229–30) ("and the entire house shines and shimmers from his face"). It is the emotional impact of the messenger that is significant; he has an immediate effect on the household, which is gladdened and cheered by his sight and "ilihtet" (229) ("freed from depression"). He announces that he is "murðes sonde.7 munegunge of eche lif.ant lives luve ihaten 7 cume riht from heovene þet ich habbe isehen" (234–35) ("mirth's messenger and reminder of eternal life and I am called love of life and I come right from heaven that I have seen"). The female reader's understanding of heaven is therefore controlled by the author through his manipulation of the reader's emotions.

The inner plays of the allegory thus evoke emotions central to the female contemplative experience. The dramatization of Fearlac and Lives Luve reinforces the emotions evoked by their descriptions of hell and heaven. The emotional intensity of both characters establishes a model for the response desired from Wit and Will and encourages the reader to participate in these emotions. The author intends the reader actually to experience fear, not merely to acknowledge it intellectually. Lives Luve's appearance and his eye-witness experience of heaven help the contemplative to shift mood, from fear to hope. The Middle English version explains that the messenger has been sent by God specifically to counteract Fearlac's effect. The messenger announces that "þe iblescede godd iseh ow offruhte 7 sumdel drupnin" (236–37) ("the blessed God sees you frightened and drooping").

We have seen that one play establishes the emotions central to the ascetic life. The method by which religious doctrine can help the ascetic contend with these emotions is then represented dramatically in the next play-within-a-play, in which the Four Daughters react to the visions. The Four Daughters first take the stage after Fearlac's account of hell ends. In the Latin version, the Four Virtues give brief advice after listening to Timor Mortis' account. Prudence advises, "Estote prudentes" (357:16) ("Be sober and watchful"). Fortitude says, "Induite vos armaturam dei, loricam iustitiae, scutum fidei, galeam salutis. Assumite et gladium spiritus" (357:22–23) ("Clothe yourself with the arms of God, the breastwork of justice, the shield of faith, the helmet of salvation. Take to oneself the sword of the spirit"). Justice adds, "Sobrie, et juste, et pie vivamus" (357:24) ("Live sober and just and pious").[8]

The drama and detail added to the English work transforms this list of exhortations into a complex emotional analysis. The Four Daughters give conventional advice, but first they indicate that their morality has arisen out of emotional responses. The English Prudence's first response goes far beyond the stiff and remote moralizing of the Latin Prudence; she calls histrionically upon God to defend them, and asks that they be taught how to "witen us on euch half under godes wengen" (155) ("keep us on each half under God's wings"). This image, drawn from Matthew 23:37, has the protective appeal of similar images of Christ as mother that one finds in many contemporary texts.[9] The primary instinct of the female ascetic apparently is to flee like a child to the protection of God. The Four Daughters thus present external expressions of the presumed affective responses of women in the religious life.

The Four Daughters also present the religious tools available to the female ascetic for regulating the potentially dangerous emotions inspired by contemplation of heaven and hell. The advice they provide differs from that provided by the Latin version, in that each of the virtues stresses the emotional aspects of her particular attribute, and her dependence on the other virtues. This interdependence of virtues is conveyed through a dramatic dialogue in which the characters respond to one another's admonitions. Prudence, anticipating the fear of weakness the contemplative is likely to be experiencing, responds, "Tis ich mei seið warschipe warnin ow of his lað 7 for his wrenches. ah ich ne mei nawt aʒeines his strengðe" (165–66) ("It is up to me to warn you of his evil and against his tricks, but I have nothing against his strength"). Strength answers this fear by reminding the audience that God will protect them: "ʒe nis godd ure scheld.7 alle beoð ure wepnen of his deore grace" (171–72) ("Is not God our shield and all our weapons from his precious grace?"). Mead (moderation) also addresses the feelings of the contemplative by warning of the dangers of self-indulgent fear: too much woe may cause one to forget the Lord, Mead says, and "for nesche ant for flesches licunge forʒemeð ham ofte" (181–82) ("for the love of the flesh, neglect him too often"). Like the anchoresses of the *Ancrene Wisse,* who also are warned of the dangers of ascetic practice, here the reader is told that excesses of ascetic practice are as dangerous as excesses of indulgence. Mead urges the contemplative to follow the middle way: "in euch wordlich þing þe middel wei ʒuldene" (184) ("in each worldly thing, the middle way is golden"); in particular, she must exercise emotional moderation when confronted by the emotional fluctuations of earthly experience. Such moderation is not sufficient in itself, however, for as Justice warns, the ascetic must also beware of complacency and continually reassess her spiritual achievements.

In order to avoid the pride that might result from spiritual complacency, the ascetic must practice all four virtues. As Justice points out,

> For þah mi forme suster war beo of euch uvel. ant min oðer strong beo toʒeines euch nowcin. ant mi þridde meaðful in alles cunnes estes. 7 ich do rihte 7 deme. bute we wið al þis milde beon 7 meoke . . . godd mei mid rihte fordemen us of al þis þurh ure prude. (210–14) (For although my former sister is careful of every evil and my other sister is strong against each distress and my third sister moderate in all kinds of ease and I do right and judge, unless I am mild and meek when doing all this, God may with justice condemn us because of our pride.)

Thus, the Four Daughters provide the contemplative with a conventional moral structure based on moderation, a moral structure which came into being through emotional experience. In the end, then, the emotions provide a connecting matrix for the virtues, one which is constituted by the interactions of the daughters and reinforced by their loving respect for one another. The work, then, provides a fundamentally relational model of Christian values. Such a relational model is particularly well suited for female readers who were often assumed to experience the world relationally.

The English work goes on to analyze how the moral precepts introduced by the Virtues are related to the day-to-day experience of the contemplative. The moral lessons presented by the Four Daughters, while easily understood intellectually, are difficult for women to put into practice. The English homily reminds the reader of this problem by returning to the earlier "play-within-a-play," the "play" of the household, in which Wit and Will take the stage. Wit and Will (characters abandoned at the corresponding stage of the Latin version) respond both to the visions and to the commentary of the Four Daughters. Wit reminds the audience that the advice of the Four Daughters must be applied to the household; he thanks God that he has learned how to guard the household and watch over God's precious possession, the soul. Further, he reclaims from Will those unruly servants who had followed her and reasserts his control. The female contemplative's experience finally is guided by wiser and more temperate male advisors. The audience thus realizes that the commentary of the Four Daughters is directly applicable to the problem introduced at the beginning of the homily: the difficulty of protecting the soul. Whereas the Latin version of the sermon simply states a moral, the English version, through the addition of a series of plays-within-plays, takes the reader step by step through a process of moral discovery. The author has lived up to his promise in the opening statement—that in his allegory, he will show the reader *how* to protect the soul.

The English work does not end with this experiential discovery of a moral, however. Returning to the drama of the Four Daughters, the homily adds yet another dimension, absent in the Latin, which suggests that the process of establishing a moral order is not a static process, but one which must be continually renewed. In the Latin version, the Four Virtues banish Fear from the house, and the household members are left secure in their vision of a blissful afterlife. The work ends with the moral: "Sic, fratres, debet monachus torporem suum excutere et a timore ad amorem caelestis patriae sese transferre" (360:29–30) ("Thus, brothers, each ought to shake off sluggishness and pass from fear to the love of the heavenly country"). This exhortation reflects the reader's experience of the Latin text, for, as he reads, he passes from fear to rejoicing. In the English version, on the other hand, the Four Virtues do not simply delight in the vision of heaven. Rather, they come to realize that there are additional issues. The Four Daughters remind Wit and Will that, despite their new-found control, they must continue to contemplate the difficulties of the soul's protection. All four Daughters warn the reader of the opening allegory, urging the contemplative to "halden his hus þet godes tresor is in aȝeines godes unwine" (359–60) ("protect his house in which God's treasure is kept against God's enemy").

The English text's return to earthly concerns is further emphasized by the author's radically different treatment of fear at the end of his work. In the Latin version, fear is cast out forever, for perfect love casts out fear. In the English version, such perfection is not of this world; for, although Prudence says, "þer as murðes sonde is. 7 soð luve of eche lif. farlac is fleme" (Royal 368–69; Bodley ending missing) ("Wherever there is mirth's messenger and true love of eternal life, fear is put to flight"), Fearlac counters her comment with: "þah hit muri nere nes na lessere mi tal þen wes murhðes sondes ne unbihefre to ow. þah hit ne beo so licwurðe ne icweme" (Royal 371–72) ("Though my tale is not as cheerful as that of mirth, it is not less profitable to you though it is not so pleasant or pleasing"). Mead halts the ensuing quarrel between Fear and Love, saying, "Eiðer of ow haveð his stunde to speokene . . . þu warnest of wa. he telleð of wunne. muche neod is þet me ow ba ӡeornliche hercni" (Royal 373–75) ("Each of you has had his time to speak . . . You warn of woe; he tells of joy. There is much need to hearken to both"). Fearlac is told to leave while Lives Luve is there, but he is also told, "þu schal ful bliðeliche beon underfon in as ofte as Lives Luve stutteð forto spekene" (Royal 377–78) ("You shall be eagerly received as often as Lives Luve stops speaking.") Fear is as important as hope to the contemplative who reads this homily.

The English version of "Sawles Warde" thus concludes by returning yet again to the drama of Wit and Will. Here the author explains that the concerns of this homily are with the fluctuating emotions of the ascetic life rather than with the celebration of rewards to come. The homilist summarizes his lesson:

> þus ah mon te þenchen ofte ant ilome. ant wið þulliche þohtes awecchen his heorte. þe i slep of ӡemeles forӡet hire sawle heale.efter þeos twa sonden. . . . to habben farlac of þet an.luve toward þet oðer" (Royal 386–90) ("Thus, according to these two messengers, a man ought to think often and with thoughts awaken his heart that in the sleep of negligence forgets his soul's health . . . to have fear of that one and love toward that other.")

The servants of the household must obey Wit:

> Lustneð nu his lare. 7 fondeð ever euchan efter þet him limpeð to. þurh þeos twa sonden. þet ha iherd habbeð. 7 þet fowr sustren lerden þruppe for euch unþeawes inӡong his warde to witene. (Royal 382–85) (Listen now to his teaching and experience what belongs to each of the two messengers that he has heard, and listen to what the four sisters taught to protect [the soul] securely against the entrance of sin.)

For the woman reader, intellectual truths continually must be discovered through emotional experiences of both fear and hope.

The English text has maintained both the inner frame (the Four Daughters and the two messengers) and the outer frames (Wit, Will, and the reader) of the allegory. The consistency of the allegory makes its moral especially dynamic: Will again will be tempted to lead the senses astray, the household again will need Fearlac, and Lives Luve again will need to bring the household back under Wit's control. This concern for the vulnerability of the contemplative and the precariousness of the mystical vision of God is one shared by other AB texts. "Sawles Warde" shares with these other texts a concern with the difficulties of escaping the world entirely, difficulties reinforced by a woman's inescapable rootedness in the body.

Through this analysis of "Sawles Warde," we see clearly that the allegorical techniques present in this Middle English sermon were introduced at least in part to address the perceived needs of a specialized group, female contemplatives. Concerned about the emotional demands of the female anchoritic life, the English male author chose to translate a homily that provides a guide for understanding those emotional pressures. This text, like the other AB texts, is temporal and interactive; it forces the reader's attention away from consideration of an abstract and hypothetical Christian hierarchy and toward the very real problems of integrating fluctuating daily emotions into the Christian scheme. The differences between "Sawles Warde" and its Latin source suggest that male contemplatives were assumed to need texts that celebrated the abstract order, while women were assumed to need texts that helped them understand and regulate their unruly and willful emotions as they pursued Christian goals. The new version also suggests that women can understand Christian ideals only relationally and not hierarchically; the author assumes his readers to be in need of a dramatic and personalized realization of Christian truths. He assumes further that those readers are characterized by a willfulness that limits their ability to retain the final lesson of the work; rather, the realization of Christian truths must be repeated daily. Differences between the styles of the English work and its Latin source parallel the differences between women's and men's approaches to moral problems discussed by Carol Gilligan. This "feminized" experiential theology was not, however, restricted to literature written for women. As we shall see in the next chapter, this style also occurs in English works written for audiences that, whether male or female, were assumed to share the perceptual limitations of female audiences. "Sawles Warde," then, is not simply a vivid translation addressed to women. It is instead a new work which expresses a distinctively "feminine" experience of Christian theology, in that it arises because of male attitudes toward, first, the needs and circumstances of women and, second, the experience of women in the religious life. As we shall see in the next chapter, however, this very unusual style also occurs in literature written for men who were in circumstances similar to those of the anchoresses and to whom the same theories of Christian training were applied.

CHAPTER 8

The AB Texts and
the Anglo-Saxon Tradition

The AB texts, we have seen, due to their authors' consideration of their female audience, are characterized by a style that is pragmatic, non-teleological, and emotional and that stresses the concrete and personal over the abstract and universal—qualities often associated today with women's style generally. Some of these stylistic features reflect the influence of continental concepts of the self in relationship to the physical world, a subject addressed in the next chapter. The particularity and pragmatism of the AB texts, however, had their origins in a native English prose tradition. In order to appreciate the English tradition that informs the AB texts, we must consider Anglo-Saxon sources in terms of their audiences. However, given the obscurity that surrounds the production of Anglo-Saxon literature, identifying the precise audience of a given work is virtually impossible. We must rely primarily, then, on internal evidence—that is, on a consideration of the style of Anglo-Saxon works—as a measure of their audiences. Recurrent stylistic features suggest that many Anglo-Saxon works were intended for audiences uneducated in Latin. The variations of style found in the works suggest that early English religious writers varied their emphasis on the pragmatic or the theoretical according to the needs and education of the specific audience. Like the female audience of the AB texts, the audiences of many of the Anglo-Saxon prose religious works probably were uneducated in Latin and living far from the Latin centers where a privileged, educated elite controlled access to power and learning. These marginal audiences were thought to require a different training in religious ideals, one that emphasized the apprehension of Christian religious ideals through the experiences of the body rather than the comprehension of such ideals through the exercises of the mind.

Critics generally have either overvalued or undervalued the AB texts' "Englishness." Chambers raised the question of the nature of early English prose style, when, in 1934, he argued that the English prose tradition does not begin in the Renaissance but rather is a full and continuous tradition beginning in the ninth century with the prose translations of King Alfred.[1] To Chambers, the AB texts are simply points on a continuum of a homogeneous tradition, a tradition which he nonetheless declines to define with any precision. Tolkien similarly praises the AB texts for their "Englishness" and similarly fails to tell us what that "Englishness" is.[2] Owst, in his study of sermons, perhaps came closest to identifying this Englishness in his praise of the "spirit of realism in the pulpit which loved to play with examples from ordinary life."[3] Commenting, for example, on the Blickling and Lambeth homilies, he writes, "The characteristic features of English medieval preaching . . . exhibit this same desire to escape as far as possible from the abstract and the universal in religion, and to be 'at home with particulars.' "[4] Even so, Owst too fails to analyze the Anglo-Saxon tradition in any detail.

Another group of critics, sharing Chambers' celebration of the "Englishness" of the AB texts, criticizes them as examples of a declining tradition. Dorothy Bethurum argues that the majority of the works poorly imitate earlier homilies; of "Sawles Warde" she writes, "The alliterative phrases in the description of hell only ring the changes on a vocabulary well known to readers or hearers of the Blickling homilies or Wulfstan's homilies."[5] In Bethurum's view, the English tradition stopped developing after the Conquest and resumed its progress only much later. She nonetheless cannot deny the literary distinctiveness of one of the AB texts, the *Ancrene Wisse.* She writes of the *Wisse:* "It marks for English works a new sort of prose for which there is no antecedent in Old English writing."[6] But she sees this work as an anomaly rather than as a product of English developments. Margaret Hurley attributes the alliterative style of the AB texts to the influence of the homilies of Ælfric and Wulfstan, but she, like Bethurum, sees the AB texts on the whole as simplified versions of earlier, more successful texts.[7]

Most critics, including the most recent ones, prefer to attribute literary innovation in the AB texts to Latin influences. Geoffrey Shepherd, for example, scrupulously annotates the Latin sources of most of the passages of the *Ancrene Wisse* but rarely mentions English precedents.[8] In her recent edition of *Hali Meidenhad,* Bella Millett, on the basis of her identification of Latin sources for passages previously considered unattributable to Latin, denies the work any English originality.[9] In her recent article, Millett reexamines the question of the continuity of English prose and criticizes earlier praise of the Englishness of the AB texts as overly motivated by patriotism.[10] She writes, "Tolkien and Chambers attached a high value to the AB group largely because they saw it as a symbol of native English resistance to alien culture."[11] While admitting some native influence, she nonetheless reasserts a traditional critical habit of assessing English style in terms of Latin influence. She concludes, "There is no doubt that it [the AB texts] draws on a native tradition of prose writing which can be traced back beyond the Conquest; but some of its works at least look outwards as well as backwards for their models, and one of the formative influences on their styles is the Latin prose of their own time."[12] Because Latin sources are often more sophisticated stylistically than English sources, they are often viewed as the measure of an author's style. Such analyses implicitly subordinate English influences to Latin ones.

Latin influences are clearly significant. Still, to analyze style only in terms of Latin influences suggests that there is a hierarchy of style and that texts written by a supposed intellectual elite are the fulfillment of stylistic development and that other texts are simply inferior imitations. I argue that works written by and for those uneducated in Latin are on a different hierarchical scale altogether. Anglo-Saxon style, although influenced by Latin works, had its own relatively independent developments. Therefore, if we are to understand these works correctly, an attempt must be made to ground Anglo-Saxon texts in their native literary soil.

Confusion about the influence of the Anglo-Saxon prose tradition on the AB texts arises in part from viewing the prose tradition as stylistically homogeneous. The religious prose tradition is made up of several different parts. It includes: (1) the prose translations of Alfred and his school in the 890s; (2) the tenth-century homilies and saints' lives of Ælfric; (3) the tenth-century homilies of Wulfstan; (4) the early anonymous homilies represented in the Blickling and Vercelli collections; and (5) the late anonymous homilies of the twelfth and thirteenth centuries (many of which are copies of earlier Ælfrician homilies, but many of which are independent works).

What most critics have failed to acknowledge is that the style of these groups of works varies depending on the needs and circumstances of the intended audience. The relationship of audience to style has been overlooked in part because of the difficulty of identifying or characterizing Anglo-Saxon audiences with any precision. The texts that remain are only a small sample of what was written, and they are difficult to date. Yet we can, with caution, make some generalizations. English audiences differed from vernacular audiences on the continent, because the Latin tradition did not always develop side by side with the vernacular as it did on the continent. Throughout the Anglo-Saxon period, English audiences were considerably removed from Latin learning. Their access to Latin learning varied, however, depending on the stability of the kingdom and the condition of the monasteries. The earliest prose writer of the period, Alfred, wrote at a time of political and religious upheaval. He told readers of his concern for an audience whose members were no longer able to read Latin texts.[13] Turning to the works of Ælfric and Wulfstan, we find that political and religious circumstances had stabilized. As a result of the tenth-century monastic revival, the religious hierarchy was firmly established. Furthermore, Latin learning was flourishing. Despite the fact that Ælfric wrote in the vernacular, his prose clearly reflects his position as a member of the educated elite writing for those well established within the religious hierarchy—that is, for his fellow monks and priests. Wulfstan, on the other hand, stood between the elite and nonelite. Although writing from within the elite, he was a bishop preaching to the masses and writing for an uneducated audience.

We know little about the audience for the anonymous homilies of the ninth to the thirteenth centuries. Yet, dialectal peculiarities of these texts, as well as Ælfric's campaign against them, suggest that they were popular, pervasive, and written far from the religious centers controlled by Ælfric and Wulfstan. After the Conquest, the audiences for English literature presumably were removed even further from centers of Latin learning, since at that time, literature for the court tended to be written in French and literature for the learned, in French or Latin. Literary English was threatened with extinction; at this period it survived primarily in literature produced for those who had no access to the centers of power and learning.

It is probable that the majority of English religious prose works were addressed to audiences whose members were located far from centers of power, uneducated in Latin, and in most cases of the lower class. Therefore it is worthwhile to explore the question of authorial attitudes towards such audiences. The style of the English works seems to reflect political attitudes towards the uneducated that are similar to the attitudes we have discovered in texts written for women. That is to say, male Christian writers viewed the uneducated as they did women—as willful, sensual, rooted in the body, and therefore capable of being taught abstract Christian ideals only through a concrete, pragmatic style. John of Salisbury's twelfth-century political theories summarize attitudes towards the uneducated that may well have been current in the Anglo-Saxon period. Using notions that have their origins in Roman political theory, John writes of the body politic:

> The place of the head in the body of the commonwealth is filled by the prince, who is subject only to God and to those who execute His office and represent Him on earth, even as in the human body the head is quickened and governed by the soul. The place of the heart is filled by the Senate, from which proceeds the initiation of good works and ill. The duties of eyes, ears and tongues are claimed by the judges and governors of provinces. Officials and soldiers correspond to the hands. . . . the husbandmen correspond to the feet, which always cleave to the soil, and need the more especially the care and fore-sight of the head, since, while they walk upon the earth doing service with their bodies, they meet the more often with stones of stumbling, and therefore de-serve aid and protection all the most justly since it is they who raise, sustain, and move forward the weight of the entire body.[14]

Because John of Salisbury was a monk, his political model reflects his commitment to an encompassing hierarchical religious model. This politi-cal theory directly parallels the theological theories about women we have discussed in earlier chapters; like the prince, Adam is the head; like the husbandmen, Eve is the body; like the prince, Adam represents divinely directed reason; like the husbandmen, Eve is earthbound. That assump-tions about women are similar to those held generally about the uneducated is suggested by Ian Maclean's summary of medieval commentaries: "Women are associated with a privation of meditative powers (*contempla-tionis defectus*) which makes them, with rustics and the simple-minded, well suited to devoutness, but ill suited to intellectual disciplines."[15] In-deed, women and the laity were often seen as interchangeable. Thus Bynum argues, "As Georges Duby has pointed out, women were outside the 'three orders' of medieval society: those who pray, those who fight, and those who till the soil. Even in the church, although nuns were 'clergy' in one sense (that is, they were 'regular,' they took vows), in another sense all women were laity—that is, outside orders."[16] Gilbert and Gubar have shown how women were often associated with those outside the privileged elite.[17] It is possible, then, to reverse the analogy of women to laity, and to argue that in some senses the laity were viewed as women.

There is no explicitly political theoretical work surviving from the Anglo-Saxon period, but in his translations, the ninth-century King Alfred similarly views spiritual and secular leaders as closer to God and having a higher percentage of "gewiss andgit" (clear understanding) than the unedu-cated, whom he sees as being both willful and prevented from the acquisi-tion of reason through the distractions of the flesh. The tenth-century homilists Ælfric and Wulfstan also see correct teaching as necessary to control the willfulness and sensuality of their audiences. These authors' stylistic choices are shaped both by their conscious consideration of the circumstances of their audience and by their unconscious assumptions about the nature of that audience.

Although a direct correspondence between such theories and the style chosen for moral teaching is difficult to prove, it is nonetheless suggestive that texts written for audiences whose members are seen as willful and rooted in the body make use of a quotidian style designed to evoke emotional and physical reactions. The idea that the uneducated are earthbound effects a radical change in an author's view of an audience's experience of Christian ideals in relationship the experiences of the world. In texts written for the educated, the reader is taken through a hierarchical process that mimics John of Salisbury's hierarchical social system; that is, the reader's attention is moved away from the feet to the head, from the earth to heaven, and from consideration of the experiences of the world toward contemplation of an unchanging ideal. In works written for the uneducated, however, because the audience is perceived to be closer to the soil, the reader is presumed to be unable to transcend the experiences of the world. These differences suggest that, within the general Christian frame, different codes operated for the intellectual and the uneducated. In their contemplation, the educated were seen as ascending a ladder that leads ultimately to union with God. The ascent was impeded by the soul's embodiment, and, except for mystics, complete union was possible only at death. Yet, as the educated contemplative ascended the ladder, he left the concerns of the body—the world—behind. The uneducated, however, like women, were inescapably trapped in the body and so could never forget the world. Their contemplation of God, therefore, had to be realized through worldly experiences. Their mental movement was horizontal rather than vertical, and their realization of the soul was conditioned by the temporal. Rather than deny the experiences of the world, the authors of works for the uneducated transformed the mundane into experiences charged with religious meaning.

These different codes surely influenced an author's style—the congruence of such features as vocabulary, syntax, method of argumentation, imagery, and figures of speech. Although many elements of style can be difficult to identify or to characterize precisely and much stylistic analysis is often finally impressionistic, nevertheless we can isolate some specific features characteristic of Anglo-Saxon style. Some of the concreteness of Anglo-Saxon prose for the uneducated might be attributed to its native vocabulary, and much of the particularity of the AB texts could well be seen as a function of its high percentage of Anglo-Saxon words. Because of the peculiar circumstances surrounding the development of English, Anglo-Saxon vocabulary is inherently more concrete than Latin or French, and one of its features is that its vocabulary developed by the compounding of concrete nouns. The necessity of using a native vocabulary in texts for the uneducated here reinforced an emphasis on the concrete and mundane.

Yet the particularity and concreteness of the AB texts also resulted from other stylistic features which flourished in Anglo-Saxon writing intended for those who were uneducated and located far from the centers of Latin learning. Here we may extend Owst's description of a distinctive English "spirit of realism" by investigating those elements of English style which produce what I shall call "quotidian realism." Two distinct styles emerge from an analysis of extant Anglo-Saxon prose texts. In one set of texts— those written by the educated and usually for the educated, that is, texts primarily by Ælfric and his imitators—a style predominates which is syntactically complex and teleological and which focuses on the abstract and universal. In another set of texts, written for those uneducated in Latin and located far from stable religious centers, a style predominates which is syntactically simple and nonteleological and which focuses on the particular and the individual. In the following pages, I shall analyze the latter style, as it developed in response to the circumstances and perceived needs of English audiences.

The following analysis will show that the "Englishness" which Chambers and Tolkien praise as peculiar to the AB texts and Anglo-Saxon religious works is manifested in stylistic techniques that cannot be attributed to Latin sources. These techniques instead were the result of, and a response to, the relationship of the English audience to the Latin Christian establishment. Rather than present a chronological analysis, I shall consider Anglo-Saxon texts in order of the degree of certainty about the circumstances of their production. First we turn to the authors we know most about: Alfred, writing in the 890s, and Ælfric and Wulfstan, writing in the tenth century. Then come the anonymous homilies, written from the 890s to the thirteenth century. The argument traces the following stylistic developments. Alfred, writing for the uneducated, introduced a radical shift in style away from his Latin sources through his use of quotidian imagery. Ælfric, writing for the educated, retained the abstract emphasis of the Latin tradition and eschewed quotidian realism altogether. Wulfstan followed Ælfric when he wrote for the educated, but when he addressed the laity, he made use of affective syntactical devices.The anonymous homilists, sharing an address to the uneducated, made use of both the quotidian imagery found in Alfred and the affective rhetoric of Wulfstan. They also utilized improved dramatic techniques.

Neither an independent English tradition nor the dependence of English works on Latin sources can account for the habitual pragmatism of the English religious tradition; rather, the English tradition appears to have exhibited relative stylistic independence, depending on its distance from the Latin establishment. Although Brian Stock has demonstrated persuasively the important implications of literacy in the development of medieval literature, illiteracy had just as significant an influence on the development of style.[18] This chapter shows that a characteristic English quotidian style may well have developed in relationship to the perceived needs of the illiterate.

ALFRED'S TRANSLATIONS

English quotidian realism has its origins with the earliest English prose writer, King Alfred. Although Alfred's works were primarily translations of major Latin Christian texts, his consistently pragmatic style reveals an aesthetic different from that of his Latin sources. Unlike his neo-Platonic sources, which emphasize stillness, stability, perfection, and timelessness, Alfred's translations illustrate his concern for mutability, the vicissitudes of daily life, and the natural imperfections of the individual—precisely the differences that we found between later Latin sources and the AB texts. Alfred expressed his attitudes in his stylistic choices, particularly in his diction, his concrete and practical imagery, and his use of story—all features prominent in Anglo-Saxon literature written for the uneducated.

Alfred's poetics sprang from his deliberate consideration of the nature and needs of his uneducated audience. His preface to his translation of Gregory's *Pastoral Care* provides unusually clear evidence of authorial consideration of audience. There Alfred tells us that, in response to the decline of learning in England, he intends to translate Latin works. He writes:

Swæ clæne hio wæs oðfeallenu on Angelcynne ðæt swiðe feawa wæron behionan Humbre ðe hiora ðeninga cuðen understondan on Englisc oððe furðum an ærendgewrit of Lædene on Englisc areccean; ond ic wene ðætte noht monige begiondan Humbre næren . . . ond ða swiðe lytle fiorme ðara boca wiston, for ðæm ðe hie hiora nanwuht ongiotan ne meahton, for ðæm ðe hie næron on hiora agen geðiode awritene . . . ða ic ða gemunde hu sio lar Lædengeðiodes ær ðissum afeallen wæs giond Angelcynn ond ðeah monige cuðon Englisc gewrit arædan, ða ongan ic . . . ða boc wendan on Englisc ðe is genemned on Læden *Pastoralis* and on Englisc "Hierdeboc," hwilum word be worde, hwilum andgit of andgiete. (So completely had it [Latin learning] fallen off in England that there were very few of those below the Humber who could construe the divine service into English or further could translate a message from Latin into English; and I think that there were not many beyond the Humber; and they knew so little of the form of these books, because they in no way might understand them since they were not written in their own tongue . . . when I considered how the teaching of the Latin tongue had before this fallen off and that nevertheless many could read the English language, then I began to turn this book into English, which is named in Latin "Pastoral Care" and in English "Shepherd's Book," sometimes word for word, and sometimes sense for sense.)[19]

From this preface we gather that Latin literacy was on the decline in England. While we know little about who in fact read or heard Alfred's translations, we certainly can assume that many of those in his audience were untrained in Latin. When writing for people uneducated in Latin, Alfred focuses continually on the concrete and particular rather than on the abstract and general.

The style of Alfred's translations differs significantly in many respects from the style of the later homilies. Alfred does not depend on alliterative pairs to link concepts, nor does he use such affective techniques as heaping up emotional evocative adjectives or simulating dialogue. In part, this style reflects the influence of the genres of his sources; nonetheless, it incorporates features that became crucial in the development of writing intended for readers who were uneducated in Latin. Because of his concern for an audience continually exposed to war and religious upheaval, Alfred chose to confront the nature of the world directly. Using mundane imagery and vocabulary drawn from standard Anglo-Saxon rather than from Latin as signs and symbols of a mutable, transient world, Alfred was able to evoke a reality full of potential Christian meaning. The firmly-established abstract, hierarchical model of his sources was transformed into a fluid model of Christian society, a model that depends on continual change rather than on a progressive movement away from mutable things. Although Alfred clearly was an intellectually sophisticated, conservative writer who upheld the values of the Church, his technique was radical in that, through his use of quotidian imagery and vocabulary, he allowed the common man to invest the objects and experiences of everyday life with religious significance. Thus, the temporal and the mutable, rather than constituting distractions from Christian contemplation, became a means to understanding. It is Alfred's focus on the value of the mundane that makes his writing "realistic" in a way that the writing of the Church Fathers is not. Just such an emphasis on integrating the fluctuations of everyday life with abstract, re-mote religious goals characterizes the AB texts, too.

Early commentators on Alfred's translations assumed that he did not fully understand the abstract philosophy of his sources. His homely, prag-matic translations were seen as reflecting a limited, uneducated perspec-tive.[20] This view has been contested by more recent commentators, who have demonstrated that Alfred's translations are not inferior but rather are different.[21] Since Anne Payne has provided a subtle and extensive analysis of Alfred's style, the following discussion focuses on only those aspects of his work that contributed especially to the development of English quoti-dian realism. To demonstrate the role of quotidian realism in Alfred's work, I shall discuss his translations of one work, Boethius's *Consolation of Philosophy*, with occasional reference to his translation of Augustine's *Soliloquies*.[22]

Often it is a single word in Alfred's translations that results in major shifts in meaning. For example, in his translation of Boethius's *Consola-tion,* Alfred substitutes for the figures of "Boethius" and "Lady Philoso-phy," two characters named "Wisdom" and "Mod." These two pairs of names reflect the different epistemological views of the two authors. Boe-thius develops a consistent Platonic argument: God's knowledge is differ-ent from man's because God lives in a different time frame, a continual present. Man, affected by time and so preoccupied with the acquisition and maintenance of worldly goods, is distracted from true contemplation of God. For the Latin Boethius, a mystical, transcendent contemplation of God, free from the cares of the world, is the way to knowledge. Alfred's translation, on the other hand, is determined by his contrasting belief in practice rather than theory. The distance between Alfred's and Boethius's visions of God is seen in the contrasting figures of Wisdom and Philoso-phy; to Alfred, wisdom is practicing philosophy.

Unlike Boethius's ideal state, in which an individual can forget the world entirely, in Alfred's view the individual never can completely escape involvement in the world. This idea is encapsulated in Alfred's image of the Boethian eagle, which Alfred calls "Mod." To compare the mind to an eagle is a conventional *topos*. Unlike Boethius, who in his aquiline image praises the power of the mind to ascend, Alfred stresses the importance of both the ascent and descent of the mind. Alfred describes the ascent of the mind as an eagle's ascent, but extends the image, suggesting that the eagle must return to earth just as the individual must bring knowledge back to earth in order to put it into practice: "Swa ic wolde, la Mod, þæt þu fore up to us, gif þe lyste, on þa gerad, þæt þu eft mid us þa eorðan secan wille for godra manna þearfe" (18) ("So I wish, oh, Mod, that you travel up to us, if you desire, in your travels, but that you afterwards with us will seek the earth for the need of good men"). This image is not dissimilar to that of the sparrow in the *Ancrene Wisse*, another image used to address the contemplative's inevitable return to earth. As for the authors of the AB texts, for Alfred, transcendence has no hierarchical relation to practice. Alfred is concerned with immanence rather than transcendence. He denies that a person can completely hold fast to God, and therefore he does not advocate dismissing temporal things; indeed, it is the continual interplay between temporal and eternal that interests Alfred. In his translation of Augustine's *Soliloquies*, for example, he implies that in fact the divine can be understood only through the world; he writes:

> "We naðer (ne myd þam lychamlican eagum) ne myd þaes modes eagan nanwiht ne magon of þisse weorulde geseon eallunga swa swa hyt is. Ac of ðam dæle þe we hys geseoð, we sceolun gelifan þane dele þe we hys ne geseoð." (III:93) (We cannot with the bodily eyes nor with the eyes of the mind, see the world as it is, yet from the part of it we see, we must believe the part we do not see.)

Typical of Alfred's style is his rendering of Boethius's abstract geometrical image of the relationship of God's foreknowledge and man's knowledge in his translation of the *Consolation of Philosophy*. Instead of describing two spheres, as does Boethius, Alfred employs an image of a wheel with all its parts to symbolize the relationship between God and man:

> Swa swa on wænes eaxe hwearfiað þa hweol 7 sio eax stint stille 7 byrð þeah ealne þone wæn 7 welt ealles þæs færeltes: þ hweol hwerfð ymbutan 7 sio nafu next þære eaxe sio færð micle fæstlicor 7 orsorglicor þonne ða felgan don, swelce sio eax sie þ hehste god þe we nemnað god 7 þa selestan men faren nehste Gode swa swa sio nafu færð neahst þære eaxe 7 ða midmestan swa swa ða spacan; forðæmþe ælces spacan bið oðer ende faest on ðære nafe, oðer on þære felge. Swa bið þæm midlestan monnum; oðre hwile he smeað on his mode ymb ðis eorðlice lif, oðre hwile ymb þæt godcundlice, swilce he locie mid oðre eagen to heofonum, mid oðre to eorþan. Swa swa þa spacan sticiað oðer ende on þære felge oðer on þære nafe, middeweard se spaca bið ægðrum emnneah ðeah oðer ende bio fæst on þære nafe oðer on þære felge; swa bioð þa midmestan men onmiddan þam spacan 7 þa betran near þære nafe, 7 þa mætran near ðæm felgum; bioð þeah fæste on ðaere nafe 7 se nafa on ðære eaxe. Hwæt, þa felga þeah hongiað on þæm spacan, þeah hi eallunga wealowigen on þære eorðan; swa doð þa mætestan men on þæm midmestum, 7 þa midmestam on þæm betstan 7 þa betstan on Gode. (129–30) (Just as the axle of a wagon turns the wheel and the axle stands still and bears nonetheless the entire wagon and turns all the fellies, the wheel turns all about and the nave next to the axle moves more securely and less painfully than do the fellies, so is the axle the highest good that we name God, and the best men go nearest God just as the nave goes nearest

the axle and the midmost just as the spokes; because the spokes of the axle are fastened on the other end of the nave or on the felly. So are the middlemen; sometimes either he considers in his mind about this earthly life or sometimes about the divine life, as he looks with one eye to heaven and with the other to the earth, just as the spokes stick each end either in the felly or the nave; in the middle the spokes are equidistant, each end being fastened either in the nave or the felly; so are the middlemen in the middle of the spokes and the better near the nave and the unimportant near the felly; they are secure in the nave, and the nave on the axle; yet the fellies nonetheless hang on the spokes, though they completely wallow in the earth; so do the unimportant men depend on the middlemen and the middlemen on the best and the best on God.)

Here God, ever still and unchanging, emblematically becomes the axle of a wheel; though unmoving, the axle motivates the movement of the wagon. Men and women are distributed along the spokes of the wheel; although they can never achieve the stillness of the axle, the closer they are to the axle, the less they will be exposed to the mud of existence. In this passage, as throughout Alfred's translation, Alfred renders the abstract, divine principle of Boethius's text, *amor*, as a more personal figure, personifying it as God. This personified principle is also actively and directly engaged in the operation of the world. Boethius's *simplicitatem meditatem* of the divine becomes more active in Alfred's image of the axle which "stint stille"; the active verb "stint" implies not simply that God is still and unchanging, but that he has *decided* to stand still. Alfred's different conception of God's active involvement in the world is more fully developed in his later image of God as a "ship steerer" who alters the course of the ship of human events according to his anticipation of the weather. Such images of God, both as axle and as helmsman, imply that God, like man, is subject to time. The association of God with objects and people from ordinary experience, as well as the figuration of God as a person wrestling with the vicissitudes of daily, temporal experience, brings God closer to the common man and further suggests that the temporal and the divine are intertwined. And the axle of the wagon, though different in kind from the nave, felly, and spokes of the wheel, is no more important to the movement of the whole wagon than are those parts.

Such a vision of mutual cooperation and interdependence is underscored in Alfred's further elaboration of the wheel image. Although he postulates a hierarchy of position on the wheel, in which the best men are closest to the nave, all positions, whether on the nave, spoke, or felly, are interconnected, and the spoke is fixed firmly in both the felly and the nave. Elsewhere in this translation, in his famous tripartite view of social structures Alfred restates his vision of a cooperative society. There are, he says, those who work, those who pray, and those who fight. For Alfred, none of these groups is superior to another; individuals are distinguished only according to their degree of understanding. Understanding, "gewiss andgit," or discrimination, "gesceadwisness," is what distinguishes men from God and from the angels. Angels lack the perfect understanding of God, but they share with God "gewiss andgit buton tweon" ("clear understanding without doubt"). Doubt inspired by the mutability of the world and anxiety produced by excessive attachment to worldly goods are what prevent individuals from proper understanding. God is distinguished from mankind not so much because he is immutable, as in the Boethian original, but rather because he is less susceptible to doubt.

Despite Alfred's conservative acceptance of Christianity, his concept of society is relatively fluid: he allows the possibility that men are able to move along the wheel according to their degree of "gesceadwisness." Although the individual is placed on the spokes of the wheel according to his level of understanding, his position is not fixed. Caught between the mundane and the divine, individuals oscillate between two realms. In this fluid, nonhierarchical model of society, all individuals can, as Alfred writes later, sin like cattle or rise like angels.

Although Alfred values the Latin tradition, his superior training does not lead him to set himself or to set teachers above those who learn. Alfred is deeply aware of and sympathetic to the limitations of his audience. Such sympathy may spring from his own experience of illiteracy; Alfred did not learn to read and write until he was in his teens. Alfred often states throughout his writing that each person must act according to the measure of his understanding. Yet that level of understanding can be increased through proper education. Throughout his translations, Alfred stresses the importance of proper teaching. He does not, however, suggest that teachers are in a particularly privileged position. Even though Alfred was more gifted intellectually than those around him, he does not propose a hierarchical system of learning in which churchmen would become superior to common men and Latin would be seen as more valuable than the vernacular.

In the *Consolation,* Alfred conveys his notion of the process of learning in concrete diction drawn from everyday life: "Forðy we scoldon ealle mægen spyrian æfter gode þæt we wissen hwæt he wære" (72) ("Therefore we must with all our strength track after God that we might know what he is"). The word *spyrian,* "to track," is most often applied to hunting dogs following the track of a scent. It is an overdetermined, multivalent image that both compares men to animals and evokes the elusive presence of God on earth as one who can be sensed though not seen. In addition, the image emphasizes the discipline that must be practiced in order to reach understanding. The teacher leads the learner to the scent, but both share equal responsibility in the pursuit of learning.

Alfred's egalitarian view of education leads him to value reading and writing as means rather than as ends in themselves. Because books, stories, and parables help men to learn, Alfred adds or expands stories and parables in his translations. For example, in the *Soliloquies,* using a story about a lord and his friends, he explains faith and tells us that books provide models of wise men whose example we should follow. To Alfred, stories are valuable above all because they help people to learn. Alfred's praise of stories contributes to the development of quotidian realism in the English tradition, because it is through stories that everyday circumstances can be recreated. Alfred's praise of stories, like his evocation of images drawn from everyday experience, bespeaks his commitment to, and consideration of the needs of, an uneducated audience struggling to integrate Christian ideals amid the fluctuations of daily life in a period of religious and political turmoil.

Although Alfred was a sophisticated and intellectual writer, he was not an elitist. While supporting the conservative ideals of Christianity, he centered his attention on the common man. Because of his concern for the individual's realization of Christian values even in the most mundane circumstances, Alfred used everyday imagery to invest common sensory experience with Christian immanence. The "this-worldliness" of Alfred's writing constitutes a radical shift from the traditional Christian view of the world as something to be avoided altogether. Early in the English religious tradition, then, at a time when the Latin Christian tradition was unstable, attempts to meet the perceived needs of an uneducated audience helped to create a literature emphasizing the concrete and the pragmatic rather than the abstract and the theoretical.

ÆLFRIC AND WULFSTAN

Ælfric and Wulfstan, the well-known homilists of the tenth century, wrote their homilies during a time of relative religious stability. As members of the clergy, both were representatives of the tenth-century monastic revival set in motion by Æthelwold.[23] Critics often speak of Ælfric and Wulfstan together, partly because Wulfstan often simply transcribed or abbreviated Ælfric's homilies. However, they had different social roles: Ælfric was a monk, while Wulfstan was a bishop. In writing, their missions clearly differed in accord with the responsibilities of their offices. Even so, the two shared one basic intention: to instill securely in the minds of readers the basic precepts of the church in terms of a clear hierarchical model. The styles of Ælfric and Wulfstan were conditioned by their commitment to the central goal of the Benedictine revival, the integration of church and state. Both homilists emphasized the meaning of church rituals, the need to attend church, and the importance of supporting the Church financially. To both writers, the proper functioning of the Church meant the proper functioning of society.[24] Both had a clear sense of their responsibility to "illustrate . . . the importance of adherence to the moral teachings of the church."[25] The homilies of Ælfric and Wulfstan provided their audiences with theological explications related to the author's goal of integrating monasticism with secular society.

The Chain of Being sketched out in Alfred's work had become rigidly fixed by the time of these authors. Whereas authors such as Alfred had asserted the importance of education, the model of society presented by Ælfric and Wulfstan was more fundamentally conservative: to them, education was the responsibility of the clergy, who already occupied a fixed, superior place in society. Alfred's writing proposed a social mobility which, through education, allowed people to move closer to God. This fluid social context was not available to the readers of Ælfric and Wulfstan. The model they propose in their pages is static and hierarchical: each individual must shoulder the responsibilities of the position he or she already occupies, in order to save the world from chaos and damnation. In the "Sermo Lupi," Wulfstan reflects this static vision when he complains that the different ranks of society have failed to perform their duties. As Stafford summarizes Wulfstan's position: "A dislocation of the essential order of society has caused the troubles of the English."[26]

Ælfric and Wulfstan's writings generally reflect the security of the Latin Christian tradition from which they emanate. The emphasis on the abstract and anagogical, found in Ælfric, and on the hierarchical, found in Wulfstan, was determined by the relative stability of the Latin Christian establishment in England at the time they wrote. In their writing, unlike Alfred's, the mundane is despised. As writers, Ælfric and Wulfstan are easily as sophisticated as Alfred, but both are writers of the elite. Entirely denying the value of worldly experience, they prefer the neoplatonic ideals of traditional Christianity over the mutability of the world. Both eschew the stylistic choices which Alfred and the AB texts employ to recreate the particular circumstances of everyday life. Wulfstan, however, writes his homilies for a broader audience than does Ælfric; as we shall see, this broader aim leads Wulfstan to use some stylistic features—in particular, affective stylistic techniques—that contributed to the development of quotidian psychological realism.

Although the styles of Ælfric and Wulfstan were determined in part by their shared conservative viewpoint, these styles were most probably further shaped by the needs and circumstances of their audiences. It is difficult, however, to establish the nature of those audiences firmly, although we can speculate on the basis of the authors' clerical positions. As an abbot, Ælfric presumably wrote for monks—that is, as a well-educated representative of the elite, he wrote for other members of that elite who had less training in Latin than he, but who nevertheless belonged to a privileged group. Although Ælfric well may have written originally for devotional and monastic audiences alone, his homilies sometimes did address larger audiences. Indeed, some of his sermons were intended to be read during mass. While Ælfric shows an obvious preference for monastic life, he also wrote homilies that were, as Gatch observes, "explications of the gospel pericopes for selected occasions of the liturgical year."[27] Despite the fact that Ælfric's homilies presumably were addressed to a general audience, they consistently assume that the audience shares the concerns of a narrower devotional group, perhaps a monastic audience. Wulfstan, a bishop, presumably wrote most often for the laity. Originally it was the duty of bishops alone to preach; among Wulfstan's major responsibilities would have been delivering sermons to the general public. His surviving sermons are largely "public discourses on religious topics."[28] He sometimes simply adopted parts of Ælfric's sermons or, finding them suitable for a general audience, transcribed them completely. Yet he often wrote original homilies shaped more specifically for his lay audience. While most often seeming to address the general public, sometimes, as in "Antichrist 1b," Wulfstan seems to address only members of the clergy who themselves will become teachers. This discussion of the styles of Ælfric and Wulfstan will concentrate on those homilies by Ælfric that most probably were addressed to his monastic peers and those homilies of Wulfstan that most probably were addressed to a broader, less educated lay audience.

Ælfric's style contrasts vividly with the style of the AB texts. As has been discussed by Peter Clemoes and Gatch, Ælfric's intricate syntax reflects his sense of order; he alliterates, for example, across grammatical segments rather than simply alliterating pairs or phrases. The structure of his homilies also reflects his anagogical interests and his commitment to the neoplatonic Christian hierarchy. His arguments focus on the top of the hierarchy—salvation and the nature of the afterlife in heaven. His homilies are intellectual celebrations of Christian order. If that order is followed, then a positive end is assured. This is not to say that Ælfric's works are not emotional, but, Ælfric, unlike the authors of the AB texts, is not interested in the fluctuations of emotion inherent in temporal experience. Instead he emphasizes the fixed, static emotion of joy that awaits the saved. As Ælfric was a monk writing for monks who are imitating the angelic life ahead, it is not surprising that this should have been his focus.

Ælfric's anagogical interests influenced his use of imagery. His avoidance of the literal meaning of an image can be seen in his homily for the Second Sunday in the Lord's Advent, a homily on the gospel pericope outlining the signs of the Second Coming. Here, Ælfric, following standard biblical exegetical technique, is not concerned with the particularity of the signs themselves. Although he does mention that nation has risen against nation, other harbingers, such as falling stars, are dismissed because they are not yet manifest. Rather than urging his listeners to look for those signs, he suggests a more abstract interpretation: "þæt ure mod þurh wærscipe wacole beon" ("that our minds may be heedful through vigilance").[29] Preoccupied with a progressive vision of an ascending ladder that takes his religious audience toward an ultimate vision of heaven, Ælfric rarely connects divine sayings with the literal things of this world; instead, he eschews the literal in favor of the allegorical. This emphasis on the metaphorical meaning even of the Eucharist has led some to point to Ælfric as a forerunner of Protestantism. Ælfric's interpretations ultimately are intellectual and hierarchical, in that he assigns a single meaning to an image. For example, in his sermon for the Nativity of the Virgins, Ælfric explains away the metaphorical overtones of Christ's words: "Ic beweddode eow anum were" ("I have betrothed you to one man").[30] In direct contrast to the literalization of the *sponsa christi* motif in the AB texts, Ælfric avoids exploring the interpretive possibilities available in the literal level of an actual betrothal to Christ, instead emphasizing the spiritual meaning: "Nis ðis na to understandenne lichamlice ac gastlice" ("This is not to be understood bodily but spiritually").[31] Again, in his sermon for the Second Sunday in the Lord's Advent, Ælfric discusses the specific tribulations prophesied by Christ in Matthew, making reference to the predicted earthquakes around the world and eclipses of the sun and moon, but he warns that it is a mistake to read these earthly happenings as literal signs. Rather, one should look for the signs in their allegorized representations. In his homily on Judgment Day, he tells us of these allegorical meanings. Those found in bed, for example, "ða beoð þonne on bedde þe beoð on stillnysse and fram eallum woruldcarum æmtige þonne beoð" ("those who are in bed are those who are still and empty of all worldly cares").[32] Rather than bearing a literal meaning, "Niht is her gecweden for ðære nytennysse and for ðære mycelan ehtnysse on Antecristes timan" ("Night is here mentioned because of the ignorance and the great persecution in times of Antichrist").[33] By winter, "Ne mænde he þone winter þe gewunelice cymð . . . on þam yfelan timan [but when] seo soðe lufu swiðe acolað" ("he [Christ] does not mean the winter which customarily comes, but the evil time when true love cools").[34] In his sermon on the Pentecost, Ælfric explains the meaning of the prophesied darkening of the sun and the moon: "þonne seo sunne and se mona ne magon syllan nan leoht for þam godcundan leoht ðe gæþ of þæm Hælende" ("The sun and the moon cannot give any light because of the divine light that shines from the Creator").[35] All literal images have meaning only on the allegorical and anagogical level. The last line of Homily 18 looks forward to the "unasecgendlicre" ("unutterable bliss of heaven").[36] The signified is far more important than the signifier, and the meaning of all signs dissolves into the inexpressibility of the awaited experience of heaven.

Unlike "Sawles Warde," where the purpose of the homily is to emphasize the importance of both the fear of hell and the hope of heaven in daily life, this homily inspires hope alone and ends, not with an examination of the contemplative's place on earth, but with an anticipation of his place in the afterlife. The structure of the work is teleological. Most of Ælfric's works follow the same development away from the things of this world and up towards heaven. The literal world is unworthy of contemplation. Ælfric urges his audience to turn away from love of this world and to lift the mind to heaven, because "Drihten ure Alysend us gewilnað gearwe gemetan and forþi cydde ða yfelnyssa ðe folgiað þam ealdigendan middangearde þæt he us fram his lufe gestilde" ("the Lord our redeemer is desirous to find us ready and therefore chid the evils which follow the senescent world that he might wean us from its love").[37] In other words, he urges his audience not to mourn the end of the world. Instead, "we soðlice ðe þæs heofonlican eðles gefean eallunga oncneowan sceolon anmodlice to ðam onettan" (I:612) ("we, who well full know the joys of the heavenly country should singlemindedly hasten to it"). Here Ælfric assumes that his audience shares his security and joy at an anticipated salvation in heaven. Such security most likely would be shared by an audience of monks, whose life on earth mimicked their anticipated angelic life after death. This earthly life is only a path to God: "Hwæt is ðis deadlice lif buton weg?" (I:614) ("What is this deathlike life but a way?") The insignificance of earthly time, in the context of salvation history, is emphasized: "þeah þe gyt wære oðer þusend geara to þam dæge, nære hit langsum" (I:618) ("Though there were yet another thousand years to that day, it would not be long"). This world, he reminds us, is not even suited to be the place of judgment: "Ne bið se dom on nanum eorðlicum felda gedemed ac bið swa swa se apostel her wiðufan on þyssere rædinge cwæð þæt we beoð gegripene on wolcnum togeanes Criste geond þas lyft" (I:616) ("The doom will be deemed on no earthly field, but will be as the apostle here above in this lesson said, that we shall be seized up in clouds towards Christ through the air"). Like the later *Cloud of Unknowing* and most male mystical literature, Ælfric's homilies express a distaste for, and deny the significance of, earthly experience. In Ælfric's work, then, we see techniques diametrically opposed to those of the AB texts. Where the AB texts are pragmatic, concrete, and nonteleological, his works are theoretical, hierarchical, abstract, and teleological (anagogical).

Wulfstan, while sharing Ælfric's commitment to a static hierarchy, shows a concern for the education of the laity which leads him to a different assessment of the individual's relationship to worldly experience. Like the authors of the AB texts, Wulfstan explores the nature of temporal vicissitude, presumably assuming that his audience finds such experience inescapable and that its members are willful, sensual, and prey to temptation. In order to address such problems, he makes use of affective techniques to check his audience's delight in the distractions of the mundane. Unlike Ælfric's highly wrought, intellectually balanced sentences so closely connected to doctrine, Wulfstan's sentences characteristically consist of a series of alliterative phrases. This technique renders his evocation of fearful things more powerful, as a means of inspiring a desire for repentance in an audience presumed to be unruly and sinful. His style, dependent on the use of parataxis, climax, and descriptive nouns and adjectives, is designed to inspire emotional rather than intellectual realizations of Christian truths. Many of these features are tailored for a listening rather than a reading audience. These affective techniques reinforce the individual's personal commitment to Christian goals.

Despite these techniques, Wulfstan's writing lacks the developed realism of the AB texts. He does not employ the full range of techniques found in the AB texts, because, unlike the AB authors and Alfred, he writes from the center of the establishment, the position of the privileged, educated elite. The emotion evoked through his imagery reflects his intent to impose his Christian scheme on his audience; he inspires Christian commitment not by recreating the experiences of the individual, but by evoking corporate guilt.

Although Wulfstan was a member of the same elite group as Ælfric, Wulfstan's work represents the voice not of those at the top of the socioreligious scale, but rather of those at the bottom. Both authors write about the end of the world. Indeed, many of Wulfstan's homilies are based on those by Ælfric. Yet, where Ælfric emphasizes the joy of the approaching end of the world, Wulfstan emphasizes its terror. Throughout his homilies, Wulfstan examines the interplay between sin, affliction, and repentance; his "Sermo Lupi" contains the most intricate development of these themes. Like Ælfric's, Wulfstan's vision of the world and the role of the individual within it is fundamentally conservative. Wulfstan exhorts sinners to repentance by outlining the vast number of ills common in the world, including war, famine, deceit, manslaughter, and fraud. For him, the end of the world has already come, and Antichrist is already present. In Bethurum V, "Secundum Marcum," he imposes a sense of urgency on his audience by repeating, "Nu is se tima" ("Now is the time").[38] Such repetition inspires both terror and the desire for repentance. Because of the security of his faith, Wulfstan reiterates a single theme, the warning that we must not be corrupted despite the presence of evil in the world. This urgency is perhaps intensified because of the need to reassert the prominence of the Christian system at a time of social upheaval, namely the shift from Æthelwold to the supremacy of the Danes. An accumulation of vices is the natural result of the coming of Antichrist, equated with the Danish invasions, and the only proper response to this event is repentance. As Wulfstan asserts in his "Sermo Lupi," "to micelan bryce sceal micel bot nide" (20; 261) ("so great an offence needs a great remedy"). Since Wulfstan's sense of his audience is corporate rather than individual, he attempts to sway his audience as a group. Thus his images do not inspire identification with individual protagonists, nor do they help the reader to analyze her or his individual susceptibility to sin or temptation. Rather, they consistently evoke an eagerness to accept the moral of the text: the need for repentance.

Wulfstan's narrow view of a perpetually sinful audience shapes his use of imagery. In contrast to Ælfric, whose discussion of the signs of the end of the world emphasizes allegorical meanings, Wulfstan emphasizes the literal meaning of the signs. In his view, these prophesied signs are either already present or will occur soon. Furthermore, they are the direct result of the irresponsibility of his audience. Thus, "ealswa flod com hwilum ær for synnum, swa cymð eac for synnum fyr ofer mancynn, 7 ðærto hit nælæcð nu swiðe georne" (3; 123) ("just as before long a flood will come because of man's sins, so also will come a fire over mankind because of his sins and that time approaches very rapidly"). Just as the uneducated lay populace generally is viewed as earthbound and incapable of perceiving the higher truths of God, so too are Wulfstan's images earthbound. Even when Wulfstan adds an allegorical level of meaning to the signs, the allegorical level remains rooted in everyday experience. In his discussion of the falling of the stars and the darkening of the sun, Wulfstan assigns meaning in the everyday world: these signs result from humanity's evil behavior—the sun's darkening indicates God's withdrawal from the world during the time of Antichrist; the moon's darkening signifies that God's angels no longer can help people as they once did; the falling of the stars signifies a human fall from correct belief. For Ælfric, the sun darkens only in comparison to the brightness of the light cast by Christ.

Wulfstan's Christian lessons are conveyed primarily through affective techniques. The negative images of Homily III pave the way for Wulfstan's climactic description of the terrors of hell: "þær is granung 7 wanung 7 aa singal heof" (3; 126) ("there is groaning and lamentation and ever continual wailing"). The assonance and rhythm of this sentence animate the lament of those in hell, setting the stage for the urgent appeal for repentance presented in the last paragraph of the homily: "Utan don swa us þearf is . . . lufian God . . . 7 his wyllan wyrcan" (3;126) ("Let us do as our need is . . . love God . . . and work his will"). This conclusion reflects a consideration of the passivity of the members of his audience. There is nothing they can do for themselves; rather they must depend on help from their superiors.

The only remedy—admittedly partial—for sin offered by Wulfstan in many of his homilies is proper "lage 7 lare" ("law and teaching"). As with Alfred, with Wulfstan education can lead to salvation. Unlike Alfred's more egalitarian and hopeful image of the power of teachings, however, Wulfstan's vision of teaching is pessimistic. As Wulfstan's technique implies that his audience is easily swayed by the rhythm and climax of a phrase, so he warns listeners against being too easily swayed by bad teachers. In "De Antichristo I," Antichrist is the one who lets go of God's law and teaching. Through the devil's teaching, Antichrist drags others down. There should be more good Christian teachers so that fewer will be lost through "larleste" (Ib; 118) ("want of instruction"). In Homily II, "Lectio Sancti," Wulfstan warns readers to beware of "leaslicre lare" (2; 120) ("deceitful teaching").

The disparate visions of Judgment Day in Ælfric and Wulfstan reflect their different audiences. Ælfric urges his audience, probably a group of monks, to look forward to Judgment Day, while Wulfstan urges his audience—lay society—to fear the approaching day. Whereas Ælfric shows little or no concern for the experiences of daily life, Wulfstan focuses consistently and repetitively on experiences widely known to his audience—famine, corruption, war, and murder. For Ælfric, the everyday world is an insignificant place doomed to destruction, a place of waiting soon to be replaced by a better world. Thus, Ælfric's work, literature written for and by the elite, celebrates an accepted Christian order. Wulfstan's work, literature written by the elite for the uneducated, also endorses the abstract Christian scheme but focuses particularly on those who fail to uphold the order. Such a focus is affective rather than intellectual in its insistent use of alliterative patterns designed to inspire terror. As a bishop, Wulfstan in his writing reflects a concern for corporate social recognition of his audience's sinful nature. We see in Wulfstan's work early experimentation with affective stylistic techniques. However, it is not until we turn to the anonymous homilies—literature presumably written by those less firmly established in the Christian orders than Ælfric and Wulfstan and presumably written for the uneducated—that we see techniques capable of exploring the full range of affective, pragmatic, interactive, and psychological levels as the AB texts do.

THE ANONYMOUS HOMILIES

Despite the fact that Ælfric's and Wulfstan's homilies were both popular and influential and that rewrites of Ælfrician homilies are found in the majority of post-Conquest sermon collections, it is a mistake to view either Ælfric or Wulfstan as setting the stylistic norms of the period. Indeed, the vast majority of extant homilies—all anonymous—exhibit a quotidian style that is important to understand as an antecedent to the AB texts. This style also is quite distinct from the abstract and intellectual style of Ælfric and from the general and tropological style of Wulfstan. The anonymous homilies span the long period from the ninth to the thirteenth centuries. Many of the later collections are interspersed with transcriptions of Ælfrician sermons. Despite the facts that the collections vary from one another and that some of the anonymous homilies occur side by side with Ælfrician sermons, the anonymous works nonetheless share a style that is distinct from that of Ælfric. I have chosen for discussion two representative collections—one early collection, the Vercelli homilies, and one late, the Lambeth homilies—although I shall make some references to other collections.

It is important to remember, of course, that the anonymous homilies are not a homogeneous group, since they differ widely in date and provenance. However, despite their differences, these homilies share circumstances of production that suggest that they were written by the relatively less educated for the uneducated. Clues in several of the collections suggest that many of them were written far from the established monastic centers of Britain. In investigating the provenance of the Vercelli manuscript, for example, Szarmach argues, citing Sisam, that it is not the product of " 'a great monastery, with flourishing scriptorium, trained scribes, and large library, but rather the product of a small house,' such as perhaps the restored nunnery of Barking Abbey, where a vernacular book was needed for private reading." [39] It is also probable, though difficult to prove, that many of the homilies, especially those written after the Conquest, were written for the laity. After the Conquest, texts written for the educated upper classes tended to be written in French or Latin. English survived as the language used in the literature of the marginal, uneducated, lower-class audiences who resided far from the centers of power. We can assume, then, that despite differences between the collections, the anonymous homilies as a group are shaped by two factors: they were written by those outside established centers of Latin learning, and they were written for those who were removed from those centers.

That the authors of the anonymous homilies used techniques which challenged the authority of the establishment is suggested by the condemnation of them by Ælfric and others. These writers especially criticized the popular vision of St. Paul which occurs in several collections and is referred to in many of the anonymous homilies. Antonette di Paolo Healey summarizes the establishment's criticism of this vision: "Aldhelm places it under the category of 'fevered fancies' and exhorts the faithful to repudiate it. Three centuries later Ælfric takes the same orthodox position . . . [and] marvels at the gullibility of men who read the 'false composition' called the *Vision of St. Paul*." [40] Ælfric was clearly distressed by the popularity and by the emotionally dangerous appeal of such apocryphal works. That Ælfric takes such a strongly orthodox stand suggests the popularity of a concurrent tradition which employed such material. The distinguishing characteristics of the anonymous homilies might be accounted for by their authors' presumably limited training, as well as by those authors' concern for the needs of uneducated audiences. These homilies share the following distinctively non-Ælfrician features: (1) they are syntactically simple, relying primarily on the heaping up of parallel paratactic clauses; (2) they use native vocabulary and themes that place Christian concepts firmly within the everyday world of Anglo-Saxon society; (3) they repeatedly use the dual "uton" ("let us"), allying the speaker of the homily with the audience; (4) they delight in apocryphal stories; (5) they use descriptive adjectives and nouns; (6) they use figures of speech based on common, everyday experience; and (7) they introduce dramatic characters, events, and simulated dialogue. Clearly, some of these features, such as repetition and syntactic simplicity, like the rhetorical devices of Wulfstan, are tailored for a listening rather than a reading public. This fact increases the likelihood that these homilies were intended for the laity. Not unlike the sermons of contemporary twentieth-century evangelists, similarly addressed to the uneducated, the homilies are repetitious, hypnotic, theologically simplistic, and intellectually undemanding, yet they are persuasive and emotionally powerful.

While each anonymous collection makes use of a different combination of these stylistic techniques, all share with the AB texts an emphasis on the particular and the individual rather than on the abstract and the universal. All recreate Christian ideals from the point of view of the audience. Through the use of affective rhetorical devices combined with quotidian imagery, the homilies create a theological drama of the common person. The homilists make use of themes drawn from earlier heroic and elegiac poetry, such as the celebration of deeds, the "ubi sunt" theme, the theme of the transitoriness of earthly experience, and the image of the hero as an exile. But, rather than dismissing earthly experience, they integrate it into a new Christian scheme. Thus, for example, these authors represent the body as a character or present a "witness" who stands in for the reader and mediates between the abstract perfection of heaven and the assumed corruption of everyday life. All Christian ideals, in other words, are mediated through the individual's earthly experiences. These works thus emphasize the experiences of the body, often explicitly in such techniques as the soul-and-body debate. Such techniques reveal the authors' assumptions that the lay audience is swayed by emotion rather than by reason and can apprehend the soul only through the body.

The Vercelli Homilies. Among the earliest collections of homilies is that known as the Vercelli homilies. The manuscript contains six Old English poems, including the famous "Dream of the Rood," as well as twenty-three homilies. The collection includes a number of Judgment Day homilies and a series of homilies that feature soul-and-body debates. The manuscript has been dated generally to the second half of the tenth century. Its association with a small house, perhaps a double house of men and women, significantly isolated from theological centers, would account for its stylistic distinctiveness.

John Sala, in his discussion of the Vercelli homilies, observes: "As one analyzes the special appeal of the Vercelli, he realizes that much of it lies in the fresh and vivid earthiness of its illustrative material and the commonsense view of life's processes."[41] The freshness and vividness of the Vercelli homilies are produced in part by the author's use of Wulfstanian rhetorical technique and partly by the use of concrete description. Despite a range of subjects, the Vercelli homilies are stylistically homogeneous. They are alliterative—for example, often a sermon begins with the following alliterative phrase: "Men ða leofestan, manað 7 myngaþ þeos halige boc" ("Beloved men, be mindful and take heed of the holy book").[42] They use doublets, such as the commonly occurring phrases "manað 7 myngaþ," "behydan 7 behelian," "lybban 7 rixian" ("be mindful and take heed of," "take heed of and behold," "to love and to rule"). The syntax of the homilies usually follows a pattern such as: "and þær bið unrotnys buton gefean 7 þær bið biternys buton swetnysse 7 þær bið hungor 7 þurst 7 þær bið granung 7 geomrung ("and there is sadness without joy and there is bitterness without sweetness and there is hunger and thirst and there is groaning and lamentation"). Here the sentence is made up of repetitive clauses that vary only in the object of the verb; these objects are usually sensorily evocative descriptive nouns. Such techniques contribute to the emotional involvement of the reader.

Homily II, a discussion of Doomsday, makes use of both affective syntactic devices and concrete description. Like the description of hell in "Sawles Warde," which inspires terror in its audience by particularized description and emotional appeal, the Vercelli homily's description of Doomsday helps to fulfill its opening prophecy that Doomsday "bið swiðe eges-lic 7 andryslic eallum gesceaftum" (II:44) ("will be very terrible and dreadful for all creatures"). The author lists the signs of the coming Judgment Day in a long series of syntactically simple sentences beginning with "on þam dæge." The parataxis and repetition emphasize the inevitability of the event. Like Wulfstan, the author uses intensifiers such as "swiðe" (very) to heighten the effect. Visual images increase the terror of the vision: the light of the sun and the moon "gewit" ("dies"); "On þam dæge bið Dryhtnes rod blode flowende betweox wolcnum" (II:44) ("On that day, the Lord's cross flowing with blood will be amidst the clouds"). (Notice this echo of "The Dream of the Rood.") Christ will be there "on þam hiwe þe he wæs þa hine Iudeas swunʒon 7 ahenʒon 7 hiora spatlum him on spiwon"

(II:44–45) ("in the same form that he was when the Jews beat him and hung him and spewed their spit on him"). The representation here of a suffering, human Christ rather than a triumphant, divine Christ enhances the reader's ability both to identify with Christ and to take responsibility for his suffering.

The horrors of Judgment Day are conveyed through additional sensory and affective descriptions, reinforced by syntactic devices. The homilist climaxes his discussion of hell with a cumulative list of horrors dominated by such words as "hryre" ("destruction") and "for-wyrht" ("ruin"). As in "Sawles Warde," all the senses are assailed in a description of the noise of the fire on Judgment Day, the color of the bloody stream, and the feel of fire and rain. The description is interspersed with such words as "groaning" and "trembling," experiences the description itself inspires. In a long series of sentences prefaced by "La" ("alas"), the author warns the audience to be afraid:

> La hwæt men him eallinȝa ne ondrædaþ hu þæt dioful him onstælaþ ealle þa un-
> rihten weorc . . . La, hwæt men him ne ondrædaþ þæt mycle dioful Anti-Crist
> . . . La hwæt we us ne ondrædaþ þone to-weardan eȝe domes-dagas . . . se is
> yrmþa dæȝ 7 . . . wanunȝe dæȝ 7 sares dæȝ. (II:46–47) (Alas that men don't
> completely fear how the devil completely establishes evil work; alas, that men
> don't fear the great devil Anti-Crist; alas, that we do not fear the approaching
> terror of Doomsday . . . that is a day of wretchedness, a day of lamentation, a
> day of sorrow.)

The progression of this sentence heightens fear and pity by first condemning those who do not fear the devil and then collapsing the distance between those sinners, the listener, and the speaker of the homily by substituting "we" for the repetitive subject, "men." The repetition of "La" suggests the dismay of the judge of the sinner at the sight of lamentable and regrettable but nonetheless unforgivable sins; it also echoes the word that the sinner himself is most likely to utter on Judgment day. The urgency of repentence is highlighted by the repetition of the word "dæȝ" ("day"), qualified by a series of adjectives, all unpleasant. The author ends the passage with an image of the frail rotting body eaten by worms:

> þa lichoman bið lað-lic leȝer ȝeȝyrwed in þære cealdan cealdan foldan gebros-
> nodan 7 þæt læne lic þær ȝe-rotaþ to fulnesse 7 þam wælslitenden wyrmum to
> æte. (II:50) (For the corrupted body a hateful grave will be prepared in the cold,
> cold ground and that transitory body will rot to foulness and be as meat for the
> corpse-eating worms.)

As in "Sawles Warde" and many other passages of the AB texts, such as the description of the dragon in *The Life of St. Margaret,* this passage deliberately evokes in the audience an intense emotional response—that is, fear—through its hyperbolic, concrete description.

The structure of the homily similarly works to create an emotional rather than an intellectual realization of a Christian truth. As in "Sawles Warde," where the reader learns affectively that fear must be balanced with hope, the listener learns in this homily that he or she must transfer the intensity of fear inspired by the first half of the homily to the earnest devotion and hope of heaven inspired in the second half. In heaven, "þaer bið ece leoht 7 blis 7 ece wuldor 7 ece ჳefea mid urum Dryhtne" (II:53) ("there is eternal light and bliss and eternal glory and eternal joy with our Lord"). Having drawn listener and speaker together through the fear they both experience as "we," the author now exhorts the listener to join him in reparations: "Utan we beon ჳemyndiჳe ussa sawla þearfe" (II:51) ("Let us be mindful of our soul's need"); "Utan we nu forþan efstan to ჳode 7 . . . sien we snotre 7 soðfæste 7 mild-heorte" (II:53) ("Let us now therefore hasten to God and let us be wise and true and merciful"); "Lufiჳen we urne Dryhten mid ealle mod 7 mæჳene" (II:51) ("Let us love our Lord with all our mind and might"). These moral exhortations have special significance for the audience because they occur after the reader or listener has experienced the emotional highs and lows inspired by the discussions of heaven and hell.

Homily IX, also a sermon on the nature of Judgment Day and the rewards and punishments awaiting the soul, is more fully developed stylistically than Homily II. Its sentences are syntactically more complex, and its structure is more formally balanced than that of Homily II. The homily consists primarily of a debate between the soul and the body, followed by a balanced description of heaven and hell. The author states his purpose at the beginning of the homily: "Forþan we habbað micle nyd-þearfe þa hwile þe we her syndon on þis laenan life and on þyssum ჳewitendlicum þæt we þonne on þære toweardan woruld mæჳen 7 moton becuman to life þæs heofoncundan rices." ("For this reason we have much need while we are in this transitory life and in this perishable life that we may and must come alive to that future world of the heavenly kingdom.")[43] In the course of the homily "maeჳen" ("may") becomes "moton" ("must"), for the author proves the necessity of choosing a life that will lead to heaven. The structure of his argument is apparently intellectual: he divides the discussion into several parts and further subdivides his areas of discussion into threes, describing three deaths—death on earth, separation of the body and the soul, and death of the soul; and three lives—the life of the body, life "þæt bið on ჳodes wuldre" (IX:103) ("that is in God's glory"), and life in heaven. After death on earth, the guilty are shut in hell. The author compares the torments of hell to five things on earth: pain, senility, death, the grave, and torture.

Although the structure is logical, the rhetoric is emotional. The homily reaches a climax in a simile designed to convince the reader of her or his personal responsibility for sinful deeds. In his description of hell, for example, the author uses the following comparison:

> ȝif hwylc man bið on helle ane niht þonne bið him leofre ȝif he þanon mot þæt he hanȝie siofon þusend wintra on þam lenȝestan treowe ufe-weardum þe ofer sæ standeð on þam hysthan sæ cliffe. (IX:110) (A man would rather spend seven thousand winters hanging on the highest tree that stands over the sea on the highest sea cliff than spend a single night in hell.)

Hyperbolic description, sprinkled with superlatives and couched within the conceit of a preference, reinforces the sense of horror at the vision of hell—a suggestion rather than a vision, which is hinted at rather than shown. The author then says that if seven men, speaking 270 languages with seven tongues, attempted to describe hell, they could not do it. This statement disrupts the intellectual order of the previous part of the homily; division, so popular in scholastic theology, is exaggerated, and the sermon is tipped from an intellectual vision of order into multiplicity and chaos. Like the discussion of hell, the discussion of heaven also depends finally on the force of a simile:

> Se man . . . hæbbe Salemanes wlite 7 wisdom 7 him sie eal middan-ȝeard on ȝeweald ȝeseald mid þam ȝestreonum . . . 7 ælc stan sy ȝylden 7 ealle þa streamas huniȝe flowen . . . þonne ȝif he wære her ane niht on heofonarices wuldre. (IX:114) (If the man had Solomon's splendour and wisdom and if all the earth with all its riches were in his control and each stone were golden and the streams were flowing with honey . . . then if he were in the heavenly kingdom for a single night, [he would scorn a life led in this world.])

Where Homily II evokes terror by describing horrifying events that will occur, Homily IX uses a different rhetorical technique, suggesting terror by not describing things. A general description of hell is given, but it depends on the word "buton" ("without"): "þær is wop buton frofre 7 hreow buton reste 7 þær bið þeowdom buton freodom 7 þær bið unrotnys buton gefean 7 þær bið biternys buton swetnysse" (IX:111) ("There is weeping without comfort and sorrow without rest, and there is servitude without freedom and sadness without joy, and there is bitterness without sweetness"). This description lacks adjectives and depends on negatives such as "unrotnys" and absence conveyed by the repetition of the word "buton." The following description of heaven similarly depends on the preposition "buton": "þær

bið lif butan deaþe 7 ʒod butan ende 7 ylde butan sare 7 dæʒ butan nihte
. . . gefea butan unrotnesse (IX:112) ("There is life without death and
good without end and old age without sorrow and day without night . . .
joy without sadness").

In this homily, as opposed to Ælfric's homilies, moral choice is determined by emotional response. The anticipation of joy replaces the anticipation of terror which had been inspired by the vision of hell. As the homily progresses, the reader is drawn inevitably to choose hope over fear. As
Szarmach writes of Homily IX:

> The audience will be ready to see things in terms of only two alternatives, the
> unspeakably horrible one and the inexpressibly joyful one, because the homilist
> arranges his material whenever he can so that the rhetorical order reflects moral
> choice . . . direct exhortation, the subtle inculcation of dichotomous thinking
> and the incremental list lead the audience to the heart of the homily, the choice
> between heaven and hell.[44]

Szarmach argues that the inevitability of the choice is supported even
within the sentence structure; for example, the author speaks of the joy of
earning heaven and of "gesæglice" ("blessedly") fleeing hell, with the ad-
jective reinforcing the choice.[45] Szarmach continues, "the incremental list
heightens the emotional tension that is part of the moral choice the homilist
wishes his hearers to make . . . the emphasis on hell effectively inspires a
ready identification with and acceptance of the vision of heaven."[46]

Another stylistic feature of the Vercelli homilies which is characteristic
of the anonymous homilies in general—and is conspicuously absent in the
homilies of Ælfric and Wulfstan—is the use of a dramatic debate, most
often a soul-and-body debate. We must question why such a motif would
have been common in popular literature. The motif depends on two features: first, the author's assumption that the reader is attached to the body
and, second, the emotional process created by the dramatization of a debate between two figures. The first figure answers the likely concerns of
the second, who also represents the voice of the listener. The recurrence of
this motif, with its constituent parts, suggests that the author assumes that
the reader can fully realize the meaning of the soul only through the body.
We can see how this motif works in Homily IV, for example, where the
soul praises the sinless body for not being a glutton, a miser, or false or
wicked in any way, but reprimands the sinful body as follows:

> Wa me, þæt ic þin æfre owiht cuðe swa unsofte swa ic on þe earðude. La, ðu
> eorðanlamb 7 dust 7 wyrma gifel . . . þæt wæron þine mæstan sorga, hu þu þine
> ceolan mid swet-mettum a-fyllan meahstan. (IV:93) (Woe to me that I ever in
> any way knew you as harshly as I did when I dwelled in you. Alas you are

earthloam and dust and worms' meat . . . your greatest concern was how you might fill your gorge with sweetmeats.)

This rhetorical passage achieves its power in part through the commitment of the soul to the body and through its paternal disappointment at the body's irresponsibility. In addition, the focus on a common quotidian indulgence, overeating sweets, from the perspective of death heightens the moral significance of seemingly meaningless everyday occurrences. The soul-and-body debate, here as elsewhere, introduces an idea that reaches its fullest development in Dante, that is, the notion that the experiences of the body on earth determine the kind of punishment the soul will receive in hell. The soul, speaking like a betrayed friend, laments:

þa he fedde his lichoman orenlicost mid sweamettum, þe ȝeernode he me þæs ecan hungres. Þa he swiðost his lichoman drencte unriht-tidum, þa earnode he me Þæs ecan þurste. Þa he his lichoman in idelnesse ȝlendȝde mid hraȝle þa earnode he me þære ecan næcede. (IV:96–97) (Because he fed his body excessively with sweetmeats, he earned for me eternal hunger. Because he often drenched his body at the wrong times, he earned for me eternal thirst. Because he in idleness adorned his body with clothes, he earned for me there eternal nakedness.)

Everyday experiences are transformed into morally determinant ones. Indeed, everyday desires are seen to be part of a larger plan of the devil, who we are told, uses his bow and arrows daily, launching such weapons as the arrows of drunkenness. All these examples assume that the audience, incapable of subordinating momentary desires to larger, more abstract goals, can be kept from satisfying the desires of the flesh only through the evocation of corresponding sensory privation. Through such stylistic devices as drama or the use of concrete description, the Vercelli homilies, like the AB texts, stimulate the individual's emotional realization of Christian values as they apply to daily experience.

After the Conquest, English vernacular literature apparently waned. Because courtly literature was dominated by the French and much religious and legal literature was composed in Latin, English literature came to be composed primarily for those removed from the monastic and religious centers of Britain. As the contents of the majority of late sermon collections suggest, many homilists were content simply to collect and transcribe earlier sermons, especially those of Ælfric. Sometimes they simplified Ælfric's sermons, either shortening them or omitting detailed exegesis. Homilies continued to be composed, however. Inevitably, the homilists were influenced by new ideas from the continent, especially the development of interest in the idea of the self and in the affective dimension presented in meditations on Christ's passions. The homilists also were influenced by the highly significant twelfth-century Lateran Council decree that required each individual to confess yearly. This decree created an urgent need for explanations of confession. Despite these influences, the homilies retained the emphasis of the earlier anonymous homilies on the quotidian and on the common person's pragmatic realization of Christian goals.

In addition to simplified explanations of confession, twelfth-century homilies are sprinkled with quotidian metaphors drawn from the everyday experience of their audiences.[47] Homily X, for example, compares three kinds of fasting to the work of a washerwoman. Just as the sinner fasts to cleanse himself of sin, the righteous man fasts to approach holiness, and the holy man fasts to increase holiness, so the washerwoman bears soiled clothes for washing, carries clothes for bleaching, or carries clean clothes. In Homily XXVII, the disgrace of not keeping altar cloths clean is brought home by contrasting the clean, expensive clothes of the priest's wife to the old, torn altar cloth and the soiled mass cloth. A more domestic scene is evoked in Homily V, which compares the devil's whisperings to the effect of a mirror on a woman: as the reflection in a mirror teaches a woman to make herself lovely, so a devil comes into a man's heart and holds secret conversations with him. These images, although relatively conventional, nonetheless focus the listener's attention by rendering numinous the objects and experiences of everyday life. Even the nature of the inner life is explained with reference to quotidian images. For example, Homily VIII compares the heart to the invisible wick within the visible wax of the candle.

The Lambeth Homilies.   A later collection of homilies, edited by Morris, is dated 1185–1225 A.D., although the sermons are believed to be based on eleventh-century collections. This collection is of particular interest for an investigation of the origins of the prose style of the AB texts because it is associated with Llanthony Priory, a convent near Wigmore Abbey, the supposed home of the AB texts. Indeed, the first half of the Morris collection is based on Lambeth MS 487, a manuscript that also includes a version of "Sawles Warde."

Lambeth 487 includes a homily, "In Diebus Dominicis," that is based on one of the most popular medieval sermons, "Visio S. Pauli" ("Vision of St. Paul"), an apocryphal legend mentioned earlier which is found in a number of English homily collections. Paul visits hell and, in this English version, describes in detail what he sees: souls hanging by their feet from high trees before hell's gates; hell as a burning oven; a well of fire guarded by devils; a sea with seven bitter waves of snow, ice, fire, smoke, blood, stench, and adders; animals with eyes like fire who torment the bodies of those who have not repented; and seven enclosures of noxious vapors. The high percentage of descriptive nouns and adjectives in this account heightens the emotional response of the reader. The homilist conveys the unpleasantness of hell by calling up images of the most unpleasant experiences of medieval life: unpleasant smells, bad weather, and dangerous animals, including the English adder. The social dimension of morality in this vision is explicitly stated. For example, Paul observes individual sinners, such as a bishop, now an old man, being led by the devil, or a maiden suffering because, although she had kept her purity in the world, she had never done any good for anyone else. The general lesson of the homily is also socially oriented: its purpose is to explain how, because of Paul's intercession on behalf of sinners, Sunday came to be a day of rest and prayer.

The homily's power, however, like the passage in the Vercelli homilies which is also based on the "Visio S. Pauli," rests primarily on its development of a theological drama in which a character, Paul, appears within the text. Paul, as the observer of the events, like the narrator of a novel authenticates the experience and provides an ally for the reader. This dramatic technique is common in many of the apocryphal stories used so often by the anonymous homilists. In addition to the soul-and-body debates of the Vercelli homilies, another characteristic of fundamental English style is the presentation of a drama which clearly is developed taking into account the point of view of the common person. Such a drama forms the essence of *Piers Plowman*, it informs the *Canterbury Tales*, it shapes the drama including "Everyman," and it influences even later allegories such as *Pilgrim's Progress*, in which the common individual learns Christian lessons and gains authenticity by retelling his or her experience. The creation of a character, often a dreamer, who tells the story was a distinctive feature of medieval dream visions especially, a genre that was particularly popular in England.

These homilies, like those in Morris's previous collection of earlier homilies, also use a number of animal images to reinforce their argument. Like the *Ancrene Wisse* (which is sprinkled with many animal images), Homily V compares animals to everyday sins. Backbiters are compared to spotted adders: "þas faȝe neddre bitacneð þis faȝe folc þe wuneþ in þisse weorlde. þe speket alse feire biforen heore evencristene . . . and swa sone se hi beoð iturned away from heom. heom to-twickheð and to-draȝeð mid ufele wordes" ("These spotted adders betoken the deceitful folk that dwell in this world, that speak as fair before their fellow Christians as if they would embrace them, and as soon as they have turned away from them they slander and detract them with evil words").[48] Rich men are compared to toads:

þos blaca tadden þet habbeð þet atter uppon heore heorte. bitacneð þes riche man þe habbeð þes mucheles weorldes ehte and ne maʒen noht itimien þar of to eten ne to drinken ne na god don þer of for þe luve of god almihten þe haveð hit heom al geven. ah liggeð þer uppon alse þe tadde deð in þer eorðe þet neure ne mei itimien to eten hire fulle swa heo is afered leste þeo eorþe hire trukie. (V:53) (These black toads that have the venom in their hearts betoken the rich men that have much of this world's goods and cannot moderately eat and drink, nor therewith do any good for the love of God almighty, who have given it them all, but lie upon it as the toad does in the earth that never can be so moderate as to eat her fill, because she is afraid lest the earth deceive her.)

The explanation of yellow frogs that follows is corrupt in the manuscript, but the author's probable intention was to compare yellow frogs to women who dress in fine clothes: "Wimmen heo smurieð heom mid blanchet þet is ðes deofles sape and claþeð heom mid ʒeoluwe claþe þet is þes deofles helfter" (V:53) ("women smear themselves with blanchet that is the devil's soap and clothe themselves with yellow clothes, that is the devil's covert"). These women are called "þes deofles musestoch" (V:53) ("the devil's mousetrap"). The moral lesson of this passage depends on the evocation of everyday images and experiences which are then closely linked with Christian concepts.

Another distinctive image from everyday experience also occurs in Homily XXV—the image of Christ as mother. Caroline Bynum has discussed the unusual affective qualities of this pervasive image. Although this image may have originated in a Latin source, this homily provides a notable early examples of such an image in English texts. Here the homilist writes:

Muʒe we ahct clepeian hine [God] moder wene we. ʒie muʒe we. hwæt deð si moder hire bearn formes hi hit cheteð and blissið pe þe lichte. and seþe hi dieð under hire arme oðer his hafed heleð to don him slepe. and reste. þis deð all ʒiure drihte. he blisseð hus mid dʒeies licht. he sweveð hus mid þiestre nicht.) (XXV:233) (May we, ween we, call him at all our Mother? Yea, we may. What doth the mother to her child? First she showeth and blesseth it by the light, and afterwards she putteth her arm under it, or covers his head, that he may sleep and rest. This does the Lord of you all. He rejoices us with the daylight; he sends us to sleep with the dark night.)

Here the homilist encourages the audience's dependence on Christ by inspiring desires for protection and comfort.

The Lambeth homilies, like the earlier homilies, share with "Sawles Warde" a focus on the realization of Christian goals through the experiences of the body. In an image similar to that of the household in "Sawles Warde," Homily II compares man to a castle:

And þah an castel beo wel bemoned mid monne and mid wepne. and þer beo analpi holh þat an mon mei crepan in. Nis hit al unnet. hwet itacnet þe castel þe mon seolf. hwet þa men þe beoð in þe castel and hin ȝemeð.þet beoð þes monnes eȝen. and his fet. and his honden. and his muð. and his nesa. and his earen. (II:23) (And though a castle be well garrisoned with men and with weapons, yet if there be a single hole whereby a man may creep in, is it not all in vain? What betokeneth the castle but man himself? What are the men who are in the castle and defend it but man's eyes, feet, hands, mouth and ears?)

Like corresponding passages in "Sawles Warde," this passage emphasizes the individual's need to control the senses. Unlike "Sawles Warde," however, which develops the image to include a discussion of the emotions experienced by the contemplative, this homily finally looks outward, rather than inward, and concludes with general social precepts: a man can protect his castle by giving alms, by going to church and by feeding the poor. Nonetheless, this homily, like so many of the anonymous homilies, assumes that its audience is easily swayed through the senses.

The Lambeth homilies, like the AB texts, also emphasize the audience's identification with Christ's suffering, a feature owed to the continental affective movement. In the English texts, Christ's suffering is related directly to the personal life of the listener. The details of the crucifixion abound in descriptions like the one in Homily XI, in which the Passion is described: "Mid irenen neilen he wes on þere rode ifestned and mid speres orde to þere heorte istungen and mid þornene crune his heaved wes icruned. swa þet þet rede blod seh ut on iwulche half" (XI:121) ("With iron nails he was fastened on the cross, and with the spear's point pierced to the heart, and with a crown of thorns his head was crowned so that the red blood flowed out on every side"). Homily VII—like the *Ancrene Wisse,* which urges the contemplative to avoid the sins of the senses because of the suffering that Christ experienced through the senses—equates the wounds of Christ with the five senses through which men sin:

He is ihaten helende for he moncun helede of þan deþliche atter.þet þe alde deovel blou on Adam.and on Eve.and on al heore ofsprinke. swa þet heore fiffalde mihte hom wes binumen. þet is hore lust. hore loking. hore blawing. hore smelling. heore feling wes al iattred. ac he hom helde mid his halie fif wunden þa he þolede for us on þe halie rode. (VII:75) (He is called Saviour for he healed mankind of the deathly venom that the old devil blew into Adam and Eve and all their offspring, so that their fivefold powers were taken from them; that is, their hearing, their sight, their breathing [blowing], their smelling, and their feeling were all poisoned, but he healed them with his five holy wounds when he suffered for us on the cross.)

Such an explanation assumes that the soul is defined through the body. Sinning through the body leads to the destruction of the body—the death earned by the sin of Adam and Eve. The salvation of the body comes through Christ's experience of suffering through the same senses by which Adam and Eve sinned. The experiences of the body are directly related to Christian concepts, as in Homily II, which tells the audience that "Crist þrouwede deð for us and alesde us of helle grunde mid his derewurðe flesse and mid his blode . . . we hit sculen beote and pinian þene wreche lichome imececheliche þer aʒein" (II:19) ("Christ suffered death for us and delivered us out of the abyss of hell through his precious blood . . . we should repent and mortify the body meetly in return").

As in the AB texts, in the Morris homilies contemplation of Christ's suffering leads not away from the experiences of the world but towards them. Homily V equates man's sinning through the senses with the suffering Christ experienced on the cross:

> Mon him biþenchþ þet he haveð sunful ibeon.and to fele sunne idon. þenne wule his heorte ake alse his heved wolde.if he hefde þer uppon þornene helm . . . hwenne . . . þe mon him biþengþ þet he haveð to selde igan to chirche. and ilome mid his honde idon þet he don ne sculde. þenne wule his heorte ake also his fet and his honde.if he þurh irnene neile were þurh-strunge. (XV:149). (When a man remembers that he hath been sinful, and committed very many sins, his heart then aches as his head would if he had thereon a helmet of thorns . . . when the man remembers that he has too seldom gone to church and often with his hands done what he should not have done; then will his heart ache, and his feet and his hands as if they had been pierced with nails.)

Here Christ's suffering becomes the suffering of every individual who sins, and the senses of the listener merge with Christ's senses. The senses must be controlled daily, as the homilist in Homily XII goes on to command:

> Mid his blode we sculan deihwanliche þa postles and þet overslaht of ure huse þet is of ure heortan gastliche bispringan . . . we sculon ure foreheafod and þa vii ʒeade ures lichomes mid þere halie rode tacne seinian . . . ðet beoð ure eʒan and ure neose and ure muð and ure earen. (XII:127) (With his blood we should daily besprinkle spiritually the posts and the lintel of our houses that is of our hearts; we shall cross our foreheads and the seven gates of our body with the sign of the holy cross . . . they are our eyes and our nostrils and our mouth and our ears.)

Thus, in these homilies, not only are everyday experiences and objects filled with religious meaning, but also the senses used to perceive them are similarly transformed.

We have seen in this chapter that the circumstances and perceived needs of uneducated audiences had an important influence on the development of style. Because these audiences had little contact with Latin intellectual centers and because the members of such audiences also were assumed to be rooted in the experiences of the body, literature written for them abandoned logical, teleological, and abstract argumentation and focused instead on the particularity and fluctuation of everyday experience. That focus inspired the use of particular stylistic techniques, including affective syntactic devices such as parataxis, climax, and alliteration; concrete description; and figures of speech, including metaphors, similes, and analogies, in which the bases of comparisons were drawn from everyday experience.

Literature, unlike theology, is not simply prescriptive or admonitory. Nor does it simply describe or celebrate an abstract, otherworldly system. Rather, literature focuses the attention of the reader on the fluctuations and distractions of everyday life that frustrate or disrupt an abstract system of ideals. Furthermore, in addition to looking outward, literature looks inward in order to sharpen a reader's understanding of the self as it grapples with the world's disruption. We see in Alfred's writing and in the anonymous homilies the development of stylistic techniques that are crucial to the development of literature as distinct from theology. Alfred's work manifests a concern for those uneducated in Latin, which led him to make use of quotidian imagery that is fluid and multivalent. In Ælfric we have discovered an author who, more theologian than literary writer, desired to escape the temporal world altogether. His writing, therefore, is abstract and teleological, and his imagery is static. Although Wulfstan shared with Ælfric a theological denial of the value of worldly experience, his concern for lay audiences led him to focus on the experiential rather than the theoretical. Yet, because Wulfstan, as a bishop, was primarily concerned with the needs of the group rather than of the individual, his techniques are ultimately simply rhetorical. The works of anonymous homilists, concerned with the average lay individual's realization of Christian truths, are stylistically richer. They employ a fuller range of stylistic tools, using such devices as concrete description and figures of speech based on everyday experience, in addition to the rhetorical techniques of parataxis and alliteration. These methods focus the individual's attention simultaneously inward and outward, so that the objects and experiences of daily life can be filled with Christian immanence.

The quotidian psychological realism of the AB texts thus arises within a tradition of English religious prose texts that probably were addressed to audiences uneducated in Latin. Use of the stylistic techniques described above varies according to the author's conception of his audience. The more an audience was perceived as earthbound, the more experiential the focus of the text becomes. Texts written for women—the AB texts—are the most fully experiential texts of the period. Christian theory clearly informs literary practice, however. We have observed how, late in the Anglo-Saxon tradition, scholastic ideas concerning the nature of the self in relationship to the physical world, as well as scholastic investigations of self-scrutiny as a means of understanding confession, informed the themes of the late anonymous homilies. Yet these new ideas always were integrated into the English tradition through an experiential filter, by the use of realistic techniques. Some of these new ideas had special significance for a woman's experience of Christianity. It was the integration of native quotidian realism with larger scholastic theoretical developments that produced the distinctively feminine style of the AB texts. The ways in which scholastic developments influenced a native English quotidian style is the subject of the next chapter.

CHAPTER 9

The Female Reader and Twelfth-Century Notions of the Physical

The focus of the AB texts on the integration of everyday experiences with abstract Christian ideals, I have argued, owes a debt to a tradition of English prose that concentrates on the pragmatic and the experiential. The quotidian realism of English texts is comprised of several elements, one of them being a close scrutiny of the self in relation to the physical world. The portrayal of that relationship was conditioned by the authors' belief that it is the nature of an uneducated self to be rooted in a willful body that must be instructed through the senses and the emotions. Yet the authors' conception of the self was determined not only by their consideration of the essentially physical nature of the works' audience, but also by the authors' views of the nature of the physical more generally. Because texts written for women and for the uneducated are permeated by the idea that readers are rooted in the body, attitudes towards matter—as it is embodied both in the individual and in the outside world—must have conditioned the authors' representation of the contemplative's experience of the world. Reevaluating the nature of the physical world in relationship to the Christian self was one of the major concerns of twelfth-century theology. Therefore, the physicalized spirituality of the AB texts can be understood fully only by recognizing the influence of twelfth-century theological developments upon those texts.

Critics, of course, have recognized the twelfth-century continental renaissance's contribution to the representation of spirituality in the AB texts.[1] Yet most of those critics, because they failed to recognize the overriding importance of the physical in the AB texts, have misconstrued the AB texts' relationship to continental thought. Widely varied individual theological texts have been named as sources of the AB texts, but the implications of those theological texts for literature that is focused on the body have not been fully acknowledged. Because the exact circumstances of the composition of the AB texts are unknown, it is difficult to state precisely what continental writers the authors of the AB texts read. Dobson argues convincingly that these works should be associated with an Augustinian rather than a Dominican house.[2] Manuscript tradition, he points out, makes Wigmore Abbey a likely home of the texts, and Limebrook Priory, a nearby nunnery of Augustinian canonesses, a likely home for the anchoresses to whom the texts were most likely addressed.[3] Dobson further suggests that because of similarities of thought in many of the works, we might be dealing with a school of writers rather than with a few isolated individuals. Dobson argues that the texts arose from "a centre of scholarship [that] . . . had a good library" located in Herefordshire.[4] We know very little about the exact contents of the thirteenth-century libraries of Herefordshire Cathedral and Wigmore Abbey.[5] However, scholars have done some work on manuscripts associated with the Abbey. Southern, for example, has shown that the dialogue "De Custodia Interioris Hominis," the alleged source of "Sawles Warde," is a part of a Herefordshire Cathedral manuscript that also includes Anselm's *De Moribus* and *De Incarnatione Verbi*.[6] Further work on Herefordshire as a potential literary center should reveal additional specific works likely to have been known to the authors of the AB texts, in which case we may be able to determine whether or not there was a literary school in Herefordshire and what kind of theological bias that school had.

Most of what we know about the reading of the AB authors comes from internal evidence—that is, from references to writers within the works themselves. Those references indicate that the authors were familiar with twelfth-century theologians who are generally well represented in manuscript collections throughout England, namely, Bernard, Anselm, Ailred, and Hugh and Richard of St. Victor. Geoffrey Shepherd argues that the largest influence on the *Ancrene Wisse* is Bernardine, but he qualifies his assertion by pointing out "it owes more to Anselmian piety than the half dozen quotations might suggest."[7] The influence of specific Anselmian works surely deserves reconsideration. In addition, because Wigmore Abbey was a Victorine Abbey whose twelfth-century abbot, Andrew of St. Victor, was both prolific and influential, specific Victorine texts also may well have had a major influence on the AB texts.

The thought of the AB texts is determined by more than specific sources, however. The authors of the AB texts must have been acquainted to some degree with most of the major developments of scholastic thought as they percolated throughout English monasteries. In recent years, critics have devoted much attention to the influence of twelfth-century theology on the development of literature, and they argue that most major literary genres, as well as the extensive philosophical and scientific developments of post-Reformation movements, actually have their roots in this fertile period. Critics studying these theological developments generally fall into two groups. One consists of those interested in exploring the development of notions of the self and emotions and/or moral theology—that is, the development of affective piety; among them are Sir Richard Southern, Linda Georgianna, and R.W. Hanning. The second group, interested in the development of naturalism, the implications of literal exegesis, and/or the rise of science, is exemplified by Beryl Smalley, Brian Stock, M.D. Chenu, and Winthrop Wetherbee.[8] Theologians of importance for the first movement include Bernard, Abelard, and Anselm; for the second, the so-called Chartrians—Bernard Sylvestris, William of Conche, Thierry of Chartres—and the Victorines.[9]

Those interested in literary developments such as those found in the AB texts have focused their attention primarily on the affective movement. By explaining the origins in twelfth-century psychology of the *Ancrene Wisse's* conception of the solitary self, Linda Georgianna has explained the importance of the affective movement for the development of thought in the *Wisse*. These psychological developments had important implications for the development of medieval literature in general, as a number of critics have discussed.[10] Georgianna's conclusions clearly apply to the other works of the AB group. Let us summarize her analysis. R.W. Southern, Georgianna observes, was one of the first to point out the ways in which Anselm and Abelard's interest in moral theology led to a shift away from a static, communal vision of humanity and toward an emphasis on the personal and the individual. Both Anselm's concept of juridical atonement, which celebrates the personal debt that the individual owes Christ, and Abelard's *Scito te Ipsum*, which argues that sin is manifested in intention as much as in deed, cast new responsibility on the individual. Such analyses, in conjunction with the Fourth Lateran Council's decree that each individual had to confess regularly, resulted in the proliferation of confession manuals designed to help the Christian discover the motivations of sinful thoughts and acts. These movements contributed to the development of affective piety, which involved an analysis of the emotions necessary for self-scrutiny. The affective movement, then, centered as it was on the exploration of the nature of the self, can be seen as having had far-reaching effects on the AB texts and on the development of Middle English texts in general.

Twelfth-century theology was marked not only by psychological investigations of the nature of the self, but also by investigations of the nature of the world itself, investigations known loosely as a scientific movement. As we review twelfth-century contexts of the AB texts, it will emerge that we cannot fully understand these works by understanding only their affective context, an understanding that Georgianna provides; in addition, we must also consider their scientific context. We shall find that the analyses of the physical world in the AB texts were conditioned by the authors' absorption of Anselmian, Chartrian, and Victorine notions of the nature of the self as it interacts with the physical world. We shall then reassess the special implications that these notions had for literature addressed to the audience most defined by the physical, the female audience.

With their shared interest in a general investigation of the relationship of the Christian self to the physical world, both the affective and scientific lines of philosophical investigation were clearly interrelated. Furthermore, they sprang from an earlier development in theology: the humanization of Christ, a movement represented by Anselm's seminal work, *Cur Deus Homo*. It was this development, as it contributed to the later parallel schools of the affective and the scientific, that determined notions of the physical that then crystallized in texts written for those audiences seen as most conditioned by their physical natures—that is, women and the uneducated. In terms of its influence on the development of notions of the self in interaction with the physical world, the humanization of Christ (a movement represented by Anselm's *Cur Deus Homo*) was possibly the single most significant development of the twelfth-century renaissance. The importance of this movement for literary developments perhaps has been insufficiently recognized. Critics comment most often on the importance of works by Anselm other than *Cur Deus Homo*. Philosophers, for example, cite the significance of Anselm's proof of the existence of God in his *Proslogion*. Southern has stressed Anselm's role in the rise of medieval humanism, but literary critics who follow Southern's line of thought tend to concentrate primarily on the importance of Anselm's *Prayers and Meditations* in the development of affective piety. These examinations, as important as they are, ignore the crucial position of *Cur Deus Homo*, written in 1097, in Anselm's canon and in the development of twelfth-century thought. It is a seminal work in the development of attitudes toward the physical, because, in its celebration of the humanity of Christ, it newly legitimizes all human experience.[11]

Because Anselm's *Cur Deus Homo* is so important in the development of a new valuation of the physical in both human beings and the world at large, it is necessary to consider this work in some detail. In response to a habitual theological concentration on Christ's divinity, Anselm set out to answer the question raised by a celebration of divinity: "qua necessitate scilicet et ratione deus cum sit omnipotens humilitatem et infirmitatem humanae naturae pro ejus restauratione assumpserit" ("for what necessity and cause God who is omnipotent should have assumed the littleness and weakness of human nature for the sake of its renewal").[12] According to Anselm, only a human being could atone for original sin: "Nam deus non faciet quia non debebit; et homo non faciet quia non poterit. Ut ergo hoc faciat deushomo necesse est eundem ipsum esse perfectum deum et perfectum hominem" ("For God will not do it, because he has no debt to pay and man will not do it because he cannot. Therefore, in order that the God-man may perform this salvific act, it is necessary that the same being should be perfect God and perfect man").[13] In Anselm's scheme of juridical atonement, God's assumption of humanity is proof of his great love for mankind, because it was a free choice. Therefore, mankind owes a corresponding debt of love to God. Moreover, because God did not *have* to suffer, his suffering on the cross is all the more pitiable.[14]

Anselm's argument had multiple implications for the development of medieval literary technique. To begin with, God's suffering became a legitimate arena for meditation. Meditation on Christ's passion inspired both compassion and pity. In addition, a focus on Christ's passion led to a simultaneous fascination with blood and tears. Such explorations led to the development of affective piety, already noted as a crucial development for literary representations of the self.

Anselm's discussion allowed the Christian tradition not only to value humanity as it is figured in Christ, but also to value humanity itself. John Bugge observes, "As Anselm writes in the *Cur Deus Homo,* Christ's assumption of humanity is not simply a lowering of God but an exaltation of humanity that gives new respect to all human behavior."[15] The influence on literature of such a shift in interest from Christ's divinity to his humanity is profound, since, for the first time, common human experience was viewed as powerful. Because Christ triumphed through the assumption of the weakness of humanity, even the weakness of humanity was to be valued. Such a concept clearly influenced the introduction into literature of common people as protagonists. Furthermore, the idea that ordinary people could triumph through human experience allowed literature to focus on process rather than conclusion, hence the rise of pilgrimage literature. Finally, the fact that Christ's humanity was valued encouraged individuals to imitate the example offered in Christ's human incarnation. In chapter 8 of

Cur Deus Homo, Anselm explains that by the sufferings he endured, Christ set man an example. The Franciscans finally institutionalized the *vita apostolica;* the influence that their interest in such a life, involving as it did an imitation of Christ's life on earth, had on literature is well documented.[16] Clearly, a focus on the individual's ability to realize Christian values in her or his daily life through imitation of Christ had its origins with Anselm. The effects of that influence can be seen even in the English sermon and dramatic literature that preceded the arrival of the Franciscans in England.

The explosion of interest in the humanity of Christ influenced more than the development of notions of literary character; it had an even more subtle and far-reaching effect on the development of medieval realism—that is, on the kind of quotidian realism we have identified in the AB texts and in their Anglo-Saxon homiletic ancestors. Its effect was obvious in art, where the shift away from Christ's divinity and towards his humanity was reflected in movement away from representations of Christ the military hero, characteristic of the early medieval period, and toward the suffering, vulnerable images of the later period.[17] Such realistic descriptions also occur in eleventh-century prayers. As Sister Benedicta Ward writes, "This personal relationship to Christ evolved rapidly after Anselm, but it is there in other eleventh-century prayers, such as those of Peter Damian—in his prayer to the cross, for instance, the idea of personal commitment in regard to the passion of Christ, and the immediateness of the scenes are very striking."[18] Gradon argues that the humanization of Christ encouraged visually realistic representations of human experience as well.[19] Numerous meditations on Christ, including those by Peter Damian, pseudo-Bernard, pseudo-Anselm, Rolle, Julian of Norwich, and St. Edmund, Gradon observes, are saturated with visually realistic details.

It is not just humanity that is imaged in realistic detail, however. Because God chose to manifest his divinity in matter, all matter becomes a reflection of the glory of God. The humanization of Christ thus also allowed for the development of the second aspect of twelfth-century thought, so often analyzed by critics as a separate movement—the rise of science. This valorization of the entire physical world reached its fullest expression in the works of the Chartrians and the Victorines, theologians who, like Anselm, had an indirect but profound influence on the kind of imagery found in the AB texts. Southern emphasizes the importance of this movement on the development of the modern world, describing it as a "new range of scientific inquiry in which England took a leading part."[20] The rise of scientific inquiry broadened the contemplative arena. As Brian Stock summarizes: "There was a growth within medieval culture as a whole of a certain existential naturalism, a this-worldliness which balanced the tendency towards mysticism in the Augustinian tradition . . . there was interest in the visible, empirically definable world."[21] The new attentive observation of reality, as Chenu writes, "in the schools and in the streets and fields" initially did not conflict with Christian ideals, though such a focus clearly carried within it the potential for undermining the asceticism of Christianity.[22] But, as Chenu points out, at this stage of theological development, "Nature, discovered now in its earthly reality, would acquire . . . religious significance and lead men to God."[23]

The so-called Chartrians were among the most significant theologians in the rise of naturalism. As Wetherbee and Nolan have observed, the new interest in the outside world was, like Christ's humanity, imaged in art. For example, at the cathedral at Chartres, animals, birds, and flowers, all encompassed by the controlling figure of Christ, reflect a celebration of the natural world as a manifestation of God's glory. The Chartrians attempted to reconcile the natural world with abstract ideals. Their attempts to reconcile the creation accounts in Plato's *Timaeus* and in Genesis reflect their preoccupation with the relationship between mental and physical worlds. Their focus was outward rather than inward. As Thierry of Chartres writes, "Wisdom is the coherent understanding of the true nature of existence," that is, of the outside world.[24]

The tension between the rise of scientific interest in nature and the doctrine of contempt for the world led to different emphases in theological reflection in which, as Chenu writes, "the Christian contemplating the world is torn by a double attraction: to attain God through the world, the order of which reveals its creator, or to renounce the world from which God is radically distinct."[25] The School of St. Victor, which existed concurrently with the school of Chartres, wanted particularly to reconcile a Chartrian curiosity about nature with a conservative hierarchical vision of God's plan. The Victorines further developed a consideration of the relationship between man and the created world, asserting that "the immense unity of all things was knotted up together in man who stands at the paradoxical borderline of matter and spirit."[26] Yet, rather than deny the material world for the sake of the spiritual, the Victorines argued that, "connatural with matter, a man's intelligence had to work through matter."[27] Such an attitude towards matter clearly underlies the *Ancrene Wisse* if not all of the AB texts.

The Victorines well may have exerted a major influence on the AB texts. As mentioned earlier, Wigmore Abbey, the religious house closest to the possible home of the anchoresses for whom some if not all of the AB texts were written, was both a Victorine abbey and the home of the influential Andrew of St. Victor. Whether or not the authors of the AB texts were Victorines themselves, it is likely, given the popularity of Victorine texts in England generally, and their probable prominence in Herefordshire more particularly, that the AB authors were well acquainted with Victorine thought.[28]

A previous chapter illustrated the differences between the exegesis of Hugh of St. Victor and that of the *Ancrene Wisse*, but it is important to recognize that the focus of the AB texts—and of many English texts—on the literal and sensual may well have been fueled by Victorine thought. The Victorines were known especially for their development of biblical exegesis that favored literal interpretation of the Bible over allegorical interpretation. Of course, Victorine concern with the literal level of exegesis is not necessarily equivalent to the AB texts' interest in the literal level of Christian experience in the world. Yet the method of Hugh's commentary on Noah's ark, for example, shares with the AB texts a theological bias that privileges the physical as a means of understanding the spiritual. Andrew of St. Victor has particular relevance for our investigation of the theological context of the AB texts, because he was the abbot of Wigmore Abbey in about 1147, and he even may have been British. Andrew shared with authors of the AB texts a particular attitude towards the world; Smalley describes him as a "rationalist . . . explaining Scripture in terms of everyday life."[29] Smalley praises Andrew for his "sense of concrete reality."[30]

These twelfth-century theologians' celebration of both corporeal and mundane physicality clearly had important implications for literary texts meant for people seen as inescapably conditioned by their identification with the body—namely, women and the uneducated. Because English texts in particular addressed such audiences, in English works the ideas of continental theologians took on new dimensions. As we have observed in connection with Anglo-Saxon homilies, in English texts the meditative arena includes not only the physical world of the Bible, but all physical creation. Moreover, English works focus in detail on the literal plane itself rather than on the possible allegorical meanings, because the authors needed to make the literal meanings immanent for the ordinary reader. Furthermore, the ordinary person is often the protagonist in English texts. The rise of popular drama and pilgrimage literature cannot be attributed solely to continental influences. Both Chaucer's and Langland's representations of the common person's integration of Christian ideals and everyday experiences owed a debt to this peculiarly English emphasis. Yet, it cannot be denied that English pragmatism received new impetus from continental developments.

The idea that spirituality can be realized through meditation on the outside world had further implications for literature written for women. The celebration of the redemption of the flesh through the flesh, inherent in the new emphasis on the humanity of Christ, had special meaning for women, who were perceived as quintessentially the flesh. It is not surprising, then, as Caroline Bynum has demonstrated, that the Eucharist played a more significant role in female than in male meditation.[31] In this context, Anselm's work takes on new importance in the history of literature written for women, because women's nature could be seen as allowing them a fuller identification with the humanity of Christ than was available to men. Because women's bodies were thought to contain more moisture than men's, tears were believed to come more easily to them, and their own blood would make it possible for them to meditate with compassion on the blood of Christ. Blood, tears, and a celebration of weakness were key features of Anselmian piety; these features surely would have special significance for women, whose very nature was perceived as constituted by weakness and excess moisture.

Besides allowing a woman to identify more fully with Christ through his female-like humanity, Anselm's work also allowed a woman to meditate upon Christ as her literal lover. We have seen in an earlier chapter that a woman's experience of the *sponsa christi* motif was concretized. Much of that concretization was made possible by the eleventh-century humanization of Christ. If Christ was human, then he also was sexual. As Bugge writes, the humanization of Christ "permitted the believer to focus on what the unerring fixation upon his divinity had all but obscured, the fact of Christ's human sexuality . . . it opened the way to speaking of Christ in the metaphorical terms of human sexual love."[32] As Leo Steinberg has demonstrated, such a "sexualization" of Christ influenced artistic representation of Jesus.[33] Women could not imagine Christ as their lover, and, further, the image of Christ as sexual allowed for inevitable comparisons between Christ and other human beings. As Bugge writes, "The portrayal of Jesus as the rival with other men for the affections of holy women was a unique by-product of the Anselmian atonement;" Bugge observes further, "It also put the marriage of Christ on an equal footing with human marriage."[34] The consideration of Christ as a lover to be compared with human lovers even extended into the legal and secular world. For example, Thomas Head has demonstrated that Christina of Markyate defended her childhood commitment to Christ as a legally binding marriage that could not be violated by a secular marriage.[35]

The literalization of the *sponsa christi* motif allowed a new range of sensual experience to take prominence in meditative writing. As Bugge argues, "In the twelfth century the *sponsa christi* metaphor attracted to itself the suggestive dress of a thinly veiled literary eroticism which was to characterize the testimony of female mystics throughout the remainder of the Middle Ages."[36] We have seen how the authors of the AB texts describe the virgin's relationship to Christ in frankly sensuous terms. For example, St. Katherine talks of Christ with what Bugge calls a "hazy, dreamlike softness," and to Margaret, Christ is "leoflukest to loken upon 7 swotest to smellen" ("Christ is most lovely to look upon and sweetest to smell").[37] The sensuality of Christ as a bridegroom appears in texts written for men, but in such works the erotic emphasis is less explicit than in texts written for women.

Anselm may have had a more profound influence on female spirituality than is generally recognized, for, from early in his career, Anselm showed a particular interest in the needs of both female and lay audiences. As Southern points out, "He (Anselm) also wrote to meet the increasingly articulate needs of lay people, especially women in great positions who had the time, inclination, and wealth to adopt the practices of the monastic life. Such women were among the earliest recipients of his prayers."[38] Scholars often point to Anselm's prayers and meditations as among the earliest texts of the affective movement, but they rarely mention that a woman, Mathilda of Tuscany, not only was among the recipients of the prayers, but also, as Southern notes, was "one of the main agents of their dissemination."[39] Surely Anselm's emphasis on emotions in these prayers was shaped by his consideration of his female audience. In addition to the prayers, Anselm also wrote a large number of letters to women, letters notable for their sympathy and concern for feminine spiritual needs.

Anselm's prayers focus particularly on compassion, weakness, blood, and tears. Since these attributes had traditionally been viewed as "feminine," such a focus suggests that femininity itself might have been reevaluated and revalued in this early period of affective piety. Indeed, Caroline Bynum has argued that feminine imagery such as that found in Anselm inspired a reevaluation of the feminine.[40] She has shown that numerous paintings from this period show Christ as a feminine figure. In some, for example, he is shown presenting his wound as if it were a breast. In another painting, the Christ child is represented as a child with two fully formed female breasts. Such representations, Bynum suggests, clearly value the female body in a new way. Yet such images more often appropriated the feminine rather than serving to redeem women. For example, the last image is so jarring that the viewer is forced to make an allegorical leap. The twin breasts do little to value breasts; instead, they force the viewer past any physical reality present in the image to an allegorization of the breasts as the Old and New Testaments. However, the fact that Anselm praised feminine emotions does seem to have redeemed some qualities specifically associated with women. In later affective works, however, the feminine qualities of such emotions are subsumed within the traditional male heirarchical model. These later works divorce emotions of tenderness and mercy or images of tears and kisses from their literal meaning and place them in a logically progressive argument that mimics the ascent of the mind to God. This treatment results in a very different stylistic quality in these later affective works. Commenting on Bernard, for example, Chenu describes "a certain failure to give physical actuality, natural or historical, its due; a viewing of all things in an essentially transcendent light."[40] Such an emphasis subordinates the literal to the transcendent and so suggests the ultimate insignificance of earthly—and female—experience. Female corporeality, far from being revalued, then, ultimately was either allegorized or made the requirement of female meditation.

If we look at other twelfth-century writers associated with the affective movement, we find that a very clear distinction was made between female and male spirituality. What was implicit in Anselm—the inescapable corporeality of lay or female audiences—became explicit in Abelard's leters to Heloise. Abelard was among the first to call attention to the unique advantages of the religious life for women who followed the models that the Gospels provided for them. In his sixth letter of direction to Heloise, for example, Abelard celebrates the unique favor that Mary's role as the mother of God bestows upon women, and further describes the privileged position that both Maries occupied during the Crucifixion and afterwards as figures of consolation.[42] For instance, Mary Magdalene acted as a nurse in anointing Christ's wounds and had the special honor of being allowed to see the newly resurrected Christ. Although Mary McLaughlin argues that one might construe Abelard as an early feminist, it seems to me that Abelard's praise of women and of women's roles in the Gospels reasserts and enhances his underlying misogynistic assumptions about woman's corporeal nature. Because women's bodies are assumed to contain more moisture than men's, blood and tears become the special prerogative of women. Abelard, emphasizing the symbolic and meditative importance of blood, ignores Heloise's objection that Benedictine clothing rules made no provision for menstruating women. Abelard's concentration on the symbolic implications of women's blood lets him ignore the literal implications of women's actual blood. Nonetheless, Abelard does justify the development of an especially feminine strand of affective piety which exaggerates compassion for suffering and stresses the female identification with blood.

In art, the feminization of affective piety is reflected in representations of the tenderness of Mary and even more pointedly in the efflorescence of artistic representations of Mary Magdalene. These visual representations of Mary Magdalene reflect misogynistic concepts of women by emphasizing their physical natures; in this tradition, Mary Magdalene represents the lowest form of humanity, whom Christ nonetheless redeems. Often she appears clothed only in her long hair, suggestive of pubic hair. The aura of sexuality which surrounds Mary Magdalene because of her past as a prostitute is transcended through her compassion for and care of Christ. Abelard similarly responds to Heloise's impassioned longing for her former sexual relationship with Abelard by urging her to replace her physical, carnal, and sinful love for man with love of God. As in so many of the texts written for women, women are to achieve a love of God not by overcoming desire but by transferring it to a more appropriate object. In male texts, compassion or pity is divorced from the body, whereas in female texts it is linked to the body.

Even within the Latin tradition, then, a woman's corporeality determined her Christian role. While the mundane took on an abstract value in texts for men, we have seen in the works of the Chartrians and the Victorines, it remained a necessary component of texts for women. The primary theological movements of the twelfth-century renaissance, the praise of the physical world and the celebration of Christ's humanity in emotional meditation, then, had special implications for texts written for uneducated audiences and especially for women. That is, works written for women emphasized the latter's supposedly unique ability to identify with and to comfort Christ in his suffering. Furthermore, because women, as well as the uneducated in general, were perceived as rooted in the body, sensory perception was felt to be their primary means of understanding God. Thus, close scrutiny of the physical world was viewed as especially apt when addressing such audiences. It is no surprise that in texts written *by* women, as opposed to *for* them, the features we have investigated become even more exaggerated. As Bynum puts it, "Women's writing was, in general, more affective, although male writing too brims over with tears and sensibility; erotic nuptial themes, which were first articulated by men, were most fully elaborated in women's poetry. And certain devotional emphases, particularly devotion to Christ's suffering humanity and to the eucharist (although not, as is often said, to the Virgin), were characteristic of women's practices and women's words."[43] Bynum goes on to argue,

> Women writers tended either to ignore their own gender . . . or to embrace their femaleness (as did Margery Kempe) as a sign of closeness to Christ . . . Women drew from the traditional notion of the female as physical an emphasis on their own redemption by a Christ who was supremely physical because supremely human . . . To women, the notion of the female as flesh became an argument for women's *imitatio Christi* through physicality. Subsuming the male/female dichotomy into the more cosmic dichotomy divine/human, women saw themselves as a symbol for all humanity.[44]

Although affective features as well as a celebration of the physical in general did characterize women's writing, it is extremely important to remember that the focus on physicality was necessary because of more general male notions of female nature. I quarrel, therefore, with Bynum's suggestion that women were able to escape their limited gender identification and also with her argument that the celebration of the physical then compelled men to reassess the value of women's symbols generally. As Bynum herself points out, these symbols were appropriated by men. It can be argued that medieval women gained power by accepting medieval categories of male and female and then manipulating them to their own advantage. Perhaps those women would finally have been more powerful had they abandoned these categories altogether, achieving thereby what Helene Cixous would describe as a celebration of true difference rather than inferiority.[45]

Recent feminist analyses of female mysticism could have benefitted from a consideration of historical context. Feminist critics who have turned their attention to female mysticism, such as Simone de Beauvoir, Luce Irigaray, and Julia Kristeva, base their analyses on a recognition, if not an endorsement, of the centrality of a woman's sexuality to her mystical vision. Blood and tears, for example, predominate in women's mystical writing. Although these writers praise mystics such as Hildegard of Bingen, who emphasized that it is precisely female flesh—the very weakness of women—that restores the world, it is necessary to acknowledge that such a celebration assumes an original acceptance of subordination. Was such female mysticism redemptive for women or not? De Beauvoir argues that while female mystical visions, as logical expressions of a woman's sociological condition "on her knees," could redeem her body, ultimately they denied her a sphere of action in the world. As Bynum points out, "women's symbols did not reverse social fact, they enhanced it."[46] Despite the fact that such symbols reinforced a women's subordination in the social world, it is possible that they enhanced her power in the spiritual realm. Both Kristeva and Irigaray, like Hildegard, find strength in weakness. Kristeva praises the unique celebration of motherhood available to women when they meditated on Mary. Irigaray suggests that women could overcome male categories by exaggerating them. She argues that when the female mystic equated her vagina with Christ's wounds, the lips of her vagina, Christ's wounds, and her mouth were linked together, allowing her access to a distinctively feminine voice unavailable to men. All these interpretations must be qualified, however, by recognition of the fact that the feminine voice ultimately was determined by male definitions of women.

Medieval concepts of the physical are complex, and this subject poses many areas of potential research. Caroline Bynum, for example, has recently argued that medieval notions of the nature of the body's resurrection casts doubt on our usual perceptions of medieval soul-body dualism.[47] If the body was valued in the way that Bynum suggests, some of my arguments here may need qualification. Yet, even that new work should be considered within the context of gender issues. For example, the resurrected body was viewed essentially as "complete," as one that neither cries or bleeds. Such a view implies that the body is, in an Aristotelian sense, essentially male. How such notions related to views of women deserves further consideration. Nonetheless, it is clear that twelfth-century notions of the physical—both of the body and of the material world—form an essential backdrop for proper appreciation of the spirituality of those defined most essentially by the body—that is, women.

CHAPTER 10

The Question of Female Style

In the AB texts, we have identified a distinctive nonteleological and relational style that can be called "female" in that it arises out of the authors' considerations of the nature and needs of a female audience. Yet the fact that this style was created by men and also occurs in other works written for both male and female readers implies that it is a gender-linked rather than a gender-determined style—that is, it is not "female" by necessity. If we were to turn to works written *by* women as opposed to *for* women—for example, to Julian of Norwich's *Revelations* or Margery Kempe's autobiography—we would find similar stylistic strategies at work in their writing, often in exaggerated forms.[1] For example, both Julian and Kempe emphasize the concrete and sensual, both make use of hyperbolic images of blood and tears, and both employ a plethora of domestic or mundane images (think of Julian's famous use of a hazelnut to convey the meaning of God's love for the world). In addition, the structure of Julian's work, as Barry Windeatt has demonstrated so persuasively, violates expectations of linear narrative, being repetitious, contradictory, and fundamentally experiential.[2]

To what degree does this style and the similar style of other late medieval women writers reflect such writers' femininity? If the style of such women writers were considered without considering other contexts, it might well be considered *essentially* female, that is, limited to women writers alone. However, the fact that the same features occur in the AB texts renders suspect the idea that the work of such writers reflects a female essence. While a nonteleological and relational style might well reflect aspects of femininity, the fact that these aspects have their roots in male views of women suggests that the elements of femininity that permeate these women's texts are ultimately the creation of men, whatever the relationship of style to female essence. Indeed, the origin of female style in these male views suggests that many of our notions of femininity are socially constructed. On the other hand, it can be argued that the *hyperbole* of the style is unique to women writers. The effects of such hyperbole further suggest that women are adopting and adapting views about their nature to subversive effect. Indeed, for many of these female writers, the "assumption" of inferiority, humility, and moist, compassionate "essence" becomes the basis of their own "female" authority. In this respect, the style is particular to women in that it arises out of the cultural and historical circumstances that condition a woman writer's self-expression.

As we have seen in the chapter on Anglo-Saxon sermons, however, these same stylistic elements also occur in works written for audiences untrained in Latin. Although the stylistic strategies we have discussed may be central to and/or exaggerated in women's writing, they are not restricted to women's works. It is also true that similar strategies occur in works written later in the tradition, presumably for audiences of mixed gender outside the intellectual elite. Windeatt, for example, has demonstrated the affinity between Julian of Norwich's style and that of both the *Pearl*-Poet and Langland. Langland's work, like Julian's, is fundamentally experiential and relational, and his overall structure is fluid and nonteleological. Langland's allegorical figures have challenged readers of allegory for decades. They continually move in and out of the realistic, everyday world. Additionally, they act upon the reader in a way not unlike the action of the *Ancrene Wisse:* that is, they reflect the outer world but they serve as a guide to the inner life. For example, like Adam in Julian's lord/servant parable, Piers is both a simple laborer, the common man, and Christ himself. Will, of course, is the quintessential representation of multiple levels of meaning; even in name, he stands for a "real" character, the author himself, and for an abstract inner property (Will), a property significantly, from the point of view of the gender issues raised by the AB texts—most often associated with women. Haukyn, the active man, is another character who operates on several levels. He wears an allegorical coat and is quite consistently representative of the nature of the active life. Yet he bears the name of an ordinary man. Furthermore, the smoothness of his dramatic representation is disrupted by the process of his interaction with other characters, both individual and allegorical. Langland's work as a whole reiteratively concretizes and temporalizes abstractions, creating a process through which Will as a character, Will as Langland, and we the readers learn how to realize Christian abstractions in the process of time and in the context of everyday life. Like the AB texts, *Piers Plowman* celebrates the paradoxical transcendence of this world available precisely through the full experience of this world. Such complexity surely has its roots in part of Langland's concern for a lay audience removed from monastic centers yet in need of a guide in learning how this life can be a path to the other life.

The imagery in the work of the *Pearl*-poet also shares with the AB texts and with the work of women mystics an emphasis on a complex interplay between the temporal pressures of everyday life and a desire to infuse that life with the meaning of abstract Christian ideas. As Windeatt writes, "Julian's reconciling of contraries is achieved by patterns of language which recall *Pearl*, for just as the nature of the Virgin is expressed in *Pearl* by her queenship of courtesy, so Julian recurrently finds in her visions and meditations both homeliness and courtesy."[3] In *Pearl*, the *Pearl*-poet, like Julian, makes use of the idea of courtliness and yokes together earthly and heavenly meanings. *Sir Gawain and the Green Knight,* in a more secular context, also dramatizes the disjunction between the different levels of meaning evoked by the word *courtesy*.

The similarities among the AB texts, the late English mystics, Langland, and the *Pearl*-poet raise questions about the similarities in the various audiences of these works as perceived by the authors. This study suggests that a proper appreciation of the style of such works can only be reached through a consideration of perceived audience need, expectation, and circumstance, as these shaped the development of style. Gender is only one determining aspect of an audience. Each work can be understood fully only by considering it as a product of its own specific time and place. Yet, such historical contextualization is hard to achieve, given the obscurity that surrounds even the name of the author, let alone the date or events that surrounded the creation of some of these works. We must not neglect the audience issue just because we do not know precisely who that audience was. Often we may be dependent only on internal evidence—the style itself— as an aid in speculating on the nature of the audience. As we have seen with the AB texts, the author creates the reader, and that constructed reader has profound effects of stylistic choices. Central to the exploration of this book is the assumption that style can be a primary source of information about audience, although we need not be limited to stylistic considerations alone, of course. In the case of at least one of the AB texts, the *Ancrene Wisse,* we are fortunate in knowing precisely for whom the work was written, as well as many details about that audience's circumstances. In addition, we also have been able to consider another context, that of the age's likely view of such women readers. Style, when considered in relationship to general ideas about audience, can broaden our understanding of a text.

Sometimes, as we have seen in this study of the AB texts, the style of a given work can be misunderstood if the nature of the audience is not taken into account. If we consider style in conjunction with the idea of audience we can gain a broader understanding of lesser-known mystical works. We may also, however, gain a new perspective on better-known works, such as those by the Ricardian poets.

Notes

The title of this book indicates that, for the purposes of this investigation, I consider the texts of the Katherine Group to be prose rather than poetry. I have never made a scholarly study of this particular matter, however, and leave the final nomenclature of these works open.

ABBREVIATIONS

EETS   Early English Text Society
OS   Original Series
JEGP   *Journal of English and Germanic Philology*
SS   Supplementary Series
NS   New Series

CHAPTER I

1. J. R. R. Tolkien, *"Ancrene Wisse* and *Hali Meidenhad," Essays and Studies by Members of the English Association* 14 (1929): 104–26.

2. Linda Georgianna, *The Solitary Self: Individuality in the Ancrene Wisse* (Cambridge, Mass.: Harvard Univ. Press, 1981).

3. See E. J. Dobson, *The Origins of Ancrene Wisse* (Oxford, England: Clarendon Press, 1976).

4. For bibliography on prose works from this period, see A. S. G. Edwards, ed., *Middle English Prose: A Critical Guide to Major Authors and Genres* (New Brunswick, N.J.: Rutgers Univ. Press, 1984) and A. S. G. Edwards and Derek Pearsall, eds., *Middle English Prose: Essays on Bibliographical Problems* (New York: Garland, 1981).

5. R. M. Wilson, ed., *Sawles Warde, Leeds School of English Language Texts and Monographs,* no. 3 (Leeds, England, 1938), vii.

6. R. W. Chambers began the debate about the continuity of English prose with his "The Continuity of English Prose from Alfred to More and His School" in Nicholas Harpsfield, *The Life of Thomas More,* EETS, OS 186 (1932; rptd. London: Oxford Univ. Press, 1963). For more recent discussions and challenges to this argument, see Elizabeth Zeeman, "Continuity in Middle English Devotional Prose," *JEGP* 55 (1956): 417–22; and Bella Millett, " 'Hali Meiðhad,' 'Sawles

Warde,' and the Continuity of English Prose," in *Five Hundred Years of Words and Sounds*, ed. E. G. Stanley and Douglas Gray (Cambridge, England: D. S. Brewer, 1983), 100–108.

7. D. W. Robertson, Jr., *A Preface to Chaucer: Studies in Medieval Perspective* (Princeton: Princeton Univ. Press, 1962), 55.

8. Ibid., 55–56.

9. Ibid., 16.

10. Georgianna, *Solitary Self*.

11. See R. W. Hanning, *The Individual in Twelfth-Century Romance* (New Haven: Yale Univ. Press, 1977); R. W. Southern, *The Making of the Middle Ages* (1953; rptd. New Haven: Yale Univ. Press, 1970); and Southern, *Medieval Humanism* (New York: Harper and Row, 1970). Michel Foucault, in a lecture given at the University of Colorado in 1983, argued that, because of its importance for psychology, the twelfth century deserves more critical attention than it has received.

12. See Chambers, "Continuity of Prose"; Dorothy Bethurum, "The Connection of the Katherine Group with Old English Prose," *JEGP* 34 (1935): 553–64; and Margaret Hurley, "The Katherine Group: Manipulation of Convention in Conventional Narrative" (Ph. D. diss. Syracuse Univ., 1974).

13. For a summary of Alfred's life, see Simon Keynes and Michael Lapidge, trans., *Alfred the Great, Asser's Life of King Alfred and Other Contemporary Sources* (Middlesex, England: Penguin, 1983).

14. For a discussion of the audiences for Ælfric and Wulfstan's works, see Milton McC. Gatch, *Preaching and Theology in Anglo-Saxon England: Ælfric and Wulfstan* (Toronto: Univ. of Toronto Press, 1977).

15. See Brian Stock, *The Implications of Literacy: Written Language and Models of Interpretation in the Eleventh and Twelfth Centuries* (Princeton: Princeton Univ. Press, 1983).

16. For a discussion of these categories, see Ian Maclean, *The Renaissance Notion of Woman: A Study in the Fortunes of Scholasticism and Medical Science in European Intellectual Life* (Cambridge, England: Cambridge Univ. Press, 1980).

17. See Carol Gilligan, *In a Different Voice: Psychological Theory and Women's Development* (Cambridge, Mass.: Harvard Univ. Press, 1982).

CHAPTER 2

1. For summaries of extant information on the personal histories of anchoresses, see Rotha Mary Clay, *Hermits and Anchorites of Medieval England* (1914; rptd. Detroit: Singing Tree Press, 1968); Lina Eckenstein, *Woman Under Monasticism: Chapters on Saint-Lore and Convent Life, A.D. 500–1500* (Cambridge, England: Cambridge Univ. Press, 1896); and Doris Stenton, *The English Woman in History* (New York: Macmillan, 1957).

2. See Doris Stenton, *English Woman*, 53.

3. Ann K. Warren, *Anchorites and Their Patrons in Medieval England* (Berkeley: Univ. of California Press, 1985), 92.

4. For a comprehensive discussion of the new religious movements of this period, see David Knowles, *The Monastic Order in England: A History of Its Devel-*

opment from the Time of St. Dunstan to the Fourth Lateran Council (940–1216) (Cambridge, England: Cambridge Univ. Press, 1940).

5. Jean Leclercq discusses this new recruitment policy in *Monks and Love in Twelfth Century France* (Oxford, England: Clarendon Press, 1979), 86–108.

6. For a discussion of the position of women in Anglo-Saxon and Anglo-Norman society, see Doris Stenton, *English Woman;* and Christine Fell, Cecily Clark, and Elizabeth Williams, *Women in Anglo-Saxon England and the Impact of 1066* (Bloomington: Indiana Univ. Press, 1984). For a discussion of the role of women in Anglo-Saxon literature, see Jane Chance, *Woman as Hero in Old English Literature* (Syracuse, N.Y.: Syracuse Univ. Press, 1986).

7. Kathleen Casey discusses the problem of sources in her "Women in Norman and Plantagenet England," in *The Women of England from Anglo-Saxon Times to the Present: Interpretive Bibliographical Essays,* ed. Barbara Kanner (Hamden, Conn.: Archon Books, 1979), 83–123.

8. For a discussion of women's legal rights in Anglo-Saxon England, see Frederick Pollock and Frederick W. Maitland, *The History of English Law,* vol. 2 (Cambridge, England: Cambridge Univ. Press, 1898), 364–66. Much of the discussion of women and English law that follows is based on Pollock and Maitland as well as on Fell.

9. Perhaps part of the reason Anglo-Saxon women had extensive legal rights to land was a response to the upheaval of war. In Iceland, women inherited land in part because the death of so many men at sea threatened the survival of newly established communities.

10. See Pollock and Maitland, *History of English Law,* 391.

11. Ibid., 391–92.

12. See discussion of marriage laws, ibid., 364–99.

13. Ibid., 403–404.

14. Ibid., 404.

15. Ibid., 405 and 447. In Chaucer's "Clerk's Tale," when Griselda is cast out by Walter, she asks only to take her necessary clothes with her. This story of her limited possessions, designed to heighten our pity for her, also accurately reflects English women's actual legal rights of possession.

16. Ibid., 434.

17. Ibid., 428.

18. Ibid., 406.

19. Ibid., 436.

20. Ibid., 436, n1.

21. Infant mortality was extremely high in the Middle Ages. See Emily Coleman, "Infanticide in the Early Middle Ages," in *Women in Medieval Society,* ed. Susan Stuard (Philadelphia: Univ. of Pennsylvania Press, 1976), 95–124. For a general discussion of medicine in England during this period, see Rubin Stanley, *Medieval English Medicine, A.D. 500–1300* (New York: Barnes and Noble, 1974).

22. Pollock and Maitland, *History of English Law,* 437.

23. Ibid., 421.

24. Ibid., 404.

25. For a full-length treatment of the life of Eleanor, see Amy Kelly, *Eleanor of Aquitane and the Four Kings* (Cambridge, Mass.: Harvard Univ. Press, 1950).

26. See Eileen Power, *Medieval English Nunneries, circa 1225–1535* (Cambridge, England: Cambridge Univ. Press, 1922), 5.

27. Ibid., 40.

28. See Pollock and Maitland, *History of English Law*, 368.

29. Stenton, *English Woman*, 53.

30. For a discussion of educational opportunities for women in nunneries see Power, *Nunneries*, 237–84.

31. Ibid., 1–4.

32. Ibid., 42–95.

33. For a discussion of Abelard's twelfth-century defense of Christianity as a positive force for women, see Mary McLaughlin, "Peter Abelard and the Dignity of Women: Twelfth-Century 'Feminism' in Theory and Practice," in *Pierre Abelard, Pierre le venerable, Les Courants Philosophique, Litteraires et Artistiques en Occident au Milieu du XIIe Siecle* (Paris: Editions du Centre Nationale de la Recherche Scientifique, 1975), 287–334.

34. For a discussion of the psychological effects of anchoritic life on men and women, see Peter Brown, *The Making of Late Antiquity* (Cambridge, Mass.: Harvard Univ. Press, 1978).

35. Warren, *Anchorites*, 19–20.

36. Ibid., see table 1, p. 20.

37. Ibid., 22 and 25.

38. Ibid., 23–26.

39. Ibid., 27.

40. Bruno Scott James, trans. *St. Bernard of Clairvaux Seen Through His Selected Letters* (Chicago: Henry Regnery Co., 1953), Letter 118, pp. 161–63.

41. See discussion of the bishop's control in Warren, *Anchorites*, 53–91.

42. Ibid., 61.

43. Ibid.

44. J. R. R. Tolkien, ed., *The English Text of the Ancrene Riwle. Ancrene Wisse* (Corpus Christi College, Cambridge 402), EETS, OS 249 (London: Oxford Univ. Press, 1962), 8.

45. The following description of an anchorhold is based both on Warren, *Anchorites*, and Clay, *Hermits and Anchorites*.

46. Warren, *Anchorites*, 97–98.

47. Ibid., 31.

48. Ibid., 32.

49. C. H. Talbot, ed., *The Life of Christina of Markyate: A Twelfth-Century Recluse* (Oxford, England: Clarendon Press, 1959).

50. Aelred of Rievaulx (Aelredi Rievallensis), "De Institutione Inclusarum," in *Opera Omnia*, ed. A. Hoste and C. H. Talbot (Turnholti, Belgium: Typographi Brepols Editores Pontificii, 1971) 638–682, see especially 638.

51. Ibid., 640:4, 93–95.

52. Giles Constable, "Ailred of Rievaulx and the Nun of Watton: An Episode in the Early History of the Gilbertine Order," in *Medieval Women*, ed. Derek Baker (Oxford, Eng.: Basil Blackwell, 1978), 205–25.

53. See Siegfried Wenzel, *The Sin of Sloth: Acedia in Medieval Thought and Literature* (1960; rptd. Chapel Hill: Univ. of North Carolina Press, 1967).

54. Quoted in Power, *Nunneries*, 248.

55. *Ancrene Wisse*, 202–203.

CHAPTER 3

1. See Martha Lee Osborne, ed., *Woman in Western Thought* (New York: Random House, 1979), 15.

2. See ibid., 16.

3. Rosemary Radford Reuther discusses this split in her essay, "Misogynism and Virginal Feminism in the Fathers of the Church," *Religion and Sexism: Images of Women in the Jewish and Christian Traditions*, ed. Reuther (New York: Simon and Schuster, 1974), 150–83.

4. In her plenary address on medieval notions of the resurrection of the body, Medieval Institute meeting, Kalamazoo, Mich., May 1988, Caroline Bynum suggested that medieval notions of the body are considerably more complex than they are usually thought to be. The relationship of medieval notions of the resurrected body to attitudes toward gender remains to be investigated, however.

5. At least one collection of Aristotelian writing, the *Parva Naturalia*, had reached England by 1200. It is possible that the Victorines, because of their interest in Arabic learning, also may have had greater familiarity with Aristotelian thought than is generally recognized.

6. For Aristotle's reproductive theories, see *Generation of Animals*, trans. A. L. Peck (London, 1953), (Cambridge, Mass.: Harvard Univ. Press, 1953), 729 A 25–34. His views are discussed by Vern Bullough in his essay, "Medieval Medical and Scientific Views of Women," in *Five Papers on Marriage in the Middle Ages, Viator* 4 (1973): 483–501.

7. Quoted by Christine Garside Allen in her essay on Aristotle, "Can a Woman Be Good in the Same Way as a Man," *Woman in Western Thought*, ed. Martha Lee Osborne, 46.

8. Maclean, *Renaissance Notion*, 30.

9. Ibid., 8.

10. Ibid., 31.

11. Ibid., 32.

12. Ibid., 8.

13. Aristotle, *Politics*, bk. 1, ch. 13. Quoted in *Woman in Western Thought*, ed. Martha Lee Osborne, 43.

14. Ibid.

15. Maclean, *Renaissance Notion*, 43–44.

16. Aristotle, *Historia Animalium*, bk. 9, ch. 1. Quoted in *Woman in Western Thought*, ed. Martha Lee Osborne, 37.

17. Isidore, *Etymologiae*, XI, ii, 17–19. Quoted in Joan Ferrante, *Woman as Image in Medieval Literature* (New York: Columbia Univ. Press, 1975), 6.

18. Bullough, "Medieval Views," 491.

19. See Ferrante, *Woman as Image*, 6.

20. Thomas Laqueur, "Orgasm, Generation, and the Politics of Reproductive Biology," *Representations* 14 (Spring 1986): 8.

21. Maclean, *Renaissance Notion*, 10.
22. Ferrante, *Woman as Image*, 17.
23. Ibid., 19.
24. George Tavard, *Woman in Christian Tradition* (Notre Dame, Ind.: Univ. of Notre Dame Press, 1973), 132.
25. Bullough, "Medieval Views," 497; see also George Tavard's comments on Philo in his *Woman in Christian Tradition*, 62.
26. Tavard, *Woman in Christian Tradition*, 104–105.
27. I Cor. 11:3 and I Tim. 2:11–14.
28. Maclean, *Renaissance Notion*, 9.
29. Ferrante, *Woman as Image*, 20–21.
30. See Eleanor McLaughlin, "Equality of Souls, Inequality of Sexes; Woman in Medieval Theology," in *Religion and Sexism*, ed. R. R. Reuther, 218–19.
31. See Gen. 3:16 and Tavard, *Woman in Christian Tradition*, 17.
32. Quoted in Marina Warner, *Alone of All Her Sex: The Myth and the Cult of the Virgin Mary* (New York: Vintage, 1976), 58.
33. Tavard, *Woman in Christian Tradition*, 133. See also his discussion of Bonaventure, pp. 132–33.
34. For a discussion of Augustine's commentaries on Genesis, see Kari Elisabeth Børreson, *Subordination et équivalence: nature et rôle de la femme d'après Augustin et Thomas d'Aquine* (Paris, 1963).
35. See the summary of Augustine's views in Osborne, *Woman in Western Thought*, 51–52.
36. Reuther, 158.
37. Tavard, *Woman in Christian Tradition*, 115.
38. See discussion of Mary in Ferrante, *Woman as Image*, 30.
39. Ibid.
40. Caroline Bynum, *Holy Feast and Holy Fast: The Significance of Food to Medieval Religious Women* (Berkeley: Univ. of California Press, 1986), 269.
41. Warner, *Alone of All*, 69.
42. Bullough, "Medieval Views," 499.
43. Ibid., 497.
44. Bynum, *Holy Feast*, 25.
45. Ibid., 29.
46. See the discussion of this subject in Warner, *Alone of All*, 71.
47. Ibid., 74.
48. Ferrante, *Woman as Image*, 17, 19.
49. See the excellent discussion of Bernard's misogyny, ibid., 27–30.
50. Ibid., 28.
51. Bynum, *Holy Feast*, 261.

CHAPTER 4

1. See Dobson, *Origins of Wisse*.
2. Janet Grayson, *Structure and Imagery in the Ancrene Wisse* (Hanover, N.H.: Univ. Press of New England, 1974).

3. Dobson, *Origins of Wisse,* 174–311.

4. For a general discussion of the affective movement, see Southern, *Making of the Middle Ages.*

5. Geoffrey Shepherd, *The Ancrene Wisse: Parts Six and Seven* (New York: Barnes and Noble, 1959), xxiii.

6. See, e.g., R. W. Chambers, "Continuity of Prose," xlv-clxxiv. For a recent challenge to such views, see Millett, "'Hali Meiðhad,' 'Sawles Warde,' and Continuity" 100–108.

7. Wolfgang Riehle, *The Middle English Mystics* (London: Routledge & Kegan Paul, 1981).

8. See M. D. Chenu, *Nature, Man and Society in the Twelfth Century* (Chicago: Univ. Of Chicago Press, 1957).

9. For a discussion of the Victorines, see Beryl Smalley, *The Study of the bible in the Middle Ages* (Oxford, England, 1952; rptd. Notre Dame, Ind.: Univ. of Notre Dame Press, 1978).

10. My comparisons will be based on St. Bernard, *De Gradibus Humilitatis et Superbiae, Patrologia Latina,* 182, 1, cc 942–72; and Hugh of St. Victor, *De Arca Noe Morali,* PL 176, 2, cc. 616–81. All quotations will be taken from these editions; column numbers are cited in parentheses in the text.

11. St. Bernard, "Sermones super Cantica Canticorum," in *S. Bernardi Opera,* vol. 1, ed. J. Leclercq, H. M. Rochais, and C. H. Talbot (Rome: Editiones Cictercienses, 1957), Sermo 9, 42. My translation follows that of Kilian Walsh in *On the Song of Songs I* in *The Works of Bernard of Clairvaux,* vol. 2 (Spencer, Mass.: Cictercian Publications, 1971), 53.

12. St. Bernard, "Sermones," Sermo 9, 43–44. My translation follows Walsh, *On the Song,* 55.

13. *Ancrene Wisse,* 32–33. All further quotations are from this edition; page numbers are cited in parentheses in the text. Following Tolkien, I have rendered the tironian ampersand as a "z" with a hyphen through it.

14. M. D. Salu, trans., *The Ancrene Riwle* (London, 1955; rptd. Notre Dame, Ind.: Univ. of Notre Dame Press, 1956), 23–24. All further English translations of the *Wisse* are from this text; page numbers are cited in parentheses in the text.

15. See discussion of the author's interest in temptation, in Georgianna, *Solitary Self,* 69–71.

16. Shepherd, *Ancrene Wisse,* lxxiii.

17. Grayson, *Structure and Imagery,* 128.

18. Ibid., 47.

19. Ibid., 75–76.

20. Ibid., 34.

21. Ibid., 30.

22. Ibid., 105.

23. Riehle, *Middle English Mystics,* 46–47.

24. John Bugge pointed out this very important feature of the use of the *sponsa christi* motif in the AB texts in his *Virginitas: An Essay in the History of a Medieval Ideal, Archives Internationales d'histoire des Idees,* Series Minor 17 (The Hague: Martinus Nijhoff, 1975).

25. I discuss this issue in an essay, "Do Wey youre book, and Rede on Holy Seyntes lyves: The Female Reader of Courtly Literature in the *Ancrene Wisse* and Chaucer's *Troilus and Criseyde*," to be included in a collection of essays on Chaucer edited by Sylvia Tomasch.

26. Grayson, *Structure and Imagery*, 205.

27. Ian Bishop, "'Greek Fire' in *Ancrene Wisse* and Contemporary Texts," *Notes and Queries*, 224 (1979): 170–99, 198–99.

28. For medieval medical accounts of moisture, see Laqueur, "Orgasm, Generation," 1–41.

29. See Simone de Beauvoir's discussion of the mystic in *The Second Sex*, trans. H. M. Parshley (New York: Bantam, 1961), 630–38; and Luce Irigaray, "La Mysterique" in *Speculum de L'autre Femme* (Paris: Editions de Minuit, 1974), 238–52. For a translation of this difficult essay, see Irigaray, *Speculum of the Other Woman*, trans. Gillian Gill (Ithaca, N.Y.: Cornell Univ. Press, 1985), 191–202.

30. Elaine Showalter, *A Literature of Their Own* (Princeton: Princeton Univ. press, 1982), 277. Many of the comments in this paragraph were the result of a discussion with James Kincaid.

CHAPTER 5

1. See summary of critical responses in Dobson, *Origins of Wisse*, 155–56.

2. d'Ardenne, xlvi.

3. Dobson, *Origins of Wisse*, 155–56.

4. Bella Millett, ed., *Hali Meiðhad*, EETS 284 (Oxford, England: Oxford Univ. Press, 1982), xxiv. My discussion of *Hali Meidenhad* is based on this edition, and all quotations are from it. In my discussion of Millett's edition I shall call the text by its longer name, *Hali Meidenhad*. Page numbers are in parentheses in the text. (I have omitted Millett's emendation brackets.) Translations follow F. J. Furnivall's translation in his earlier edition of the work, *Hali Meidenhad*, EETS OS 18 (Oxford, 1922; rptd., New York: Greenwood Press, 1969).

5. See discussion of the sources of *Hali Meidenhad*, in Millett, *Hali Meiðhad*, xxiv–lvi.

6. On the subordinate role of women, see Georges Duby, *Medieval Marriage: Two Models from Twelfth-Century France* (Baltimore: Johns Hopkins Univ. Press, 1978), 3–4. On the subject of divorce in the Middle Ages, see Jo-Ann McNamara and Suzanne Wemple, "Marriage and Divorce in the Frankish Kingdom," in *Women in Medieval Society*, ed. Susan Stuard, 95–124.

7. Coleman, "Infanticide," 95. For a discussion of children and parents in the Middle Ages, see also Mary McLaughlin, "Survivors and Surrogates: Children and Parents from the Ninth to the Thirteenth Centuries," in *The History of Childhood*, ed. Lloyd de Mause (New York: Psychohistory Press, 1974), 101–81.

8. See Jerome, "Epistola XXII ad Eustochium: De Custodia Virginitatus," PL, vol. 22, cc. 394–425.

9. For a discussion of the different implications of the terms see Mary McLaughlin, "Peter Abelard," 310.

CHAPTER 6

1. Millett, *Hali Meiðhad*, 23.

2. *Seinte Marharete: Þe Meiden ant Martyr*, ed. Frances M. Mack, EETS, OS 193 (Oxford, England: Oxford Univ. Press, 1934), 4. All further quotations from both the Middle English and Latin versions are taken from this edition. The Middle English is taken from the edited version of MS Bodley 34. Page numbers and line numbers are given in parentheses in the text. I have chosen here and in the discussion of the remaining AB texts to use the edited version of MS Bodley 34 because this is the manuscript upon which Tolkien based his analysis of the AB language, A standing for the *Ancrene Wisse* and B for the texts of MS Bodley 34—*Hali Meidenhad*, "Sawles Warde," and the three saints' lives. MS Bodley 34 is the manuscript most likely to have been associated with the anchoresses of Wigmore Abbbey. Following Mack, I have rendered the tironian ampersand as a " + ".

3. An exception to this perhaps is Aelfric's *Lives of the Saints*, in which male and female saints are treated in the same way: they are presented and discussed for their historical importance as figures who represent salvation history as manifested in England.

4. See Donald Howard, *The Three Temptations: Medieval Man in the Search of the World* (Princeton: Princeton Univ. Press, 1966).

5. See Hurley, "The Katherine Group"; and Cecily Clark, "Early Middle English Prose: Three Essays in Stylistics," *Essays in Criticism* 18 (1968):361–82.

6. *Seinte Katerine*, ed. S.R.T.O. d'Ardenne and E. J. Dobson, EETS, SS7 (Oxford, England: Oxford Univ. Press, 1981), 122. All further quotations are from this edition from the edited version of MS Bodley 34; page references are in parentheses in the text. *Þe Liflade ant Te Passiun of Seinte Iuliene*, ed. S.R.T.O. d'Ardenne, EETS, OS 248 (Oxford, England: Oxford Univ. Press, 1961), 11. All further quotations are from this edition from the edited version of MS Bodley 34; line numbers are in parentheses in the text. The symbol *7* in the text is spelled out as ant. The symbol þ is spelled out as þet.

7. Bugge, *Virginitas*.

8. de Beauvoir, *Second Sex*, 630.

9. Warner, *Alone of All*, 71.

10. See *Ancrene Wisse*, 52, and Salu, *Riwle*, 43.

11. In Clemence of Barking's *The Life of St. Catherine*, Anglo-Norman Text Society, 18 (Oxford, England: Blackwells, 1964), xiii, the editor, William McBain, writes, "It seems highly probable that the Abbey at Rouen was responsible for the wide dissemination of the cult of St. Catherine in Northern Europe."

12. As in the *Ancrene Wisse*, inner virtues are of more worth than outer virtues. Her heart, like the heart of the *Wisse* maidens, is to be directed by holy writ.

13. The Latin version is taken from Eugene Einenkel, ed., *The Life of Saint Katherine*, EETS, OS 80 (London, 1884; rptd. Millwood, N.Y.: Kraus Reprint, 1978). Translations of the Middle English follow Einenkel's text.

14. Katherine here lucidly summarizes a quite complex scholastic argument. This summary might suggest that this work was condoning female involvement in scholasticism. Yet, given Anselm's particular concern for women, as well as the

particular implications Anselm's work had for women, it is not surprising that a woman should be acquainted with Anselm's work.

15. For the warnings the *Wisse* author gives the anchoress, see *Ancrene Wisse* 33–35.

16. *Ancrene Wisse*, 62.

17. In Cynewulf's version of this saint's life, in keeping with Anglo-Saxon poetic conventions, Eleusius is criticized as an inadequate treasure-giver in comparison to Christ. Furthermore, Juliana is presented as a heroic warrior. For female readers, it is interesting to read of a woman warrior.

CHAPTER 7

1. For this attribution, see R.W. Southern and F.S. Schmitt, eds., *Memorials of St. Anselm* (London: Oxford Univ. Press, 1969). This attribution has not been sufficiently acknowledged by scholars, who continue to attribute the source to Hugh of St. Victor. All further references to the Latin source of the homily will be to this edition; page and line numbers are given in parentheses in the text.

2. For a discussion of the manuscripts of "Sawles Warde," see R. M. Wilson, ed., *Sawles Warde, Leeds School of English Language Texts and Monographs*, no. 3 (Leeds, 1938), i-xliv. Following Wilson, I have rendered the tironian ampersand as a "7". All quotations from the Middle English text are taken from the edited version of MS Bodley 34; line references are given in parentheses in the text.

3. For a discussion of the dating and localization of this text, see Dobson, *Origins of Wisse*, 237–84.

4. See *St. Bernard of Clairvaux: Seen Through His Selected Letters*, Letter 118, p. 116.

5. R. M. Wilson, *Sawles Warde*, 72, note to 288.

6. Ibid., 290–98.

7. For a discussion of congruence and detail in allegory, see Pamela Gradon, *Form and Style in Early English Literature* (London: Methuen, 1971; rptd. New York: Harper & Row, 1974).

8. From Eph. 16–17.

9. See Caroline Bynum's discussion of the image of God as mother in twelfth-century writing in *Jesus as Mother* (Berkeley: Univ. of California Press, 1982).

CHAPTER 8

1. Chambers, "Continuity of Prose," xlv-clxxiv.

2. Tolkien, "Ancrene Wisse and Hali Meidenhad," 104–26.

3. G. R. Owst, *Literature and Pulpit in Medieval England* (Cambridge, England: Cambridge Univ. Press, 1933), 12.

4. Ibid., 110.

5. Bethurum, "Connection of the Katherine Group," 556–557.

6. Ibid.

7. Hurley, "The Katherine Group."

8. See Shepherd, *Ancrene Wisse*.

9. Millett, *Hali Meiðhad*, xiii-lviii.

10. Millet, "'Hali Meiðhad,' 'Sawles Warde,' and Continuity," 100–108.

11. Ibid., 100.

12. Ibid., 108.

13. See Alfred's "On the State of Learning in England" and his preface to the translation of Gregory's "Pastoral Care," in *Sweet's Anglo-Saxon Reader in Prose and Verse,* ed. by Dorothy Whitelock (Oxford, England: Clarendon Press, 1967), 4–7.

14. John Dickinson, ed., *The Statesman's Book of John of Salisbury* (New York: Russell and Russell, 1963), *Policraticus* V, 2, 65.

15. Maclean, *Renaissance Notion,* 64.

16. Bynum, *Holy Feast,* 286.

17. See Sandra Gilbert and Susan Gubar, *Madwoman in the Attic* (Cambridge, Mass.: Harvard Univ. Press, 1981).

18. See Stock, *Implications of Literacy.*

19. Alfred, "On the State of Learning in England," 5–7.

20. For a summary of those views, see Anne Payne, *King Alfred and Boethius: An Analysis of the Old English Version of the Consolation of Philosophy* (Madison: Univ. of Wisconsin Press, 1968).

21. See ibid.

22. My discussion of these two works is based on W. J. Sedgefield, ed., *King Alfred's Old English Version of Boethius: De Consolatione Philosophiae* (Oxford, England, 1899; rptd. Darmstadt: Wissenschaftliche Buchgesellschaft, 1968); and Thomas A. Carnicelli, ed., *King Alfred's Version of St. Augustine's Soliloquies* (Cambridge, Mass.: Harvard Univ. Press, 1969). All quotations are from these two editions; page references are in parentheses in the text. Much of my discussion of Alfred's writing owes a debt to David Johnston, who worked with me to prepare discussions of Alfred's work for tutorials while we were students at Cambridge.

23. For a general introduction to the tenth-century monastic revival, see Frank Stenton, *Anglo-Saxon England* (1943; rptd. Oxford, England: Clarendon Press, 1975), 433–69.

24. See a discussion of this concern in P. A. Stafford, "Church and Society in the Age of Aelfric II," in *The Old English Homily and Its Background,* ed. Paul Szarmach and Bernard Huppe (Albany: State Univ. of New York Press, 1978), 11–32.

25. Gatch, *Preaching and Theology,* 74.

26. Stafford, "Church and Society," 19.

27. Gatch, *Preaching and Theology,* 19.

28. Ibid., 19.

29. Benjamin Thorpe, ed., *Homilies of the Anglo-Saxon Church* (London: The Aelfric Society, 1844), 1:610.

30. Malcolm Godden, ed., *Aelfric's Catholic Homilies: The Second Series,* EETS, SS5 (Oxford, England: Oxford Univ. Press, 1979), Homily 39, p. 330.

31. Ibid.

32. John C. Pope, ed., *Homilies of Aelfric, A Supplementary Collection,* EETS, 260 (London: Oxford Univ. Press, 1968), vol. 2, Homily 18, p. 594.

33. Ibid.

34. Ibid., 605.

35. Ibid., vol. 1, Homily 11, p. 430.

36. Ibid., vol. 2, Homily 18, p. 609.

37. Thorpe, *Homilies of the Anglo-Saxon Church*, vol. 1, p. 608. All further references to Aelfric's homilies are to this edition; volume and page numbers are cited in parentheses in the text. (Translations follow those in the facing pages of this edition.)

38. Dorothy Bethurum, ed., *The Homilies of Wulfstan* (Oxford, England: Clarendon Press, 1957), Homily 5, p. 134–35. Further quotations from Wulfstan's homilies are from this edition and homily and page numbers will be cited in parentheses in the text.

39. Quoted in Paul Szarmach, ed., *Vercelli, Homilies ix-xxiii* (Toronto: Univ. of Toronto Press, 1981), xx.

40. Antonette diPaolo Healey, *The Old English Vision of St. Paul* (Cambridge, Mass.: Medieval Academy of America, 1978), 41.

41. John R. Sala, *Preaching in the Anglo-Saxon Church* (Chicago: Univ. of Chicago Libraries, 1934), 117.

42. Max Forster, ed., *Die Vercelli Homilien* Bibliotek der Angelsachsichen Prösa, 12 (Hamburg: Henri Grand, 1932). All quotations from the Vercelli Homilies 1–8 are from this edition; homily numbers and page numbers are cited in parentheses in the text.

43. Homily 9 is taken from Max Forster, "Der Vercelli Codex" in *Festschrift für Lorenz Morsbach*, Studien für Englische Philologie, 50 (Halle, Netherlands: 1913), 20–179.

44. Szarmach, "The Vercelli Homilies," 242.

45. Ibid., 242–43.

46. Ibid., 243.

47. Richard Morris, ed., *Old English Homilies of the Twelfth Century*, EETS, second series 57 and 59 (London: N Trübner and Co., 1873). The homilies referred to in the following discussion of twelfth-century homilies are from this edition.

48. Richard Morris, ed., *Old English Homilies and Holiletic Treatises of the Twelfth and Thirteenth Centuries*. EETS (London: N Trübner and Co., 1868), V, 53. All further references to these homilies are from this edition; homily numbers and page numbers are in parentheses in the text. (My translations follow the facing-page translations provided in these editions.)

CHAPTER 9

1. The fullest treatment of the twelfth-century context of the *Ancrene Wisse* is Georgianna. Dobson's study of the origins of the *Ancrene Wisse* also provides information on the sources that would have influenced the *Ancrene Wisse* and the related Katherine Group. Other studies such as Shepherd, Ackerman's editions of parts of the *Wisse*, and individual essays on the works themselves identify specific sources. See Shepherd, *Ancrene Wisse*; and Robert W. Ackerman and Roger Dahood, *Ancrene Riwle: Introduction and Part One* (Binghamton, N.Y.: Medieval and Renaissance Texts and Studies, 1984). See also Millett's edition of *Hali Meidenhad* and her essay on the Katherine Group.

2. See Dobson, *Origins of Wisse*.

3. See Dobson's argument for this attribution, ibid.

4. Ibid., 122.

5. A recent study by Mary Ellen Griffin of the contents of the medieval library of Wigmore Abbey is currently unavailable to scholars because it is part of a will that is still in the process of litigation. Charity Cannon Willard is the literary executor of this material.

6. Southern and Schmitt, *Memorials of St. Anselm*, 354–60. See also Dobson, *Origins of Wisse*, 149.

7. Shepherd, *Ancrene Wisse*, xxviii.

8. See Southern, *Making of the Middle Ages, St. Anselm and His Biographer* (Cambridge, England: Cambridge Univ. Press, 1963), and *Medieval Humanism*. See also Georgianna; Hanning; Beryl Smalley, *Study of the Bible;* Stock, *Myth and Science in the Twelfth Century* (Princeton: Princeton Univ. Press, 1972); Chenu, *Nature, Man and Society;* and Winthrop Wetherbee, *Poetry and Platonism in the Twelfth Century* (Chicago: Chicago Univ. Press, 1972). For the influence of twelfth-century thought on literary developments, see also Barbara Nolan, *The Gothic Visionary Perspective* (Princeton: Princeton Univ. Press, 1977).

9. For discussion that casts doubt on the existence of the Chartrian school, see R. W. Southern, "The Schools of Paris and the School of Chartres," in *Renaissance and Renewal in the Twelfth Century,* edited by Robert L. Benson and Giles Constable (Cambridge, Mass.: Harvard Univ. Press, 1982), 113–37.

10. In addition to the critics cited above, see Rosemary Woolf, *English Religious Lyric in the Middle Ages* (Oxford, England: Oxford Univ. Press, 1968).

11. Caroline Bynum, in *Holy Feast and Holy Fast,* has also argued that the humanization of Christ had important implications for the development of female spirituality. Her work concerns the implications for literature written by women. This movement has rather different implications for literature written for women. My argument, therefore, follows a parallel but different line of thought.

12. Anselm, *Pourquoi Dieu s'est fait homme,* ed. and trans. Rene Roques (Paris: Editions du Cerf, 1963), I, 1, 212.

13. Anselm, *Pourquoi,* II, 7, 366.

14. See Southern's discussion of the significance of this work in his *St. Anselm and His Biographer,* 90.

15. John Bugge, *Virginitas,* 82.

16. See, e.g., Gradon's discussion of the Franciscans in *Form and Style,* 304–305.

17. For a summary of this change, see Woolf, *English Religious Lyric,* 1–66; and Southern, *Making of the Middle Ages,* 118–69, 219–58.

18. Sister Benedicta Ward, ed. and trans., *The Prayers and Meditations of St. Anselm* (1973; rptd. Middlesex, England: Penguin Books, 1979).

19. Gradon, 298.

20. Southern, *Medieval Humanism,* 29.

21. Stock, *Myth and Science,* 3, 6.

22. Chenu, *Nature, Man, and Society,* 10.

23. Ibid., 5.

24. Quoted in Wetherbee, *Poetry and Platonism,* 27.

25. Chenu, *Nature, Man, and Society,* 36.

26. Ibid., 25.

27. Ibid., 123.

28. See Dobson's discussion of the prominence of Victorine manuscripts in England, in Dobson, *Origins of Wisse*, 143.

29. Smalley, *Study of Bible*, 145 and 147.

30. Ibid., 119.

31. See Bynum's discussion of eucharistic piety in *Holy Feast*.

32. Bugge, *Virginitas*, 83, 87.

33. See Leo Steinberg, *The Sexuality of Christ in Renaissance Art and in Modern Oblivion* (New York: Pantheon, 1983).

34. Bugge, *Virginitas*, 83.

35. Thomas Head made this argument in a paper delivered at the Medieval Institute meetings, Kalamazoo, Mich., May 1987.

36. Bugge, *Virginitas*, 92.

37. Ibid., 99–100.

38. See Southern's foreword to Sister Benedicta Ward's translation of Anselm's letters, reprinted in Southern, ed., *The Prayers and Meditations of St. Anselm* (London: Penguin, 1973), 9.

39. Southern, *Prayers*, 10.

40. See Bynum, *Holy Feast*.

41. Chenu, *Nature, Man, and Society*, 124.

42. See *The Letters of Abelard and Heloise*, trans. Betty Radice, (London: Penguin, 1974). For a brilliant essay on Heloise's reactions to Abelard's pronouncements, see Linda Georgianna, "Any Corner of Heaven: Heloise's Critique of Monasticism," *Medieval Studies*, 49 (1987):221–53.

43. Bynum, *Holy Feast*, 26.

44. Ibid., 263.

45. See Helene Cixous and Catherine Clement, *The Newly Born Woman*, trans. Betsy Wing (Minneapolis: Univ. of Minnesota Press, 1986).

46. Bynum, *Holy Feast*, 279.

47. Bynum made this argument in her plenary address, Medieval Institute meetings, Kalamazoo, Mich., May 1988.

CHAPTER 10

1. For a study of Margery Kempe in relationship to gender issues, see Sarah Beckwith, "A Very Material Mysticism: The Medieval Mysticism of Margery Kempe," in *Medieval Literature: Criticism, Ideology, and History*, ed. David Aers (New York: St. Martin's, 1986), 34–57.

2. See Barry Windeatt, "The Art of Mystical Loving: Julian of Norwich," in *The Medieval Mystical Tradition in England*, ed. Marion Glasscoe (Exeter, England: Univ. of Exeter Press, 1980), 55–69.

3. Ibid., 64.

List of Works Cited

Ackerman, Robert W., and Roger Dahood. *Ancrene Riwle: Introduction and Part One*. Binghamton, N.Y.: Medieval and Renaissance Texts and Studies, 1984.

Ælfric. *Ælfric's Catholic Homilies: The Second Series*. Edited by Malcolm Godden. EETS 555. Oxford, England: Oxford University Press, 1979.

———. *Homilies of Ælfric: A Supplementary Collection*. Vols. 1 and 2. Edited by John Pope. EETS 259. London: Oxford University Press, 1967.

———. *The Homilies of the Anglo-Saxon Church: The first Part containing the Sermones Catholici or Homilies of Ælfric*. 2 vols. Edited by Benjamin Thorpe. London: Ælfric Society, 1844.

———. *Lives of Saints*. Edited by W. W. Skeat. EETS, OS 76, 82. London: Trübner, 1881.

Ailred of Rievaulx. [Aelredi Rievallensis] *De Institutione Inclusarum*. In *Opera Omnia*, edited by A. D. Hoste and C. H. Talbot. Turnholti, Belgium: Typographii Brepols Editores Pontificii, 1971.

———. *The Life of a Recluse*. In *Treatises and the Pastoral Prayer*, translated by Mary Paul MacPherson. *Works of Aelred of Rievaulx*, vol. 1. Cistercian Fathers Series 2. Spencer, Mass.: Cistercian Publications, 1971.

Alfred. *King Alfred's Version of St. Augustine's Soliloquies*. Edited by Thomas A. Carnicelli. Cambridge Mass.: Harvard University Press, 1969.

———. *King Alfred's Old English Version of Boethius: De Consolatione Philosophiae*. Edited by John Sedgefield. Oxford, England: Clarendon Press, 1899.

Allen, Hope Emily. "Further Borrowings from *Ancren Riwle*." *Modern Language Review* 24 (1929):1–15.

Ambrose, Saint. *De Virginibus Ad Marcellinam Sororem Suam Libri Tres*. PL 16, 2, cc. 198–243.

Anselm, Saint. *Cur Deus Homo*. In *St. Anselm: Basic Writings*, translated by S. W. Deane. La Salle, Ill.: Open Court Publishing, 1962.

———. "De Custodia Interioris Hominis." In *Memorials of St. Anselm*, edited by R. W. Southern and F. S. Schmitt. London: Oxford University Press, 1969.

———. *Orationes et Meditationes*. In *Opera Omnia*, edited by F. S. Schmitt. Edinburgh: Thomas Nelson and Sons, 1946.

———. *Pourquoi Dieu s'est fait Homme*. Edited and translated by René Roques. Paris: Editions du Cerf, 1963.

———. *The Prayers and Meditations of St. Anselm.* Translated by Sister Benedicta Ward. Middlesex, England: Penguin, 1973.

———. *Proslogion.* Edited and translated by M. J. Charlesworth. Oxford, England, 1965; rptd. Notre Dame, Ind.: University of Notre Dame Press, 1979.

Aristotle. *Generation of Animals.* Translated by A. L. Peck. London, 1953.

Baker, Derek, ed. *Medieval Women.* Studies in Church History, Subsidia I. Oxford, England: Basil Blackwell, 1978.

Barking, Clemence of. *The Life of St. Catherine.* Edited by William McBain. Anglo-Norman Text Society 18. Oxford, England: Basil Blackwell, 1964.

Bennet, J. A. W., and G. V. Smithers. *Early Middle English Verse and Prose.* Oxford, England: Clarendon Press, 1966.

Beckwith, Sarah. "A Very Material Mysticism: The Medieval Mysticism of Margery Kempe." In *Medieval literature: Criticism, Ideology, and History,* edited by David Aers, pp. 34–57. New York: St. Martin's Press, 1986.

Bernard, Saint. *De Gradibus Humilitatis et Superbiae.* PL 182, cc. 942–72.

———. *On the Song of Songs,* I. Translated by Kilian Walsh. *The Works of Bernard of Clairvaux,* vol. 2. Spencer, Mass.: Cistercian Publications, 1971.

———. *St. Bernard of Clairvaux: Seen Through His Selected Letters.* Translated by Bruno Scott James. Chicago: Henry Regnery, 1953.

———. *Sermones super Cantica Canticorum.* Edited by J. Leclercq, H. M. Rochais, and C. H. Talbot. *S. Bernardi Opera,* vol. I. Rome: Editiones Cistercienses, 1957.

———. *The Steps of Humility.* Translated by G. B. Burch. Notre Dame, Ind.: University of Notre Dame Press, 1963.

Bethurum, Dorothy. "The Connection of the Katherine Group with Old English Prose." *JEGP* 34 (1935):553–64.

Bishop, Ian. "'Greek Fire' in *Ancrene Wisse* and Contemporary Texts." *Notes and Queries* 224 (1979):198–99.

Børreson, Kari Elisabeth. *Subordination et équivalence: Nature et rôle de la femme d'après Augustin et Thomas d'Aquine.* Paris, 1963.

Brown, Peter. *The Making of Late Antiquity.* Cambridge, Mass.: Harvard University Press, 1978.

Bugge, John. *Virginitas: An Essay in the History of a Medieval Ideal.* Archives Internationales d'histoire des Idées. Series minor 17. The Hague: Martinus Nijhoff, 1975.

Bullough, Vern. "Medieval Medical and Scientific Views of Women." In *Five Papers on Marriage in the Middle Ages. Viator* 4 (1973):485–501.

Burrow, John. *Ricardian Poetry.* New Haven, Conn.: Yale University Press, 1971.

Bynum, Caroline. *Holy Feast and Holy Fast: The Significance of Food to Medieval Religious Women.* Berkeley: University of California Press, 1986.

———. "Jesus as Mother and Abbot as Mother: Some Themes in Twelfth Century Cistercian Writing." *Harvard Theological Review* 70 (1977):257–84.

Casey, Kathleen. "Women in Norman and Plantagenet England." In *The Women of England From Anglo-Saxon Times to the Present: Interpretive Bibliographical Essays,* Edited by Barbara Kanner, pp. 83–123. Hamden, Conn.: Archon, 1979.

Chambers, R. W. "The Continuity of English Prose from Alfred to More and His School." In Nicholas Harpsfield, *The Life of Thomas More*, pp. xlv-clxxiv. EETS, OS 186. 1932; rptd. London: Oxford University Press, 1963.

Chance, Jane. *Woman as Hero in Old English Literature*. Syracuse, N.Y.: Syracuse University Press, 1986.

Chenu, M. D. *Nature, Man and Society in the Twelfth Century*. Chicago: University of Chicago Press, 1957.

Cixous, Helene, and Catherine Clement. *The Newly Born Woman*. Translated by Betty Wing. Minneapolis: University of Minnesota Press, 1986.

Clark, Cecily. "Early Middle English Prose: Three Essays in Stylistics." *Essays in Criticism* 18 (1968):361–82.

Clay, R. M. *Hermits and Anchorites of England*. 1914; rptd. Detroit: Singing Tree Press, 1968.

Coleman, Emily. "Infanticide in the Early Middle Ages." In *Women in Medieval Society*, edited by Susan Stuard, pp. 95–124. Philadelphia: University of Pennsylvania Press, 1976.

Dalbey, Marcia. "Themes and Techniques in the Blickling Lenten Homilies." In *The Old English Homily and Its Background*, edited by Paul Szarmach and Bernard Huppé, pp. 221–39. Albany: State University of New York Press, 1978.

d'Ardenne, S.R.T.O., ed. *Pe Liflade Ant Te Passiun of Seinte Juliene*. EETS 248. Liège, Belgium, 1936; rptd. Oxford, England: Oxford University Press, 1961.

d'Ardenne, S.R.T.O., and E. J. Dobson. *Seinte Katerine*. EETS, SS 7. Oxford: Oxford University Press, 1981.

de Beauvoir, Simone. *The Second Sex*. Translated by H. M. Parshley. 1953, rptd. New York: Bantam, 1970.

di Paulo Healey, Antonette. *The Old English Vision of St. Paul*. Cambridge, Mass: Medieval Academy of America, 1978.

Dickinson, John, ed. *The Statesman's Book of John of Salisbury*. New York: Russell and Russell, 1963.

Dobson, E. J. *The Origins of Ancrene Wisse*. Oxford, England: Clarendon Press, 1976.

Duby, Georges. *Medieval Marriage: Two Models from Twelfth Century France*. Baltimore: Johns Hopkins University Press, 1978.

Eckenstein, Lina. *Woman Under Monasticism: Chapters on Saint-lore and Convent Life Between A.D. 500 and A.D. 1500*. Cambridge, England: The University Press, 1896.

Edwards, A.S.G., ed. *Middle English Prose: A Critical Guide to Major Authors and Genres*. New Brunswick, N.J.: Rutgers University Press, 1984.

Edwards, A.S.G., and Derek Pearsall, eds. *Middle English Prose: Essays on Bibliographical Problems*. New York: Garland, 1981.

Einenkel, Eugene, ed. and trans. *The Life of Saint Katherine*. EETS, OS 80. London, 1884; rptd. Millwood, N.Y.: Kraus, 1978.

Fell, Christine; Cecily Clark; and Elizabeth Williams. *Women in Anglo-Saxon England and the Impact of 1066*. Bloomington: Indiana University Press, 1984.

Ferrante, Joan. *Woman as Image in Medieval Literature*. New York: Columbia University Press, 1975.

Forster, Max, ed. "Der Vercelli Codex." In *Festchrift für Loren Morsbach*, pp. 20–179. Studien für Englische Philologie, 50. Halle, Netherlands, 1913.

————, ed. *Die Vercelli Homilien*. Bibliothek der Angelsachsichen Prösa 12. Hamburg: Henri Grand, 1932.

Furnivall, F. J., ed. *Hali Meidenhad*. EETS, OS 18. Oxford, 1922; rptd. New York: Greenwood Press, 1969.

Gatch, Milton McC. "Beginnings Continued: A Decade of Studies of Old English Prose." In *Anglo-Saxon England 5*, pp. 225–44. Cambridge, England: Cambridge University Press, 1976.

————. *Preaching and Theology in Anglo-Saxon England: Aelfric and Wulfstan*. Toronto: University of Toronto Press, 1977.

Georgianna, Linda. "Any Corner of Heaven: Heloise's Criticism of Monasticism." *Mediaeval Studies* 59 (1987):221–53.

————. *The Solitary Self: Individuality in the Ancrene Wisse*. Cambridge, Mass.: Harvard University Press, 1981.

Gilbert, Sandra, and Susan Gubar. *Madwoman in the Attic*. New Haven, Conn.: Yale University Press, 1979.

Gilligan, Carol. *In a Different Voice*. Cambridge, Mass.: Harvard University Press, 1982.

Glasscoe, Marion, ed. *The Medieval Mystical Tradition in England*. Exeter, England: Exeter Press, 1980.

Godden, Malcolm. "Aelfric and the Vernacular Prose Tradition." In *The Old English Homily and Its Background*, edited by Paul Szarmach and Bernard Huppé, pp. 99–117. Albany: State University of New York Press, 1978.

Gradon, Pamela. *Form and Style in Early English Literature*. London, 1971; rptd. New York: Harper and Row, 1974.

Grayson, Janet. *Structure and Imagery in Ancrene Wisse*. Hanover, N.H.: University Press of New England, 1974.

Hanning, R. W. *The Individual in Twelfth Century Romance*. New Haven, Conn.: Yale University Press, 1977.

Hollis, Stephanie. "The Thematic Structure of the 'Sermo Lupi'." In *Anglo-Saxon England 6*, pp. 175–95. Cambridge, England: Cambridge University Press, 1977.

Howard, Donald. *The Three Temptations: Medieval Man in Search of the World*. Princeton, N.J.: Princeton University Press, 1966.

Hugh of St. Victor. *De Arca Noe Morali*. PL 176, 2, cc. 618–81.

————. *De Vanitate Mundi*. PL 176, 2, cc. 703–40.

————. *Hugh of Saint Victor: Selected Spiritual Writings*. Edited by Aelred Squire. Translated by a religious of CSMV. London: Faber and Faber, 1962.

Hurley, Margaret. "The Katherine Group: Manipulation of Convention in Conventional Narrative." Ph.D. dissertation, Syracuse University, Syracuse, N.Y., 1974.

Irigaray, Luce. *Speculum de L'Autre Femme*. Paris: Editions de Minuit, 1974.

————. *Speculum of the Other Woman*. Gillian Gill, trans. Ithaca, N.Y.: Cornell University Press, 1985.

Jerome, Saint. *Epistola XXII ad Eustochium*. PL 22, 1, cc. 394–425.

Kelly, Amy. *Eleanor of Aquitane and the Four Kings*. Cambridge, Mass.: Harvard University Press, 1950.

Keynes, Simon, and Michael Lapidge, trans. *Alfred the Great, Asser's Life of King Alfred and Other Contemporary Sources*. Harmondsworth, Middlesex, England; New York: Penguin, 1983.

Knowles, David. *The Monastic Order in England: A History of its Development from the Time of St. Dunstan to the Fourth Lateran Council (940–1216)*. Cambridge, England: The University Press, 1940.

Langland, William. *The Vision of William Concerning Piers the Plowman*. Edited by W. W. Skeat, 1886; rptd. Oxford, England: Oxford University Press, 1969.

Laqueur, Thomas. "Orgasm, Generation, and the Politics of Reproductive Biology." *Representations* 14 (Spring 1986):1–41.

Leclercq, Jean. *Monks and Love in Twelfth Century France*. Oxford, England: Clarendon Press, 1979.

Letson, D. R. "The Poetic Content of the Revival Homily." In *The Old English Homily and its Background*, edited by Paul Szarmach and Bernard Huppé, pp. 139–56. Albany: State University of New York Press, 1968.

Mack, Francis M., ed. *Seinte Marharete þe Meiden ant Martyr*. EETS, OS 193. London, 1934; rptd. London, England: Oxford University Press, 1958.

Maclean, Ian. *The Renaissance Notion of Woman: A Study in the Fortunes of Scholasticism and Medical Science in European Intellectual Life*. Cambridge, England: Cambridge University Press, 1980.

McLaughlin, Eleanor Commo. "Equality of Souls, Inequality of Sexes: Women in Medieval Theology." In *Religion and Sexism: Images of Women in the Jewish and Christian Traditions*, edited by Rosemary Radford Reuther, pp. 213–66. New York: Simon and Schuster, 1974.

McLaughlin, Mary M. "Peter Abelard and the Dignity of Women: Twelfth Century 'Feminism' in Theory and Practice." In *Pierre Abélard—Pierre le Vénérable: Les Courants Philosophiques, Littéraires et Artistiques en Occident au Milieu du XIIe siecle*, pp. 287–334. Paris: Editions du Centre National de la Recherche Scientifique, 1975.

————. "Survivors and Surrogates: Children and Parents from the Ninth to the Thirteenth Centuries." In *The History of Childhood*, edited by Lloyd de Mause, pp. 101–81. New York: Psychohistory Press, 1974.

Millett, Bella. *Hali Meiðhad*. EETS, NS 24. London: Oxford University Press, 1982.

————. "*Hali Meiðhad, Sawles Warde* and the Continuity of English Prose." In *Five Hundred Years of Words and Sounds*, edited by E. G. Stanley and Douglas Gray, pp. 100–108. Cambridge, England: D. S. Brewer, 1983.

Morris, Richard, ed. *The Blickling Homilies of the Tenth Century*. EETS, 58, 63, 73. London: 1880; rptd. Oxford, England: Oxford University Press, 1967.

————, ed. *Old English Homilies of the Twelfth Century*. EETS, NS 53, pt. 2. London, England: Oxford University Press, 1873.

————, ed. *Old English Homilies and Homiletic Treatises of the Twelfth and Thirteenth Centuries*. EETS, OS 29, 34. London: 1868; rptd. New York: Greenwood, 1969.

Muscatine, Charles. *Poetry and Crisis in the Age of Chaucer.* Notre Dame, Ind.: University of Notre Dame Press, 1972.

Nolan, Barbara. *The Gothic Visionary Perspective.* Princeton, N.J.: Princeton University Press, 1977.

Osborne, Martha Lee, ed. *Woman in Western Thought.* New York: Random House, 1979.

Owst, G. R. *Literature and Pulpit in Medieval England.* Cambridge, England: Cambridge University Press, 1933.

Payne, Anne. *King Alfred and Boethius: An Analysis of the Old English Version of the* Consolation of Philosophy. Madison: University of Wisconsin Press, 1968.

Pollock, Frederick, and Frederick W. Maitland. *The History of English Law,* vol. 2. Cambridge, England: Cambridge University Press, 1898.

Power, Eileen. *Medieval English Nunneries.* Cambridge, England: The University Press, 1922.

Radice, Betty, trans. *The Letters of Abelard and Heloise.* London: Penguin, 1973.

Reuther, Rosemary Radford. "Misogynism and Virginal Feminism in the Fathers of the Church." In *Religion and Sexism: Images of Women in the Jewish and Christian Traditions,* edited by Rosemary Radford Reuther, pp. 150–83. New York: Simon and Schuster, 1974.

Riehle, Wolfgang. *The Middle English Mystics.* London: Routledge and Kegan Paul, 1981.

Robertson, D. W., Jr. *A Preface to Chaucer: Studies in Medieval Perspective.* Princeton, N.J.: Princeton University Press, 1962.

Sala, John R. *Preaching in the Anglo-Saxon Church.* Chicago: University of Chicago Libraries, 1934.

Salu, M. D. *The Ancrene Riwle.* London, 1955; rptd. Notre Dame, Ind.: University of Notre Dame Press, 1956.

Scragg, D. G. "The Corpus of Vernacular Homilies and Prose Saints' Lives before Aelfric." In *Anglo-Saxon England 8,* pp. 223–65. Cambridge, England: Cambridge University Press, 1979.

Shepherd, Geoffrey, ed. *Ancrene Wisse: Parts Six and Seven.* 1959; rptd. New York: Barnes and Noble, 1972.

Showalter, Elaine. *A Literature of Their Own.* Princeton, N.J.: Princeton University Press, 1982.

Smalley, Beryl. *The Study of the Bible in the Middle Ages.* Oxford, England: 1952; rptd. Notre Dame, Ind.: University of Notre Dame Press, 1978.

Southern, R. W. *The Making of the Middle Ages.* 1953; rptd. New Haven, Conn.: Yale University Press, 1970.

———. *Medieval Humanism.* New York: Harper and Row, 1970.

———. *St. Anselm and His Biographer.* Cambridge: The University Press, 1963.

———. "The Schools of Paris and the School of Chartres." In *Renaissance and Renewal in the Twelfth Century,* edited by Robert L. Benson and Giles Constable. Cambridge, Mass.: Harvard University Press, 1982.

Southern, R. W., and F. S. Schmitt. *Memorial of St. Anselm.* London: Oxford University Press, 1979.

Stafford, P. A. "Church and Society in the Age of Aelfric." In *Old English Homily and Its Background*, edited by Paul Szarmach and Bernard Huppé, pp. 11–42. Albany: State University of New York Press, 1978.

Stanley, Rubin. *Medieval English Medicine, A.D. 500–1300*. Newton Abbot, England: Barnes and Noble, 1974.

Steinberg, Leo. *The Sexuality of Christ in Renaissance Art and in Modern Oblivion*. New York: Pantheon, 1983.

Stenton, Doris. *The English Woman in History*. London: Macmillan, 1957.

Stenton, Frank. *Anglo-Saxon England*. 1943; rptd. Oxford, England: Oxford University Press, 1971.

Stock, Brian. *Myth and Science in the Twelfth Century*. Princeton, N.J.: Princeton University Press, 1972.

———. *The Implications of Literacy*. Princeton, N.J.: Princeton University Press, 1983.

Szarmach, Paul. "The Vercelli Homilies: Style and Structure." In *The Old English Homily and Its Background*, edited by Paul Szarmach and Bernard Huppé, pp. 241–67. Albany: State University of New York Press, 1978.

———, ed. *Vercelli Homilies, ix-xxiii*. Toronto: University of Toronto Press, 1981.

Talbot, C. H. *The Life of Christina of Markyate*. Oxford, England: Clarendon Press, 1959.

Tavard, George H. *Woman in Christian Tradition*. Notre Dame, Ind.: University of Notre Dame Press, 1973.

Thompson, W. Meredith. *'Pe Wohunge of ure Lauerd*. EETS 241. London: Oxford University Press, 1958.

Tolkien, J. R. R. "*Ancrene Wisse* and *Hali Meidenhad*." *Essays and Studies by Members of the English Association* 14 (1929):104–26.

———, ed. *The English Text of the Ancrene Riwle: Ancrene Wisse* (Corpus Christi College, Cambridge, 402). EETS 249. London: Oxford University Press, 1962.

Ward, Sister Benedicta, trans. *The Prayers and Meditations of St. Anselm*. London: Penguin, 1973.

Warner, Marina. *Alone of All Her Sex: The Myth and the Cult of the Virgin Mary*. New York: Vintage, 1976 and 1983.

Warren, Ann K. *Anchorites and Their Patrons in Medieval England*. Berkeley: University of California Press, 1985.

Wemple, Suzanne, and Joann McNamara. "Marriage and Divorce in the Frankish Kingdom." In *Women in Medieval Society*, edited by Susan Stuard, pp. 95–124. Philadelphia: University of Pennsylvania Press, 1976.

Wenzel, Siegfried. *The Sin of Sloth: Acedia in Medieval Thought and Literature*. 1960; rptd. Chapel Hill: University of North Carolina Press, 1967.

Wetherbee, Winthrop. *Poetry and Platonism in the Twelfth Century*. Princeton, N.J.: Princeton University Press, 1972.

Whitelock, Dorothy, ed. *Sweet's Anglo-Saxon Reader in Prose and Verse*. Oxford, England: Clarendon Press, 1927.

Wilson, R. M., ed. *Sawles Warde*. Leeds School of English Texts and Monographs, nos. 3 and 4. Leeds, England, 1938.

Windeatt, B. A. "The Art of Mystical Loving: Julian of Norwich." In *The Medieval*

Mystical Tradition in England, edited by Marion Glasscoe, pp. 55–71. Exeter,: Exeter Press, 1980.

Woolf, Rosemary. *English Religious Lyric in the Middle Ages.* Oxford, England: Oxford University Press, 1968.

Woolf, Virginia. *A Room of One's Own.* New York: Harcourt, Brace, 1929.

Wulfstan. *The Homilies of Wulfstan.* Edited by Dorothy Bethurum. 1957; rptd. Oxford, England: Oxford University Press, 1971.

Zeeman, Elizabeth. "Continuity in Middle English Devotional Prose." *JEGP* 55 (1956):417–22.

Index

AB texts, 1–12, 36, 42, 43, 44, 77, 94, 96, 99, 106, 112, 122, 126, 142, 143, 144, 145, 146, 150, 153, 154, 158, 160, 162, 165, 167, 169, 173, 174, 178, 180, 181, 182, 183, 184, 186, 187, 188, 190, 195, 196, 197, 198, 207n; *see also Ancrene Wisse, Hali Meidenhad, Katherine Group, The Life of St. Juliana, The Life of St. Katherine, The Life of St. Margaret,* "Sawless Warde"

Abelard, 11, 46, 183, 191, 192; *see also* Heloise

Ackerman, Robert and Roger Dahood, 210n

Adam, 8, 36–38, 41, 123, 124, 148, 178, 196; *see also* Eve

Ælfric, 2, 6–7, 11, 145, 146, 149, 150, 157–65, 166, 172, 173, 179; *Lives of the Saints,* 207n

Æthelwold, 157, 163

affective movement, 5, 11, 46, 47, 177, 183, 184, 190, 191; *see also* Anselm, humanization of Christ

affective piety, 11, 183, 192; *see also* Anselm

affective style, 4, 151, 152, 159, 162, 164, 165, 168, 169, 173, 176, 179, 184, 193; *see also* Anselm

Ailred of Rievaulx, 26, 29, 182

Alan de Lille, 78

Aldhelm, 16, 166

Alfred, 6, 11, 145, 146, 147, 148, 150, 151–57, 158, 162, 179; trans-

lation of Augustine's *Soliloquies,* 153–57; translation of Boethius's *Consolation of Philosophy,* 153–57

Allen, Christine Garside, 203n

Ambrose, 37, 78, 84

anchoress, 1, 2, 3, 8, 10, 11, 40, 42, 45, 49, 53, 60, 61, 62, 65, 67, 69, 70, 72, 75, 76, 79, 80, 90, 94, 98, 100, 104, 111, 124, 127, 128, 130, 182; anchorite, 14, 24, 27; anchoritic life, 8, 10, 14, 15, 24, 25, 26, 27, 45, 79, 127, 143; anchoritism, 8, 14, 15, 17, 24, 25, 31; hermits, 26; history and circumstances of, 13–31; recluse, 27, 42; *see also* anchorholds, *Ancrene Wisse*

anchorholds, 10, 13, 15, 17, 22, 23–31, 32, 49, 55, 58, 62, 69, 70, 94, 98; description of, 26–27; enclosure in, 26; *see also* anchoress, *Ancrene Wisse*

Ancrene Wisse, 1, 3, 5, 26, 27, 29, 30, 31, 44–76, 77, 90, 94, 98, 106, 109, 113, 121, 126, 127, 140, 145, 154, 175, 177, 182, 183, 187, 188, 196, 197, 210n; *see also* anchoresses, anchorholds

Andrew of St. Victor, 47, 182, 188

anonymous homilies, 7, 11, 147, 150, 165–80; *see also* Lambeth Homilies, Vercelli Homilies

Anselm, 11, 46, 78, 98, 104, 182, 183, 184, 186, 189, 190, 191, 207n, 208n, 211n; *Cur Deus*

Early English Devotional Prose and the Female Audience was designed by Dariel Mayer, composed by Graphic Composition, Inc., and printed and bound by BookCrafters, Inc. The book is set in Times Roman and printed on 50-lb Glatfelter Natural.